Agile Software Development with C#, Scrum, eXtreme Programming, and Kanban
Second Edition

Lynn Smith

DEDICATION

To All Readers of This Book.

CONTENTS

Preface

This book, designed for beginners, will introduce you to the field of agile software development with C#. There are many books on C# and just as many, if not more, on agile, but few teach a programming language and software development methodology in conjunction.

Agile blurs the lines between the roles of analyst, designer, programmer, and tester. Therefore, when you learn agile, you will learn to analyze, design, develop, and test. By combining C# and agile in one book, you will be able to experience all roles through a single journey. At the end of the book, you will be given several tiny C# projects to work on following agile philosophy. Working through these projects with four or five other readers (e.g., as in a college setting) would further benefit your understanding.

This book is not a reference, so content will be kept at a minimum. This book is also not an in depth cover of any specific topic, instead designed to cater to beginners. Readers may always research the web for further details.

This book requires you to type all code. We don't provide sample code downloads. Though we understand your time is valuable, we believe hands-on practice is the best way to learn.

Throughout the book, you will be given plenty of exercises under the titles of **Programming Challenge** and **Test Your Understanding**. We strongly encourage you to try all exercises as you work through the book.

This second edition uses Visual Studio 2019 Community as the development environment.

Last but not least, we thank Dr. Youlong Zhuang for reviewing this second edition and providing valuable suggestions.

Chapter 1: Introduction to C# and Agile

1.1 What is C#?

C# is an object-oriented programming (OOP) language used for developing application software. An application consists of instructions for the computer, and C# is the language that programmers use to write those instructions.

As a modern programming language, C# is often considered easier to use than other programming languages, such as C, C++, or Java.

An object-oriented programming language is a way to develop applications with reusable classes that can be used to build larger programs. A class is a container with a collection of instructions in it. A class can be used in multiple places of a program or even in another program without having to rewrite the instructions. To use instructions in a class, you create an object of that class. Then all instructions of that class are available with the object.

Before you can start to code in C#, you need to install Visual Studio 2019 Community edition. Search the web for "download visual studio 2019 community edition" and click on the "free download" link to download the software. After downloading the file to your local computer, double click to install it.

On the "Visual Studio Installer" window, make sure you check ".NET desktop development" before clicking on the "install" button.

What you have just installed is an Integrated Development Environment (IDE), which includes a text editor to type code into and a debugger to test your code.

After installation is complete, follow the instructions to restart the computer and you are on your way to becoming a C# programmer. Make sure you close all other programs before restarting to avoid losing any unsaved work.

Test Your Understanding 1.1

C# is an OOP language that programmers use to write instructions for computers.
—A. True
B. False

Test Your Understanding 1.2

An object oriented programming language is a way to develop applications such that _____ classes can be used to build larger programs.
A. any
B. useless
— C. reusable
D. small

Test Your Understanding 1.3

What is included in Visual Studio IDE?
A. A text editor for typing in code
B. A text editor for typing in code and turning in homework
— C. A text editor for typing in code and a debugger to test the code
D. A visually appealing text editor liked by many programmers

1.2 Your First C# Program

On your PC's desktop, create a new folder named 'Agile'. You will save all project files in this folder for organization purposes.

Launch Visual Studio. The first time you start Visual Studio, it will prompt if you want to sign in by creating an account. I suggest that you create an account now even though it has the option, "Not now, maybe later". If you don't create an account, it will prompt you again after 30 days without the 'not now' option. Creating an account only requires an email address.

Start a new project by clicking "Create a new project" on the launch page (Figure 1.1).

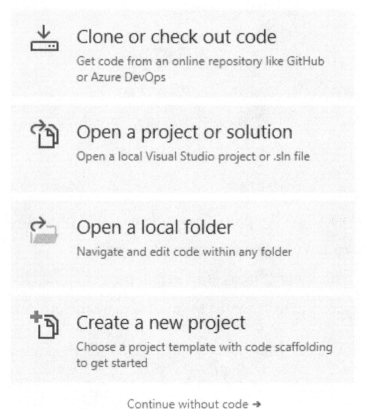

Figure 1.1 Launch page of Visual Studio 2019 Community edition.

In the "Create a new project" window, type "Console App" into the "Search for project templates" search box. Select the option that includes C# and .NET Framework (top one in Figure 1.2). Click "Next".

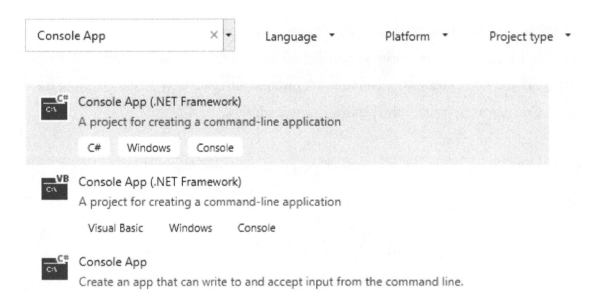

Figure 1.2 Create a new project window.

A new window, "Configure your new project", will pop up. Give a name to the project, e.g. Chapter1Program1. Browse for the location you want to save the project to by clicking on the "…" symbol on the right. Check the "Place solution and project in the same location" box (Figure 1.3). Finally, click on the "Create" button to create the project.

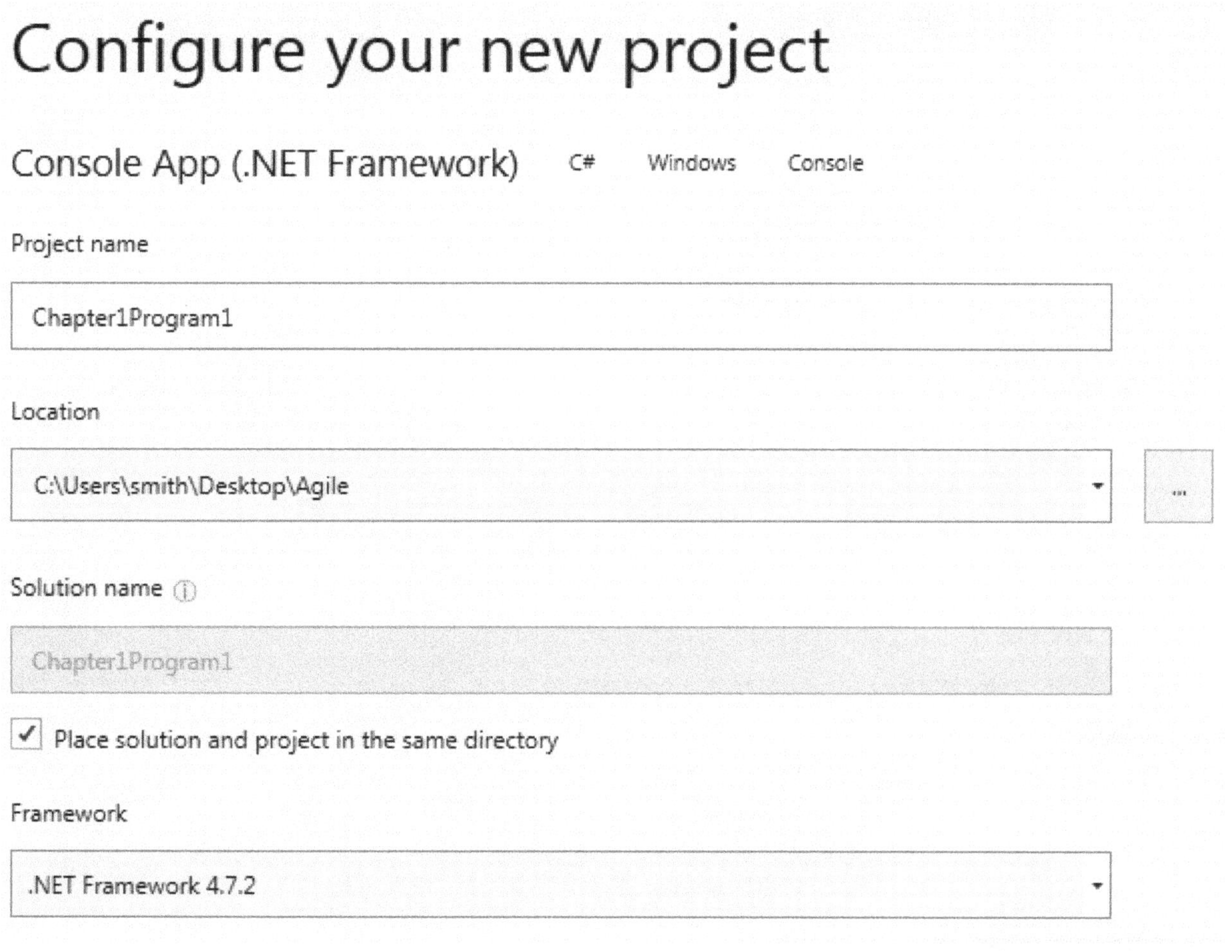

Configure your new project

Console App (.NET Framework)   C#   Windows   Console

Project name

```
Chapter1Program1
```

Location

```
C:\Users\smith\Desktop\Agile                                    ▼    ...
```

Solution name ⓘ

```
Chapter1Program1
```

✓ Place solution and project in the same directory

Framework

```
.NET Framework 4.7.2                                            ▼
```

Figure 1.3 Configure your new project.

This may take a few minutes the first time. A default program will be displayed as shown in Figure 1.4. If you don't see the default program, check the "Solution Explorer" window on the right side to see if "Program.cs" is selected (double clicking on this file name will display the code in the code window). The "Solution Explorer" window is shown in Figure 1.5.

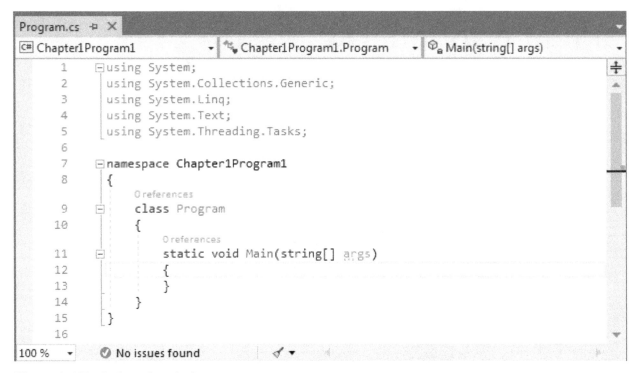

Figure 1.4 Default code window.

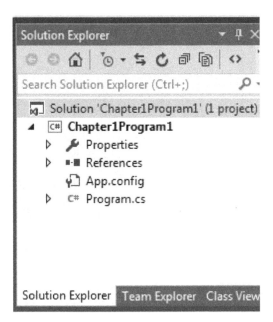

Figure 1.5 Solution Explorer window

The file has no instructions yet. Insert the code from Lines 13 to 16 as shown in Figure 1.6.

```
File    Edit    View    Project    Build    Debug    Test    Analyze    Tools    Extensions

             Debug  ▼   Any CPU          ▼   ▶ Start ▼

Program.cs*  ⌿ ✕
C# Chapter1Program1                          ▼  Chapter1Program1.Program

   1      using System;
   2      using System.Collections.Generic;
   3      using System.Linq;
   4      using System.Text;
   5      using System.Threading.Tasks;
   6
   7      namespace Chapter1Program1
   8      {
              0 references
   9            class Program
  10            {
                  0 references
  11                static void Main(string[] args)
  12                {
  13                    // display text
  14                    Console.WriteLine("Welcome to Agile!");
  15                    // pause program waiting for user to hit a key
  16                    Console.ReadKey();
  17                }
  18            }
  19      }
```

Figure 1.6 Your first C# program.

Finally, click on the little green "Start" button on the top (Figure 1.6) to run the program. The result is shown in Figure 1.7.

```
Welcome to Agile
_
```

Figure 1.7 A console window with the program running.

You have just used Visual Studio IDE to write your first application in C# and to run the program. You can now push the enter key to close the program.

1.3 Explanation for Your First Program

Refer to Figure 1.6, "Your First C# program", for this explanation.

Line 1 is called a directive, and it tells the computer that the program needs the System namespace, which someone has already developed. You can think of the System namespace as a book in a library, which someone has already written. Your program requires some instructions in that book.

Lines 2 to 5 are directives that are not used. They are greyed out. Feel free to delete them.

Line 6 is a blank line. It is not required. It is used for ease of reading.

Line 7 declares a namespace called Chapter1Program1. A namespace is just a container that includes groups of classes (as well as other stuff to be described later).

Lines 8 and 19 are a pair of braces that include all the content of this namespace. In this application, there is just one class, called Program, inside the namespace.

Line 9 declares a class named Program. Similar to a namespace, a class is a container that includes fields and methods (among other things).

Lines 10 and 18 are a pair of braces that include all the content of this class. In this application, the class contains just one method, called Main().

Line 11 declares a method named Main. A method contains all the program instructions. In this case, you have two instructions (Lines 14 and 16).

Line 12 and 17 are a pair of braces that include all instructions for the computer.

Line 13 is a comment (text for programmers, not for the computer). Comments begin with //. The computer will ignore any line which starts with //. Your program will run the same with or without comments, but writing comments may save a programmer's time when the application needs maintenance.

Line 14 tells the computer to display the text "Welcome to Agile" on the console screen. It uses a pre-developed class called Console (a class in the System namespace you imported in Line 1). The Console class has a method called WriteLine() that will display the message on the console. "Welcome to Agile" is a C# string literal and must be inside a pair of quotation marks.

Line 15 is another line of comment.

Line 16 uses the Console class's ReadKey() method, which will wait for the user to enter something from the keyboard. (You were asked to push the enter key after you ran the program to terminate it). The purpose of this line is to hold the execution of the statements until the user pushes any key on the keyboard. Without this line, the application would run the code and close the window so fast you wouldn't be able to see what happened on the screen.

You just created a program with C# by writing a few lines of code and using premade classes (Console) and methods (WriteLine() and ReadKey())!

Test Your Understanding 1.4

Namespace is a container that groups things, such as classes, together.
→A. True
B. False

Test Your Understanding 1.5

A class is a container that groups things, such as _____, together.
→A. methods
B. namespaces
C. instructions
D. statements

Test Your Understanding 1.6

A(n) _____ is a logical group of C# statements for a common objective.
A. namespace
B. class
C. method
D. instruction

Test Your Understanding 1.7

In the following statement, what is "Console"?
Console.WriteLine("Welcome to Agile!");
A. a namespace
B. a class
C. a method
D. a computer monitor

Test Your Understanding 1.8

In the following statement, what is "WriteLine"?
Console.WriteLine("Welcome to Agile!");
A. a namespace
B. a class
C. a method
D. a computer monitor

Programming Challenge 1.1

Add a line of code to the program right before Line 15 in Figure 1.6 so that, when the program runs, the console will make a beep sound.

Programming Challenge 1.2

Add a line of code to the program right before Line 13 in Figure 1.6 so that, when the program runs, the background color of the console will change to blue.

Programming Challenge 1.3

Add a line of code to the program right before Line 13 in Figure 1.6 so that, when the program runs, all the text in "Welcome to Agile" is red.

Programming Challenge 1.4

Add a line of code so that the title of the console window displays "Welcome", as shown in Figure 1.8

Figure 1.8 A console window with the "Welcome" title.

1.4 What Is Software Development?

There are several philosophies on software development. We will examine two major approaches. Let's use an example to explain the concepts.

Mr. Lincoln has been the owner of a small toy retailer since 1994. He worked in toy manufacturing for many years before being laid off when the company moved the whole manufacturing operation to China. He decided to use his experience with the toy industry and became a retailer that sold toys made in China. He was told that computers can increase his business's efficiency and effectiveness. One difficulty he has with his business is keeping track of inventory and the price of each product. He decided to buy a laptop and recently started using it. After a few days using the laptop, though, he decided that computers saved paper, but made little difference otherwise. Can you develop an efficient application to help Mr. Lincoln?

Mr. Lincoln's computer needs application software that can help him keep track of inventory and prices.

A small group of students from a local university taking a systems analysis and design course volunteered to help Mr. Lincoln.

They start by interviewing Mr. Lincoln about his business mission and strategy, business operations, budget, timeline, and scope for the software development. Following the Systems Development Life Cycle (SDLC) from their textbook, they are beginning the planning phase. In a couple of days, they turn in a business plan which includes all they can find out about the business and a feasibility study on the project. The students plan to develop an application with C# to handle the inventory with little cost to Mr. Lincoln.

The professor of the class and Mr. Lincoln approve the business plan based on the benefits and costs of the project, the manageable scope, and the timeline. The group then starts the analysis phase: determining the software requirements from Mr. Lincoln.

Mr. Lincoln wants something simple and easy to use. He wants to be able to update or enter new inventory whenever a new shipment from a supplier arrives. The application needs to be able to automatically update the inventory whenever a sale is made. He also wants to have the ability to quickly check the price for a certain toy. Finally, Mr. Lincoln wants to be able to have a print of his inventory on paper and a print of the receipt for customers. During the interview, the students ask many questions, such as the product return policy, issues regarding inventory lost or damage, and data about suppliers, products, and sales. They also want to know if Mr. Lincoln keeps a price update history. The students then write the analysis report outlining the detailed requirements from Mr. Lincoln and submit copies to the professor and Mr. Lincoln. This is the analysis phase of SDLC.

After the professor and Mr. Lincoln approve the requirements, the group begins the design phase. They draw a case diagram to show the interaction between the users and the system. It clearly defined what features the system will have and the boundary of the system. They have mock up screens for Mr. Lincoln to see if that is the user interface he wants. The specifications for all input and output forms are completed. Entity Relationship Diagrams for the business data are reviewed by the professor.

After the professor and Mr. Lincoln approve the design, the team starts to actually code. They use C# and make sure all code runs as expected. They also ask Mr. Lincoln to complete a user acceptance test to make sure he really likes the application. This is called the development phase of SDLC.

Both the team and Mr. Lincoln fully test the system and feel it is a good replacement for Mr. Lincoln's spreadsheet-based system. The team then publishes the application in Mr. Lincoln's working computer. The team also leaves a simple user manual, just in case Mr. Lincoln gets lost while using the new system. This is called the deploy phase of SDLC.

A few days later, the team meets with Mr. Lincoln and ask about his experience with the new system. Mr. Lincoln made a long list of things he wants to change. The team politely says they will discuss it with the professor and come back to Mr. Lincoln. Unfortunately, it's close to the end of the semester, and nobody wants to continue with Mr. Lincoln's change request, since the whole application may need to start all over again. They wish Mr. Lincoln told them earlier. This stage is often called maintenance, which can lead to a new round of SDLC.

Test Your Understanding 1.9

With SDLC, a feasibility study of the project is typically included in the _____ phase.
A. planning
B. analysis
C. design
D. development

Test Your Understanding 1.10

With SDLC, determining software requirements from the user(s) is typically included in the _____ phase.
A. planning
B. analysis
C. design
D. development

Test Your Understanding 1.11

With SDLC, actual coding and testing of a software project is typically done in the _____ phase.
A. planning

B. analysis
C. design
D. development

Test Your Understanding 1.12

With SDLC, drawing mock up screens for clients and developers is typically done in the _____ phase.
A. planning
B. analysis
C. design
D. development

Test Your Understanding 1.13

With SDLC, publishing the completed software project to the customer's computers is typically done in the _____ phase.
A. deploy
B. maintenance
C. design
D. development

Test Your Understanding 1.14

With SDLC, updating a currently used application is typically done in the _____ phase.
A. deploy
B. maintenance
C. design
D. development

1.5 Waterfall Approach

The team's work for the toy retailer is an example of the waterfall approach. This approach establishes well-structured phases that the developers can follow. At the end of each phase, the team produces one or more deliverables, such as the business plan and the system analysis report. There are also milestones to mark the end of each phase (usually the approval from the stakeholders). At the end of the deploy phase, the application is delivered to the customer as a whole, and the project can be closed. Figure 1.9 shows the sequence of phases in a typical waterfall approach.

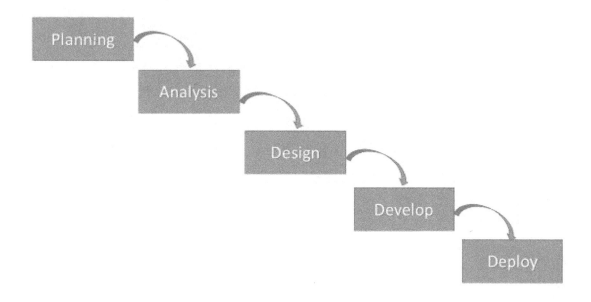

Figure 1.9 Traditional waterfall approach for software development.

Test Your Understanding 1.15

Stakeholders approving the business plan is an example of a project _____.
A. beginning point
B. closing point
C. milestone
D. deliverable

Test Your Understanding 1.16

For the waterfall approach, each phase must have one or more deliverables.
A. True
B. False

1.6 What's Wrong with the Waterfall?

The waterfall approach for systems development has been used for a long time and is still used by many businesses. However, over the years, professionals noted several problems.

The first major problem with the waterfall is the requirement for customers to know up-front what they want (Mikoluk, 2013). Customers usually have a general sense of what they want, but never a complete, detailed picture. As seen with Mr. Lincoln, many customers may know what they want at the beginning, but change their minds after seeing and running the application. By then, it is often too late for the development team to make any changes. In other words, customers won't see the finished application until it is done, which makes adjustments difficult. The Waterfall approach also assumes that all requirements have been specified in advance, which is unrealistic. That assumption, coupled with limited user involvement, reinforces the tendency of the waterfall model to lock in requirements too early, even after business conditions have changed.

The second problem has to do with the clear lines between roles in this approach. In other words, the waterfall method relies on specialists working together, which can be inefficient. System analysts do not know much about coding, and programmers may not care much about testing. A designer might plan something without knowing how difficult it is to code. As a result, it is neither realistic nor efficient to have such a team working on the same objectives. The best the team can do is cooperation. In cooperation, the role of customers was also narrowly defined (Kay, 2002). Users were often only involved in the requirements determination or analysis phases of the project. Quality assurance people also get paid according to how many bugs are found, so they are inclined towards more bugs in the product. What the team need is collaboration, not cooperation.

The third problem is that the waterfall makes it hard to backtrack. Once the next phase starts, the previous phase cannot be changed since analysts need to freeze the design at a particular point so programmers can begin to code. This becomes problematic when customers want to change with business conditions during the development process. Additionally, the amount of effort spent on implementing a specific design makes it difficult to change once it is developed (Valacich and George, 2017).

Test Your Understanding 1.17

One major problem with the waterfall is the requirement for customers to know how to program in at least one language.

A. True
B. False

Test Your Understanding 1.18

One major problem with waterfall is the clear lines between roles such as analyst, designer, and programmer.
A. True
B. False

Test Your Understanding 1.19

One major problem with the waterfall is the difficulty with working on an earlier phase once the project moves on the next phase.
A. True
B. False

Test Your Understanding 1.20

Which of the following is NOT a major problem of the waterfall approach for software development?
A. Locking in requirements too early.
B. Too much repeating work.
C. Clear lines between roles.
D. Once the next phase starts, the previous phase cannot be changed

1.7 What is the Agile Methodology?

The agile methodology is a different way to achieve the same goals as the waterfall methodology.

The agile approach breaks the project into smaller pieces and then adds the pieces together in an order similar to the waterfall phases. However, since the project is now divided into smaller pieces, phases are no longer clearly segregated, and pieces of the project can instead be completed concurrently as feasible. How does this simple change dramatically affect the success of software development?

As stated in Section 1.6, there are three major problems with the traditional waterfall approach. The first problem is that customers cannot predict everything they need before development starts. Agile, on the other hand, develops a small part of the software based on the known requirements in less time. Then the software is shown to the customers, who can give feedback and more requirements. By completing the software in small increments, customers are better able to visualize the final product and provide a more thorough list of requirements. With small pieces, there's also less documentation to work on.

The second problem concerns the clear lines between team roles, which make collaboration difficult. In waterfall, teams consist of specialists who focus solely on their own role. With agile, team members are expected to be familiar with the entire process, on top of having his or her own expertise. You can think of the team as a small business, where even the owner has multiple roles, such as procurement manager, customer service, and marketing manager. When necessary, an agile team can also seek help from a subject-matter expert (SME).

Finally, as stated in the third problem, it is difficult to go back and make adjustments in waterfall. Since the agile approach works in small pieces, fine tuning is incorporated along the way, and there is less of a need to "go back". Any changes that are needed will be reflected in the next 'pieces'.

Figure 1.10 shows such an approach. You should compare Figure 1.9 and 1.10 and see the differences between the two approaches.

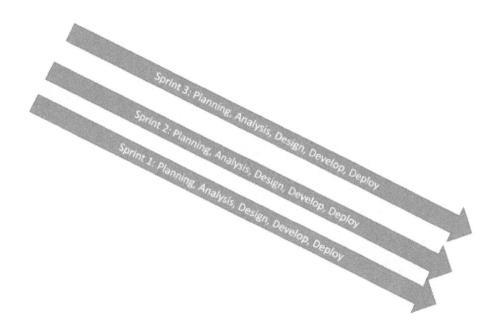

Figure 1.10 Agile approach to software development.

A sprint in agile is defined as the whole process of building one or more small "pieces" of the application. Every sprint has a deliverable. A deliverable can be any piece of functional software. Each sprint includes all planning, analysis, design, coding, testing, and delivering steps, but in a very different way than waterfall. You will see the differences throughout the book when you learn more about agile.

Test Your Understanding 1.21

How does agile solve the problem of locking in requirements too early?
A. Requirements are not necessary in agile.
B. Requirements are only needed at the end of each sprint.
C. Requirements can be added after the customers see how some features work.
D. Requirements are created by the development team.

Test Your Understanding 1.22

How does agile solve the problem of too clear lines between team roles?

A. Each member plays multiple roles.
B. Take away the lines.
C. Developing small pieces does not require more than one person.
D. All roles are played by subject matter experts (SME).

Test Your Understanding 1.23

How does agile solve the problem of "going back"?
A. In agile, each piece is so small that there is no need to go back.
B. Agile makes it impossible to go back.
C. Agile only allows one team member to go back if necessary.
D. Agile members can go back at any time.

Test Your Understanding 1.24

The agile approach has no deliverables.
A. True
B. False

Test Your Understanding 1.25

In agile, the process of working on each smaller increments of an application is called a _____.
A. method
B. sprint
C. development
D. task

1.8 Agile is an Umbrella Term

Throughout the years, different companies and developers have created their own methodologies to avoid the problems of the traditional waterfall, as you've learned in section 1.6. Eventually, these developers decided to have a meeting to exchange their ideas and philosophies. In 2001, seventeen of them held a meeting at Snowbird, Utah. They formed the Agile Alliance group, whose mission was to promote the agile software development approach. They summarized the common characteristics of their approach and came up with four values and twelve principles (http://agilemanifesto.org/), which they called the Agile Manifesto.

The methodologies the practitioners used before the meeting (some are still in use today) include Scrum, extreme programming, Kanban, lean software development, crystal methodology, Dynamic Systems Development Methodology (DSDM), and Feature-Driven Development (FDD). This book will focus on Scrum, the most popular of all, and also briefly mention extreme programming and Kanban along the way.

Test Your Understanding 1.26

Which of the following is not one of the agile methodologies?
A. Scrum
B. eXtreme Programming
C. Kanba
D. C#

1.9 What are the Four Values of Agile?

The four values actually involve eight values. The purpose of the other four values is to show the importance of the four on the left in Figure 1.11

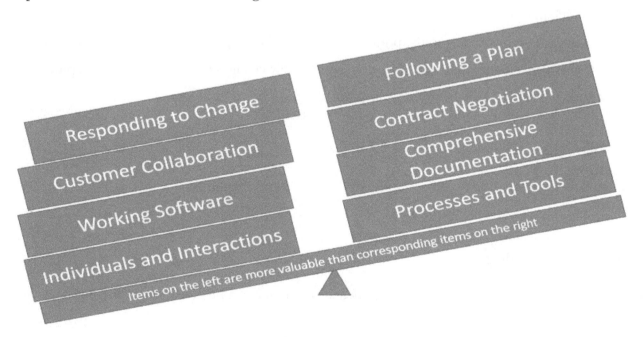

Figure 1.11 Four values of the Agile Manifesto

The first value, 'Individuals and Interactions', emphasizes the importance of the people, not the processes or the tools, that develop the software. It is equally important that the team work together through interaction and communication to reach their goal. This value suggests that people can choose their own way to develop software instead of following certain work procedures.

The second value, 'Working Software', stresses that the end product of the development is the software, not the documentation. Documentation is a helper, not the end result.

The third value, 'Customer Collaboration', highlights that customers and the development team have the same goal. The only way to achieve the goal is through collaboration. In the traditional approach, the customer requirements are usually documented in the contract and the team often wastes time negotiating the scope of the project.

The fourth value, 'Responding to Change', underlines the fact that change is not avoidable. While a plan is good, a plan is still based on a prediction of the future, which is often not accurate. In such a case, the plan needs to be updated. Continuous planning improves the chances of success. Change should be part of the plan. This allows the team to check the changes, get feedback and make revisions. Such practice delivers more valuable software for the customers. As shown in Figure 1.9, the traditional plan is made early in the project and can thus be a nightmare to follow. However, even though changes are unavoidable, agile does not support daily changes in the software development. In agile, change is typically made between sprints, not while a sprint is in progress.

Test Your Understanding 1.27

In agile, how things are done is more important than who does the things.
A. True
B. False

Test Your Understanding 1.28

In agile, teams do not need to write any documentation so time can be saved for coding.
A. True
B. False

Test Your Understanding 1.29

In agile, customers and the development team cooperate for the same goal.
A. True
B. False

Test Your Understanding 1.30

In agile, responding to change is more important than following the plan.
A. True
B. False

1.10 What are the Twelve Principles in Agile?

The complete list of the twelve principles is available at http://agilemanifesto.org/principles.html. In this section, we will summarize them in five points:

1. Working software should be delivered frequently instead of as one big software delivered at the end of the project. Using our C# example in this chapter, instead of completing the whole application at once, you would write the code that can display "Welcome to Agile" first. After you make this message display correctly, you add code to make the program beep. After you make the program beep, you add code to make the background blue. With this approach, if anything goes wrong, it is easy to identify and fix it. Also, if the customers want something different, it is easy to accommodate.

2. The purpose of software development is to meet customer requirements. We should allow customers room to change their mind. For example, when they see the background color is blue, they may want to make the font text color to be red for better contrast. The development team should have no difficulty adding that, even though the customer did not mention font color at the beginning. On the other hand, you should also work closely with the customer to cut costly changes that can be avoided.

3. The quality of the software depends on the development team. The team should be "self-organizing", meaning that they can work toward the common goal with great autonomy. The lines between the roles are blurred. Team members learn from each other. They work as a team, not as a sum of the individuals.

4. Continuous improvement is critical to the success of the team. They learn from their own experiences. What worked well? What didn't work? They learn from innovations in the field, and challenge themselves for better performance.

5. Simplicity can help one avoid many problems in software development and save money. Just make the software solve the business problems without the extra bells and whistles that the customers did not request.

Test Your Understanding 1.31

Frequent delivery of software allows better _____.
A. communication
B. rest for the team
C. customers
D. contract to be settled

Test Your Understanding 1.32

In agile, change requests from the customer are welcome.
A. True
B. False

Test Your Understanding 1.33

The agile team should be "self-organizing", meaning that they can work toward the common goal with great autonomy.
A. True
B. False

Test Your Understanding 1.34
The agile team should not be affected by the innovations in the field.
A. True
B. False

1.11 Chapter Summary

In this chapter, you learned that computers follow instructions written in a programming language. In C#, the statements are grouped into methods, methods are grouped into classes, and classes are grouped into namespace. You also learned how to use built-in classes and their methods to write your own statements.

Also in this chapter, you learned the phases in the traditional waterfall software development approach and compared it to the new agile approach. The chapter ended with a brief explanation of the Agile Manifesto.

1.12 References

Mikoluk, K. (2013), Agile Vs. Waterfall: Evaluating The Pros And Cons, Available at https://blog.udemy.com/agile-vs-waterfall/ accessed November 15, 2016.

Valacich, J. and George, J. (2017), Modern Systems Analysis and Design 8th Edition, Pearson, Boston.

1.13 Solutions to Programming Challenges

Programming Challenge 1.1

We need a method to make a beep sound. After you type in the class name and a period, all available methods will be displayed in "Intellisense." Also note that a method includes a pair of parentheses.

```
Program.cs*  +  ×
C# Chapter1Program1                      ▼  ⁂ Chapter1Program1.Program              ▼  ◐ₐ Main()
     1        using System;
     2      ⊟namespace Chapter1Program1
     3       {
     4      ⊟    class Program
     5           {
     6      ⊟        static void Main()
     7               {
     8                   // display the text
     9                   Console.WriteLine("Welcome to Agile");
    10                   Console.B
    11                   // progr  🔧 BackgroundColor        ▲ o hit a key
    12                   Console.  ◐ Beep                      │ void Console.Beep() (+ 1 overload)
    13               }            🔧 BufferHeight              │ Plays the sound of a beep through the console speaker.
    14           }                🔧 BufferWidth
    15       }                    ⚡ CancelKeyPress
    16                           🔧 CapsLock
                                  ◐ Clear
                                 🔧 CursorLeft
                                 🔧 CursorSize            ▼
```

Programming Challenge 1.2

```
Console.BackgroundColor = ConsoleColor.Blue;
```

Programming Challenge 1.3

```
Console.ForegroundColor = ConsoleColor.Red;
```

Programming Challenge 1.4

```
Console.Title = "Welcome";
```

1.14 Solutions to Test Your Understanding

1.1 A; 1.2 C; 1.3 C; 1.4A; 1.5 A; 1.6 C; 1.7 B; 1.8 C; 1.9 A; 1.10 B; 1.11 D; 1.12 C; 1.13 A; 1.14 B; 1.15 C; 1.16 A; 1.17 B; 1.18 A; 1.19A; 1.20 B; 1.21 C; 1.22 A; 1.23 A; 1.24 B; 1.25 B; 1.26 D; 1.27 B; 1.28 B; 1.29 B; 1.30 A; 1.31 A; 1.32 A; 1.33 A; 1.34 B

Chapter 2: C# Statements and Agile Characteristics

2.1 What Is a Variable?

As you learned in Chapter 1, to program is to write instructions inside the Main() method by following C# syntax. Sometimes, a value you need in the instruction may not be known at the time of programming or has changed over time. You will need a variable to hold that value thus allowing the value in the variable to be changeable. A variable is a reserved space in computer memory that is used to store things like values. It is a named memory location to temporarily store data.

In the last chapter, you displayed "Welcome to Agile" on the screen. What if you want to display "Welcome to C#"? You can write another line of statement. What if you want to display the user name but you don't know the name at the time of coding? You can write a code to display a variable value as a temporary substitute, and then let the user decide what value to put in that variable.

For example, if you want to calculate the square of a number that the user enters, you can use a variable, say x. Then you can calculate the square of x as x*x. The result value will depend on what value the user enters for x. This way your program is more powerful and flexible.

Test Your Understanding 2.1

In programming, a variable can be used to store some value for later use.
A. True
B. False

Example 2.1

Problem:

Write a program that asks the user for the name, and then displays the "Welcome to Agile, your name" message on the console screen.

Solution:

Start a new project in Visual Studio called Chapter2Program1. Save it to the Agile folder on your desktop (you followed the instructions and created the Agile folder in Chapter 1). With the default Program.cs open in the window, add instructions in the Main() method so that it looks like Figure 2.1.

```
Debug  ▼  Any CPU  ▼  ▶ Start ▼

Program.cs  ↔ ✕
C# Chapter2Program1                          ▼  Chapter2Program1.Program

1          using System;
2
3      □namespace Chapter2Program1
4       {
5      □    class Program
6            {
7      □        static void Main(string[] args)
8                {
9                    // prompt user for a name
10                   Console.WriteLine("Enter your name: ");
11                   // store the value in a variable
12                   string name = Console.ReadLine();
13                   // display the message
14                   Console.WriteLine("Welcome to Agile, " + name);
15                   Console.ReadKey();
16               }
17           }
18       }
```

Figure 2.1 Code for Example 2.1

Click on the green start button to run it. Type in your name when prompted and you should see "Welcome to Agile, your name". Push the enter key to close the program.

Variable naming rules:

A variable in C# can contain letters, numbers, and underscores only, and the first character cannot be a number. No spacing is allowed, and you cannot use the C# reserved key words, such as Main, or abstract.

Additionally, a variable name is case sensitive, e.g. 'name' and 'Name' are different.

Test Your Understanding 2.2

Which of the following is NOT a legal variable name for C#?
A. studentName
B. student_name
C. studentName1
D. 2studentName

Test Your Understanding 2.3

Variable names are case sensitive in C#, which means 'student' and 'Student' are treated as the same.
A. True
B. False

2.2 What Is Data Type?

Note that in the code example above, Figure 2.1, string (a data type) was added right before the variable 'name'. Using a data type helps the compiler reserve the right size of memory space for the variable value.

Other commonly used simple data types includes *int* (for storing whole numbers, such as 5 or 12), *double* (for storing floating point numbers, such as 3.14), and *decimal* (for storing floating point numbers with higher accuracy; you will use this type for money values). The data type *char* is used for single characters, and the data type *bool* is used to store a Boolean value, such as true or false.

A literal value, such as 3.14, will be treated as double data type. To make it as decimal data type, use 3.14m. The surfix indicates a decimal data type. See Programming Challenge 2.3 solution for an example.

One important thing to know about data type is its value range. For example, for *int*, the valid range of values is from -2,147,483,648 to 2,147,483,647. If you try to store a value out of that range, an error will occur. For a complete list of built-in data types, visit https://msdn.microsoft.com/en-us/library/ya5y69ds.aspx. Just click on the type name on the page to view more details.

Test Your Understanding 2.4

In C#, the *int* data type can be used to store any whole number.
A. True
B. False

Test Your Understanding 2.5

In C#, if you want to store the value of a student's letter grade (one of 'A', 'B', 'C', 'D', 'F', 'I', 'P'), what is the most appropriate data type?
A. int
B. double
C. char
D. string

Test Your Understanding 2.6

What is the difference between a double and a decimal data type in C#?
A. double works for integers.
B. decimal works for integers.
C. double has higher accuracy.
D. decimal has higher accuracy.

Test Your Understanding 2.7

If students take a course that can only receive the grade of pass or fail, what is the most appropriate data type for storing the grade?
A. double
B. decimal
C. char
D. bool

2.3 What is an Operator?

Computers are good at calculations, so you can use operators to add, subtract, multiply, and divide, etc., on numbers and variables. Let's see an example.

Example 2.2

Problem:

A bag holds 50 candies. The calorie information on the bag indicates that there are 25 servings in each bag and that a serving equals 100 calories. Write a program that lets the user enter the number of candies he or she ate and then display the number of total calories consumed.

Solution:

Start a new project in Visual Studio called Chapter2Program2. Save it to the Agile folder on your desktop (you followed the instructions and created the folder in Chapter 1). With the default Program.cs open in the window, change the Main() method so that it looks like Figure 2.2.

```
1      using System;
2
3      namespace Chapter2Program2
4      {
            0 references
5          class Program
6          {
                0 references
7              static void Main(string[] args)
8              {
9                  // use variables to hold values
10                 const int numberOfCandiesInBag = 50;
11                 const int servingsPerBag = 25;
12                 const int caloriesPerServing = 100;
13                 // find out how many candies per serving
14                 double candiesPerServing =
15                     numberOfCandiesInBag / servingsPerBag;
16                 // find out how many calories per candy
17                 double caloriesPerCandy =
18                     caloriesPerServing / candiesPerServing;
19                 // prompt user for number of candies he or she ate
20                 Console.WriteLine("How many candies did you eat?");
21                 // get the number from user and store it in a variable
22                 int candiesAte = int.Parse(Console.ReadLine());
23                 // calculate how many calories consumed
24                 double caloriesConsumed = candiesAte * caloriesPerCandy;
25                 // disply to user
26                 Console.WriteLine("You have consumed {0} calories.",
27                     caloriesConsumed);
28                 // pause the scren by waiting for user input
29                 Console.ReadKey();
30             }
31         }
32     }
```

Figure 2.2 Code for Example 2.2

Explanation:

Lines 14 and 15 can be in one line. It is broken here into two for a better screenshot. The "/" is a division operator used in C#.

Line 26 contains {0}, a place holder, which will be filled by the first (C# starts counting from 0, not 1) variable following the format string, which in this case is caloriesConsumed.

In lines 10 to 12, you can add the keyword *const* to make those variables constant variables. It means the value stored cannot be changed by statements later on. After adding the keyword, the three lines will look like this(you won't feel the difference in running the code, it is just a better practice):

```
const int numberOfCandiesInBag = 50;
const int servingsPerBage = 25;
const int caloriesPerServing = 100;
```

Test Your Understanding 2.8

What is the difference between the following two statements?
1) int numberOfCandiesInBag = 50;
2) const int numberOfCandiesInBag = 50;
A. 1) is a simpler statement without the keyword const and is thus recommended.
B. 2) will not allow later statements in the program to accidently change the value and is thus recommended.
C) 1) and 2) are the same.
D) 2) is incorrect.

Programming Challenge 2.1

Lynn's Pizza Restaurant needs an application to calculate the number of slices a pizza can be divided into. Your application should let the user enter the radius of the pizza in inches, then display how many slices this pizza can be cut assuming one slice is no less than 15 square inches. (Hint, the area of a whole pizza is calculated by Area $= \pi r^2$, where π is 3.14 and r is the radius.)

Programming Challenge 2.2

Replace 3.14 with a more accurate constant from C#, Math.PI, and make the number of slices a whole number. (Hint: Math.Floor(x) will return 7 if x = 7.6)

Another useful arithmetic operator is module, which is a way to calculate the remainder of an integer division.

Example 2.3

Problem:

Write a program that prints the minimum number of quarters, dimes, nickels, and pennies that a customer should get back as change. Ask the user for change amount, such as 1.23, or 0.54. Then the program should display the number of each type of coin needed.

Solution:

Start a new project in Visual Studio called Chapter2Program3. Save it to the Agile folder on your desktop (you followed the instructions and created the folder in Chapter 1). With the default Program.cs open in the window, change the Main() method so that it looks like the following:

```
1     using System;
2     namespace Chapter2Program3
3     {
4         class Program
5         {
6             static void Main(string[] args)
7             {
8                 // prompt user for amount of change and store in a variable
9                 Console.WriteLine("Enter change amount:");
10                decimal changeAmount = decimal.Parse(Console.ReadLine());
11                // make the amount into a whole number
12                int changeAmountInPennies = (int)(changeAmount * 100);
13                // calculate number of quarters needed
14                int numberOfQuarters = changeAmountInPennies / 25;
15                // calculate the remainder
16                int remainderAfterQuarter = changeAmountInPennies % 25;
17                // calculate number of dimes needed
18                int numberOfDimes = remainderAfterQuarter / 10;
19                // calculate the remainder
20                int remainderAfterDime = remainderAfterQuarter % 10;
21                // calculate number of pennies needed
22                int numberOfNickles = remainderAfterDime / 5;
23                // calculate remainder, this is the number of pennies
24                int remainderAfterNickle = remainderAfterDime % 5;
25                int numberOfPennies = remainderAfterNickle;
26                // display result
27                Console.WriteLine("Number of Quarters: {0}", numberOfQuarters);
28                Console.WriteLine("Number of Dimes: {0}", numberOfDimes);
29                Console.WriteLine("Number of Nickles: {0}", numberOfNickles);
30                Console.WriteLine("Number of Pennies: {0}", numberOfPennies);
31                Console.ReadKey();
32            }
33        }
34    }
35
```

Figure 2.3 Code for Example 2.3

Programming Challenge 2.3

Lynn's Pizza Restaurant also sells cookies. One cookie costs 10 cents. A dozen cookies cost $1. Any number of cookies less than a dozen costs 10 cents each. For example, 10 cookies would cost $1.00, 11 cookies would cost $1.10, 12 cookies would cost $1.00, 13 cookies would cost $1.10, and 30 cookies would cost $2.60. Write a program to ask the user for the number of cookies, then display the total cost.

Programming Challenge 2.4

Lynn's Pizza Restaurant needs a tip calculator for customers to calculate tips. The program will prompt the user to enter a purchase amount. Then the program will calculate and display tips at 15%, 18%, and 20%, as well as display the total cost of the meal including the tip. You should use const for those tip percentages instead of literal values. We will assume there is no state sales tax. A sample output looks like Figure 2.4:

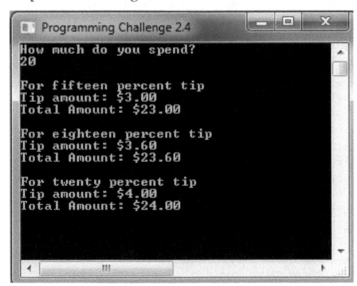

Figure 2.4 Programming Challenge 2.4 sample output.

2.4 Characteristics of Agile

Agile practice is very different from traditional practices. There are five differences (Ashmore and Runyan, 2014):

1. Self-Organizing Teams

The traditional software development team has a project manager. The agile team has no project managers and is trusted by the management to operate successfully. Unlike a non-agile project team, an agile team establishes its own norms and rules. Team members have a lot of autonomy regarding their work.

Furthermore, instead of being assigned tasks to work on, team members get to select their tasks and how they want to do it. (Of course, these tasks are to accomplish the user stories provided by customers through the product owner.)

2. Continuous Improvement (solving your own problems)

In agile, each team member is responsible for ensuring that problems from a past or current iteration are not carried into the next. This creates a higher level of engagement from employees, because they will be responsible for any problems that arise.

In the past, team members relied on the project manager to resolve issues. In agile, the team is empowered and encouraged to seek out answers and improvements on their own.

3. Quick customer feedback

In a non-agile environment, the team won't deliver the software to the customer until the whole application is finished. This makes customer feedback difficult, considering the relatively long process. Furthermore, the final delivered application might be very different from what the customers envisioned at the start. Customers may also have changed their minds during the process.

In an agile environment, the team will demo the completed part of the software to the customer at the end of each sprint. A sprint only delivers an increment instead of the whole application. Agile utilizes small increments and more frequent feedback. As a result, when all pieces are put together, the software is more likely to meet the customer's vision.

4. Blurring the lines between roles in a team

Before agile, a software development team would have needed to hire specialists, such as analysts, programmers, and testers. In the agile setting, there are no C# programmers or testers; everyone is a team member. That is one reason why this book merges agile and C#: so by the end of this book, you will be able to practice agile with actual software development as an agile team member.

For example, in a traditional setting, a tester would not start working until the programmer completed the code, and the programmer would consider his or her work completed once the tested began. This often resulted in poor quality and subsequent finger pointing.

In an agile setting, where the programmers and testers collaborate to develop high quality software, only the end result matters. It is the whole team's responsibility to complete the software.

Agile teams usually include members with a broad skill set, such as analyzing, designing, programming, and testing. However, members are expected to participate in any role the team needs them to fill (Highsmith, 2002). This situation differs from the traditional waterfall structured environments, where teams often specialize according to function (e.g., analyst, designer, developer, tester) (Nerur et al, 2005). As a result, team members often have different responsibilities and titles across organizations.

In agile, systems analysts might perform programming and design responsibilities in their job even though it is not required of them. A developer might also perform programming, testing, and configuration management tasks that would be fragmented in a traditional setting.

5. Physical Workspace

The physical workspace in agile is different by the removal of cubical borders. The close proximity of team members allows easy and quick communication. This increases efficiency and can also improve the quality of the software, though some employees may feel a lack of privacy.

Test Your Understanding 2.9

In an agile team, members get to pick any task they want, even their own project from another company.
A. True
B. False

Test Your Understanding 2.10

In an agile team, there is no project manager role.
A. True
B. False

Test Your Understanding 2.11

In an agile team, compared to a traditional team, members get more frequent feedback.
A. True
B. False

Test Your Understanding 2.12

In an agile team, every member is equally capable at analyzing, designing, programming, and testing.
A. True
B. False

2.5 Why Agile Does Not Work All the Time for All Companies

Agile methodologies have increased software development success rates, improved software quality, and shortened the time it takes to reach market. It also enhances the motivation and productivity of the development team (Ghani et al., 2015, Rigby et. Al, 2016). What makes agile so successful?

Research on agile success (Sammon et al., 2009) started with ten factors and narrowed it down to four. These factors make the difference between success and failure (Dhir et al, 2019).

1. Organizational and Reporting Structure

In agile, work cannot be done alone. Whether success is achieved can be determined by organizational structure. An example of a successful structure is organic organization (Bennis, 1969), which is identified as having little job specialisation, few layers of management, decentralized decision making, and little direct supervision. These attributes allow flexibility and adaptability. An organization with organic structure is more likely to succeed with an agile approach.

2. Organizational Process

Much like how the organizational structure can affect agile success, the organizational process does too. The organizational process includes work environment standards that support organizational learning and process improvement by promoting sharing of the best practices learned across the organization (CMMI Product Team, 2007).

Due to different mindsets, a process such as the Capability Maturity Model, which is used to develop and refine an organization's software development process, may conflict with agile methodologies.

3. Documentation Requirements

Even though agile methodologies do not prohibit documentation, the more time the team spend on documentation, the less time they have to work on the software. Thus, the documentation requirements affect the success of an agile approach. The documentation should be kept at a minimal.

4. Layout of Workspace

Similar to item 5 of the agile characteristics discussed earlier in this chapter, layout of workspace is an important factor for the success of agile. While both an open plan office and a clustered cubicle approach are popular among IT companies, some experts in agile suggest some kind of isolated room for a single team. This allows members to chat freely and promotes communication and teamwork. Furthermore, this layout facilitates bonding without the interference of other teams (Muldoon, 2014).

Test Your Understanding 2.13

Which of the following is not a success factor for agile approach?
A. Team cellphone usage policy
B. Organizational and reporting structure
C. Organizational process
D. Documentation requirement

Test Your Understanding 2.14

An organization with organic structure is more likely to succeed with an agile approach.
A. True
B. False

For organizations that are new to agile software development, Cooke (2011) suggested five steps to success.

1. Choosing the right kick-off point. Many developers switched to agile because they were struggling with their current project. That may not be the right time. They should take a step back and try to understand agile better, get prepared, and then start. The best time to start agile is when the team is well prepared and ready for the agile approach.

2. Choosing the right project(s). For example, a project that is not burdened by any legacy systems or pre-existing management techniques might be a good 'first' agile project. The success of the first project is often critical for persuading management to adopt the agile approach.

3. Choosing the right methodologies and practices. As you will learn in the next section, there is more than one flavor of agile approach. The organization culture, team member backgrounds, and the project can all affect the appropriate methodologies and practices. You can combine different types of agile or even create one for yourself as long as you follow the agile principles.

4. Choosing the right method of introduction. Like many other practices, agile can be introduced top down or bottom up. With top down, you have the organizational mandate on using agile. This approach is usually easier for the team because the champions are often the top managements. With bottom up, you might be the champion.

5. Avoiding common traps which include undermining agile principles, insufficient communication and training, and using agile as a doctrine instead of a tool.

Test Your Understanding 2.15

For organizations that are new to agile software development, Cooke (2011) suggested five steps to success. Which of the following is NOT a step?
A. Choosing the right kick-off point
B. Choosing the right project(s)
C. Choosing the right project manager(s)
D. Choosing the right methodologies and practices

2.6 Types of Agile.

As you have learned in chapter one, agile is an umbrella term. In this section, you will discover a few major types of agile methodologies, namely scrum, extreme programming (XP), and Kanban. In the rest of the book, we may not always differentiate which type of agile is used.

2.6.1 Scrum

Scrum is a lightweight framework. It is simple to understand, but difficult to master. Unlike the traditional waterfall project management methodology that requires comprehensive documentation and heavyweight processes, scrum is lightweight and focuses on working software and team collaborations. Its organization, roles, events, and artifacts are easy to understand, but applying it to the field can be difficult.

Teams are free to develop different processes and techniques as long as they follow the rules, roles, and events of the scrum framework. As a result, there are many flavors of scrum.

The term 'scrum' was introduced by Takeuchi and Nonaka (1986) regarding business operations. They explained that projects using small cross-functional teams historically produced the best results. They compared these high performance teams to "scrum" formations in Rugby.

Scrum for software development was introduced in 1993 by Jeff Sutherland at Easel Corporation, using the study by Takeuchi and Nonaka (1986) as the basis for adopting their analogy as the name of the process for software development.

Scrum is based on the empirical process control theory (Viscardi, 2013). According to this theory, knowledge comes from experience, and decisions should be made according to what is known. It has three foundations (Crisan et al., 2015): transparency, inspection, and adaptation.

The transparency foundation indicates that the software developed should be visible to all stakeholders. Inspection specifies that experienced inspectors should check the scrum artifacts against the team goals on a regular basis. Adaptation suggests that if any differences are found in the inspection, the team should adjust the related processes or materials.

Scrum includes three roles, five events, and three artifacts. These will be covered in more detail in later chapters. Scrum is the most popular agile practice. This book mostly follows the scrum practice.

Test Your Understanding 2.16

The _____ foundation indicates that the software developed should be visible to all stakeholders.
A. Transparency
B. Collaboration
C. Inspection
D. Adaptation

Test Your Understanding 2.17

Scrum is _____ and focuses on working software and team _____.
A. lightweight, collaborations
B. heavyweight, collaborations
C. lightweight, corporations
D. heavyweight, corporations

Test Your Understanding 2.18

Scrum is a very complicated framework. It is difficult to learn but easy to master.
A. True
B. False

Test Your Understanding 2.19

Which of the following is NOT a scrum foundation?
A. Transparency
B. Collaboration
C. Inspection
D. Adaptation

Test Your Understanding 2.20

Scrum framework includes ___ roles, ___ events, and ___ artifacts.

A. 1, 2, 3
B. 3, 4, 5
C. 3, 2, 5
D. 3, 5, 3

2.6.2 Extreme Programming (XP)

Extreme Programming (XP) is another popular agile methodology (Amir et al, 2013). It requires that customers be part of the team. It uses a process similar to sprint called 'iterations'. It has the following four characteristics: continuous integration, user story, team velocity, and pair programming.

1. Continuous Integration: XP requires frequent release and very short development cycles. A cycle can be as short as one day. The idea of small iterations is the same as scrum's sprints, save for the length, which is one day compared to a sprint's two weeks.

2. User story: These are software requirements written in a specific format. It is short and can fit on an index card. The story serves as a conversation between the customer and the development team, not a specification from the customer for the team. An example of a user story is "As the owner of the company, I want to be able to check the up-to-date inventory data so that I can better manage my business". Based on this user story, the development team may ask if the owner wants to see one inventory item at a time by search or display all inventory at once. This starts the conversation and helps both customers and the team understand the requirements better. The size of a user story is measured by story points. Every user story has story points estimated by the development team to reflect how much effort is needed to complete the story.

3. Team Velocity: This is a way to measure how much work can be done in a certain amount of time by the team. This velocity is measured by the number of story points. For example, a team doesn't usually say how many stories they can complete in one iteration, but rather how many story points they can complete. It is done this way because not all user stories require the same amount of effort.

4. Pair Programming: This is used to help produce high quality software. In this technique, two team members take turns controlling the keyboard. While one member types, the other one watches and brainstorms. This technique works well when a programmer and a tester form a team. Code does not need to be completed then inspected. The code is checked as it is typed into the program.

Test Your Understanding 2.21

Frequent release and very short development cycles describes which characteristic of extreme programming?
A. continuous integration
B. pair programming
C. user story
D. team velocity

Test Your Understanding 2.22

Which characteristic of extreme programming is kind of similar to a scrum sprint?
A. continuous integration
B. pair programming
C. user story
D. team velocity

Test Your Understanding 2.23

Which of the following is NOT a characteristic of XP?
A. continuous integration
B. transparency
C. user story
D. team velocity

Test Your Understanding 2.24

Two team members working on the same task to increase product quality is which characteristic of extreme programming?
A. continuous integration
B. user story
C. team velocity
D. pair programming

2.6.3 Kanban

The Kanban methodology has three characteristics (Ashmore and Runyan, 2014).

1. Visualizing the workflow: A Kanban board is used to map the workflow in columns based on the status of a task. The task is often written on sticky notes and posted on a column in the board or simply on the wall.

2. Limits on works in progress (WIP): It is easy to see how many tasks are in each stage (a stage = a column on the Kanban board). With a limited number of tasks in each stage, it is easy to identify the bottlenecks.

Limiting works in progress is good for quality, a topic in chapter 7. With a limited number of tasks, the team can focus on solving any problems they may have without working overtime. So, when the number of bugs accumulate, the whole team would stop writing new code and focus on fixing the bugs.

3. Measure the lead time: With smooth flow of work, it is easy to discover the time it takes to complete a task from start to finish.

Test Your Understanding 2.25

Which of the following is NOT a characteristic of Kanban methodology?
A. continuous integration
B. visualizing the workflow
C. limiting works in progress
D. measuring the lead time

Test Your Understanding 2.26

In Kanban methodology, it is easy to identify the bottleneck because the number of tasks in progress is limited.
A. True
B. False

2. 7 Chapter Summary

In this chapter, you learned how to write C# statements by using variables and operators. You should follow rules for naming variables and select the appropriate data type for each variable. There are many more data types and operators used in C# that can be looked up online.

You also learned the characteristics of agile and the success factors. You should know there is more than just one type of agile. In fact, there are many hybrid types, such as scrumban, which combines both scrum and Kanban.

2.8 References

Amir, M., Khan, K., Khan, A., and Khan, M. (2013), An Appraisal of Agile Software Development Process, International Journal of Advanced Science & Technology 58, pp. 57-86.

Ashmore, S. and Runyan, K. (2014), Introduction to Agile Methods 1st Edition, Boston, Addison-Wesley Professional.

Bennis, W. (1969). The Mature of Organizational Development. Reading, Mass,: Addison-Wesley.

CMMI Product Team, (2007), CMMI® for Acquisition, Version 1.2, Carnegie Mellon University, Software Engineering Institute, http://chrguibert.free.fr/cmmi12/cmmi-acq/text/index.php, Visited Nov. 18, 2016.

Crisan, E., Belieiu, I. and Ilies, . (2015), The Place of Agile in Management Science - A Literature Review, Managerial Challenges of the Contemporary Society, 8: 1, pp. 62-65.

Dhir, S., Kumar, D., & Singh, V. B. (2019). Success and failure factors that impact on project implementation using agile software development methodology. In Software Engineering (pp. 647-654). Springer, Singapore.

Ghani, I., Bello, M., and Bagiwa, I. (2015) Survey-based Analysis of Agile adoption on performance of IT organization, Journal of Korean Society for Internet Information, October, 16(5), 87-92.

Highsmith, J. (2002). Agile software development ecosystems. Boston: Addison Wesley.

Muldoon, N. (2014), Building an Ideal Agile Team Workspace, http://www.velocitycounts.com/2014/01/building-best-agile-team-workspace/, Visited November 18, 2016Nerur, S., Mahapatra, R. K., & Mangalaraj, G. (2005). Challenges of migrating to agile methodologies. Communications of the ACM, 48(5), 72-78.

Rigby, D. K., Sutherland, J., and Takeuchi, H. (2016), Embracing Agile, Harvard Business Review 94(5), 40-50.

Sammon, D, McAvoy, J, and Owens, I. (2009), Agile Teams: Reflective Debate and Shared Understanding, Proceedings of the European Conference on Information Management & Evaluation, p535-543.

Sutherland, Jeff. (1995) Business Object Design and Implementation. 10th Annual Conference on Object-Oriented Programming Systems, Languages, and Applications Addendum to the Proceedings. *OOPS Messenger 6:4*:170-175. ACM/SIGPLAN October.

Takeuchi, H.; Nonaka, I. (1986), The new new product development game, Harvard Business Review. Jan/Feb, Vol. 64 Issue 1, p137-146

Viscardi, S. (2013), The Professional ScrumMaster's Handbook: A Collection of Tips, Tricks, and War Stories to Help THE Professional ScrumMaster Break the Chains of Traditional Organizatin and Management, Packt Publishing, Birmingham, U.K.

2.9 Solutions to Programming Challenges

Programming Challenge 2.1

```csharp
static void Main(string[] args)
{
    // prompt user for the radius of the pizza
    Console.WriteLine("What is the radius of the pizza in inches?");
    // store the value in a variable
    double radius = double.Parse(Console.ReadLine());
    // calculate the area of the pizza
    double area = 3.14 * radius * radius;
    // calculate number of slices, each slice should be 15 square inches
    double numberOfSlice = area / 15;
    // display the result to the user
```

```
        Console.WriteLine("The pizza can be cut into {0} slices", numberOfSlice);
        Console.ReadKey();

    }
```

Programming Challenge 2.2

Same as the 2.1, with the lines replace as

```
        //double area = 3.14 * radius * radius;
        double area = Math.PI * radius * radius;
```

And

```
        //Console.WriteLine("The pizza can be cut into {0} slices", numberOfSlice);
        Console.WriteLine("The pizza can be cut into {0} slices",
Math.Floor(numberOfSlice));
```

Programming Challenge 2.3

```
        static void Main(string[] args)
        {
        // prompt user for number of cookies bought
        Console.WriteLine("How many cookies do you buy?");
        // store the value in a variable
        int numberOfCookies = int.Parse(Console.ReadLine());
        // divide the number by 12 to find how many dozens
        int dozens = numberOfCookies / 12;
        // module to find the remainder
        int dozenRemainder = numberOfCookies % 12;
        // calcualte the cost, m converts a double value to decimal value
        decimal totalCost = dozens * 1.0m + dozenRemainder * 0.1m;
        // display the total cost
        Console.WriteLine("The total cost for {0} cookies is {1:C}", numberOfCookies,
totalCost);
        Console.ReadKey();
    }
```

2.10 Solutions to Test Your Understanding

2.1 A; 2.2 D; 2.3 B; 2.4 B; 2.5 C; 2.6 D; 2.7 D; 2.8 B; 2.9 B; 2.10 A; 2.11 A; 2.12 B; 2.13 A; 2.14 A; 2.15 C; 2.16 A; 2.17 A; 2.18 B; 2.19 B; 2.20 D; 2.21 A; 2.22 A; 2.23 B; 2.24 D; 2.25 A; 2.26 A.

Chapter 3 C# Flow Control and Agile Roles

3.1 Recognizing syntax for conditional statements

3.2 Recognizing syntax for repeating statements

3.3 Implementing conditional and repeating statements in problem solving

3.4 Recalling types of roles in agile

3.5 Recognizing major responsibilities for each role in agile

3.1 Conditional Statements

Computers follow instructions. So far, you've seen the instructions are sequential; one statement is executed after the other in the order they are presented. This limits the use of the program, since they cannot change the execution sequence. The real world often requires different statements to be executed when certain conditions are true. For example, if a student's score is 90 or higher, you may want to display a congratulations message, while other students receive the typical response.

3.1.1 If Statements

C# has conditional statements, including the 'if' statement. If a condition is true, a block of statements will be executed. If not, different block of statements will be executed. The if statement allows you to check more than one condition with the "else if" statement.

Example 3.1

Problem:

Write an application that asks the user for a numeric score of a student's test. If the score is 90 or higher, display the message "Congratulations". Otherwise, display "Thank you for using the system."

Solution:

Start a new project in Visual Studio called Chapter3Program1. Save it to the Agile folder on your desktop. With the default Program.cs open in the code view, change the body of the Main() method so that it looks like the following:

```
1       using System;
2
3       namespace Chapter3Program1
4       {
            0 references
5           class Program
6           {
                0 references
7               static void Main(string[] args)
8               {
9                   // prompt user for a score
10                  Console.WriteLine("Enter a student score:");
11                  // store the score in a variable
12                  double score = double.Parse(Console.ReadLine());
13                  // check to see if the score is 90 or higher
14                  if(score >= 90)
15                  {
16                      Console.WriteLine("Congratulations!");
17                  }
18                  else
19                      Console.WriteLine("Thanks for using the system.");
20                  Console.ReadKey();
21              }
22          }
23      }
```
Figure 3.1 Code for Example 3.1

After typing all the code, click the green start button to run it. Type in a number less than 90 and push enter to see "Thanks for using the system" on the console screen. Push enter to end the program.

Click the green start button again. This time, type in a number greater than or equal to 90 and push enter to see "Congratulations!" on the console screen. Push enter to end the program.

Explanation:

Lines 14 through 20 are an if statement, which includes a condition on Line 14. If the condition is evaluated to be true, the statements inside the braces block (only Line 16 in this case) are executed. Otherwise, the statements inside the else block will be executed (in this case, Line 20).

The 'else' part of an if statement is optional.

You can also add an "else if" statement to the if statement. For example, if you wanted to display "Good job!" for students who scored between 80 and 90, you can add the following instructions between Lines 17 and 18:

```
else if (score >= 80)
{
    Console.WriteLine("Good job!");
}
```

An if statement usually includes all statements you want to execute under certain conditions in a pair of braces as shown in Lines 15 and 17. However, some people prefer no braces when there is only one line of statement in the block as shown in Line 19. You are encouraged to use braces so that the code is more legible.

Test Your Understanding 3.1

C# allows your program to execute a block of statements only when certain conditions are true.
A. True
B. False

Test Your Understanding 3.2

When a condition is true, an if statement can execute a block of statements inside a pair of parentheses like this: ( ). If there is only one statement in the block, the pair of parentheses is optional.
A. True
B. False

Programming Challenge 3.1

Write an application that prompts the user to enter two integers. Then display a menu like this:
Enter 1, 2, or 3
1. Addition
2. Multiplication
3. Exit

After the user enters the selection (1, 2, or 3), the application will display the result based on user inputs and the menu selection.

3.1.2 Switch Statements

The switch statement is similar to the if statement in that it executes a block of code based on certain conditions. However, there are two major differences: 1) switch can test for multiple values of a test variable in one go, and thus executes faster than an if statement. For example, if you want to display the month in letters when given a number (ex. - February in response to '2'), a switch statement is faster than an if statement. 2) a switch test is limited to discrete values. It cannot test a simple condition like x>5.

Example 3.2

Problem:

Write an application that prompts the user for an integer between 1 and 12. The application will display the corresponding name of the month in letters.

Solution:

Start a new project in Visual Studio called Chapter3Program2. Save it to the Agile folder on your desktop. With the default Program.cs open in the code view, change the body of the Main() method so that it looks like Figures 3.2 and 3.3.

```
1      using System;
2
3     □namespace Chapter3Program2
4       {
            0 references
5       □    class Program
6            {
                0 references
7       □        static void Main(string[] args)
8                {
9                    // prompt user for an integer between 1 and 12
10                   Console.WriteLine("Enter a number between 1 and 12:");
11                   // store the number
12                   int numericMonth = int.Parse(Console.ReadLine());
13                   // Declare a variable to store wordMonth;
14                   string wordMonth = "";
15      □            switch (numericMonth)
16                   {
17                       case 1:
18                           wordMonth = "January";
19                           break;
20                       case 2:
21                           wordMonth = "February";
22                           break;
23                       case 3:
24                           wordMonth = "March";
25                           break;
26                       case 4:
27                           wordMonth = "April";
28                           break;
29                       case 5:
30                           wordMonth = "May";
31                           break;
```

Figure 3.2 Code for Example 3.2 Part 1.

```
32              case 6:
33                  wordMonth = "June";
34                  break;
35              case 7:
36                  wordMonth = "July";
37                  break;
38              case 8:
39                  wordMonth = "August";
40                  break;
41              case 9:
42                  wordMonth = "September";
43                  break;
44              case 10:
45                  wordMonth = "October";
46                  break;
47              case 11:
48                  wordMonth = "November";
49                  break;
50              case 12:
51                  wordMonth = "December";
52                  break;
53              default:
54                  wordMonth = "That's not a number between 1 and 12.";
55                  break;
56          }
57          Console.WriteLine(wordMonth);
58          Console.ReadKey();
59      }
60  }
61 }
```

Figure 3.3 Code for Example 3.2 Part 2.

Explanation:

Lines 15 to 56 are a switch statement. They include switch and case .

Line 15 is a switch value; if the value matches one of the twelve cases, the block of statements inside that case will be executed. If there is no match, the default section will be executed.

Line 19 is a 'break' statement. It is used to terminate a case block. If the 'break' keyword is missing, the execution will continue to the next block.

Test Your Understanding 3.3

A switch statement is used to execute a block of statements enclosed by a pair of braces {} when a certain value is matched.

A. True.
B. False.

Test Your Understanding 3.4

One major difference between an if statement and a switch statement is that the former is limited to discrete values.
A. True.
B. False.

Programming Challenge 3.2

Write an application to prompt the user to enter an integer between 1 and 10, and have the application display the English word for that number. For example, if the user enters 5, the application will display 'five'.

3.2 Repeating Statements

In last chapter, you learned how to tell computers what to do in sequential order. In last section, you learned how to tell computers to execute only certain instructions when a condition is true. With conditional statements, you can branch the route of execution in more than one way. In many situations, sequential and conditional statements may not be enough. In Example 3.1, you might have noticed that it is inconvenient to run the program only once. How about modifying the code so that the program can run until the user wants to quit?

3.2.1 The 'while' Loop

A while loop will check a condition. If the condition is true, it will execute the statements in the block. If the condition is false, it will quit the loop. This is similar to the if statement. The difference is that an if statement only checks the condition once and executes the statement block once. The while loop will check the condition repeatedly and thus may execute the block of statements multiple times until the condition is false. It is very important that you are able to change the condition inside the execution block. Otherwise, the loop may go on infinitely.

Example 3.3

Problem:

Modify Example 3.1 so that it will prompt the user for a score and display the message based on the score. The application can repeat the prompt and display the message until the user enters a negative score.

Solution:

Start a new project in Visual Studio called Chapter3WhileLoop. Save it to the Agile folder on your desktop. With the default Program.cs open in the code view, change the Main() method so that it looks like Figure 3.4.

```
1       using System;
2
3       namespace Chapter3WhileLoop
4       {
5           class Program
6           {
7               static void Main(string[] args)
8               {
9                   // prompt the user for a score
10                  Console.WriteLine("Enter student score(-1 to terminate):");
11                  // store the score in a vavriable
12                  double score = double.Parse(Console.ReadLine());
13                  // start a loop
14                  while(score >= 0)
15                  {
16                      // check if see if 90 or higher
17                      if (score >= 90)
18                      {
19                          Console.WriteLine("Congratulations!");
20                      }
21                      else
22                      {
23                          Console.WriteLine("Thanks for using the system.");
24                      }
25                      // prompt the user for a score
26                      Console.WriteLine("Enter student score(-1 to terminate):");
27                      score = double.Parse(Console.ReadLine());
28                  }
29                  Console.ReadKey();
30              }
31          }
32      }
```

Figure 3.4 Code for Example 3.3.

After typing all the code, click on the green start button to run it. Type in a score less than 90 and see the message "Thanks for using the system." on the console screen. Next type in a score greater than 90 and see the message "Congratulations!" on the console screen. You can repeat this as many times as you want. To end the program, enter any negative number. Push enter to end the program.

Explanation:

Line 14 starts a while loop, which is almost the same as an if statement. The while loop will check the condition again after the block of statements (from Lines 15 to 28) is executed versus an if statement, which will not check the condition again after the execution of the block.

What happens if you comment out (add // before a statement to make the compiler ignore it) Lines 26 and 27 in Figure 3.4? If the score entered is more than 90, you will see "Congratulations!" running forever because that's what it is supposed to do according to the code. That is called an infinite loop and is usually not what we want. So, make sure your code contains statements that can change the condition in the while statement (like the statement in Line 27, which can be negative) and thus make it possible to terminate the program.

Test Your Understanding 3.5

C# allows your program to repeat running a block of statements as long as certain conditions are true.
A. True
B. False

Test Your Understanding 3.6

When programming, you should avoid writing statements inside a loop that can change the conditions of the loop.
A. True
B. False

3.2.2 The 'for' Loop

Before learning the 'for' loop, you need to know a type of variable called 'array' that often works with loops. In the last chapter, you learned how to use variables to hold values for calculation or display. One variable can hold only one value at a time. This can be inconvenient. For example, if a class had 10 students, and you wanted to calculate the average score for a quiz, you would need to declare 10 variables, one for each student. An array could make this process much more efficient.

What is an array? An array is just a variable that can hold many values of the same type. Each is differentiated by its index.

Let's see an example that uses an array.

Example 3.4

Problem:

A class has 10 students. The school needs an application that can ask the user to enter each student's numeric score for a test, and then display the average, highest score, and lowest score.

Solution:

Start a new project in Visual Studio called Chapter3AverageScore. Save it to the Agile folder on your desktop. With the default Program.cs open in the code view, change the Main() method so that it looks like the following:

```
1     using System;
2     using System.Linq;
3
4     namespace Chapter3AverageScore
5     {
6         class Program
7         {
8             static void Main(string[] args)
9             {
10                // declare an array that can hold 10 int scores
11                int[] scores = new int[10];
12                // using a loop to prompt user for input, one score at a time
13                for(int count = 0; count < scores.Length; count++)
14                {
15                    Console.WriteLine("Enter a score:");
16                    scores[count] = int.Parse(Console.ReadLine());
17                }
18                // Display the statistics
19                Console.WriteLine("Average: {0}", scores.Average());
20                Console.WriteLine("Highest: {0}", scores.Max());
21                Console.WriteLine("Lowest:  {0}", scores.Min());
22                Console.ReadKey();
23            }
24        }
25    }
26
```

Figure 3.5 Code for Example 3.4

After typing all the code, click on the green start button to run it. Type in a total of 10 whole numbers, each between 0 and 100. Push the enter after each number. After all 10 scores are entered, you should see the statistics on the console screen. Push enter to end the program.

Explanation:

Line 2 adds a new directive. This is because the array class for statistical methods are in the System.Linq namespace.

Line 11 declares an array that can hold 10 int values. Note the difference between 'declare' and 'initialize': a simple type variable verses an array.

int score = 90;

int[] scores = new int[10];

The array variable scores holds 10 integers, which are all 0s. The new keyword indicates that this is a reference type. The reference type means that the actual 10 integers are not stored in the array variable 'scores'. Only the memory address of the 10 integers are stored in the variable 'scores'. You will learn more about reference type in Chapter 5 when you learn classes and object oriented programming.

If you don't want to initialize an array other than the default value, you can do it like this:

int[] scores = new int[4]{3, 5, 8, 10};

The number "4" in the square bracket is optional.

To access a value in an array, use the index. For example, you can print the first value in the above array:

System.out.println(scores[0]);

Note the array index starts counting from zero, not one.

Similarly, if you want to change the value of the second score in the array, use the following statement:

scores[1] = 12;

This will change the second value from 5 to 12.

Be very careful of the index value, since they start counting from zero. In the above example, if you use scores[4], you will receive an array out of bound error because there is no element with the index of 4.

Lines 13 to 17 are a loop that repeats the statements between Lines 15 and 16 ten times. An int variable "count" is used to control the number of repetitions. Here are the steps for the loop:

Step 1. Count = 0

Step 2. Check to see if this is true: count < scores.Length; if true, continue to Step 3. If false, exit the loop. The Length property of an array holds the number of elements in the array.

Step 3. Execute the statements in the block enclosed with braces. In this case, Lines 15 and 16 are executed.

Step 4. The count++ statement increases the value in count by 1.

Step 5. Go back to Step 2 above.

This process will continue until the condition in Step 2 is no longer true.

Line 19 prints the result string with a place holder {0}. This place holder will display the average score when printed, instead of "{0}". The console uses the first argument following the print string, which is the values in scores.Average(). C#, like many other programming languages, starts counting from 0, not 1, so {0} indicates the first argument.

Lines 20 and 21 are similar to Line 19.

Test Your Understanding 3.7

When you know how many repeating loops you need in the code, the 'for' loop is a good choice.
A. True
B. False

Test Your Understanding 3.8

When you don't know how many repeating loops you need in the code, the 'while' loop is a good choice.
A. True
B. False

Test Your Understanding 3.9

An array is a variable that can hold many values of the same type. Each is differentiated by its index.
A. True.
B. False.

Test Your Understanding 3.10

What can be stored in the following variable "scores"?
int[] scores;
A. the memory address of an int array.
B. the memory address of an array.
C. a group of 10 ints.
D. an int array

Test Your Understanding 3.11

What does a reference type of variable do?
A. hold an integer value only
B. hold a floating-point value only
C. hold a string value only
D. hold memory address only

Test Your Understanding 3.12

Given the following statement about a C# array:
int[] scores = new int[4]{3, 5, 8, 10};

What will be printed on the console screen with the following statement?
Console.WriteLine(scores[3]);
A. 3
B. 5
C. 8
D. 10

Test Your Understanding 3.13

Given the following statement about a C# array:
int[] scores = new int[4]{3, 5, 8, 10};

What will be printed on the console screen with the following statement?
Console.WriteLine(scores[4]);
A. 3
B. 4
C. 5
D. Out of bound error.

Programming Challenge 3.3
Write an application that can ask the user for the inches of rainfall for each month in a year. Then the application will display the average, highest, and lowest inches of rainfall for the year.

Programming Challenge 3.4
Modify Programming Challenge 3.3 to also display the total rainfall for the year.

Example 3.5

Problem:
A class has 10 students. The school needs an application that can ask the user to enter each student's numeric test score and then display the number of As (score between 90 and 100 inclusive), number of Bs (score between 80 and 89), number of Cs (score between 70 and 79), number of Ds (score between 60 and 69) , and number of Fs (score under 60).

Solution:

Start a new project in Visual Studio called Chapter3ClassStatistics. Save it to the Agile folder on your desktop. With the default Program.cs open in the code view window, change the Main() method so that it looks like the following:

```csharp
static void Main(string[] args)
{
    // crete an int array that can hold 10 student scores
    int[] scores = new int[10];
    // using a loop to prompt user for score, one at a time
    for (int count = 0; count < scores.Length; count++)
    {
        Console.WriteLine("Enter a score:");
        scores[count] = int.Parse(Console.ReadLine());
    }
    // variables to hold number of As, Bs, Cs, Ds, and Fs
    int numberOfA = 0;
    int numberOfB = 0;
    int numberOfC = 0;
    int numberOfD = 0;
    int numberOfF = 0;
    // using a loop to check each score to find letter grade
    for (int count =0; count < scores.Length; count++)
    {
        if (scores[count] >= 90)
            numberOfA++;
        else if (scores[count] >= 80)
            numberOfB++;
        else if (scores[count] >= 70)
            numberOfC++;
        else if (scores[count] >= 60)
            numberOfD++;
        else
            numberOfF++;
    }
    // Display the result
    Console.WriteLine("Number of As: {0}", numberOfA);
    Console.WriteLine("Number of Bs: {0}", numberOfB);
    Console.WriteLine("Number of Cs: {0}", numberOfC);
    Console.WriteLine("Number of Ds: {0}", numberOfD);
    Console.WriteLine("Number of Fs: {0}", numberOfF);
    Console.ReadKey();
}
```

Programming Challenge 3.5

Body Mass Index (BMI) is used to determine weight status.

BMI value	Weight Status
Below 18.5 (<18.5)	Under Weight
Between 18.5 and 25 (>=18.5 and < 25)	Normal Weight
Between 25 and 30 (>=25 and < 30)	Overweight
30 or more (>=30)	Obese

A class has 15 students. The school needs an application that can let the user enter each student's BMI and display the number of students in each weight status and the class average BMI value.

3.3 Logical Operators

Logical operators evaluate two Boolean expressions (except for the NOT operator) and return with true or false. In this section, you will learn these operators: AND, OR, and NOT.

The AND operator, represented by &&, only returns true when both operands are true. The OR operator, represented by | |, returns true when at least one of the operands is true. Unlike the AND and OR operators, which work on two operands, the NOT operator has a single operand. The NOT operator, represented by !, returns true when the operand is false and returns false when the operand is true.

Example 3.6

Problem:
This problem is similar to Example 3.3. Create a program that will ask the user for a test score. If the score is 90 or higher, display "Congratulations!" on the console screen. Otherwise, display "Thank you for using the system" on the console screen. This process will continue until the user enters a negative score or a score above 100. (The difference from Example 3.3 is that, in this problem, the message is only displayed when the score is in the range of 0 to 100.)

Solution:

The application code is almost identical to that of Example 3.3. Just change Line 14 of Figure 3.4 (shown below)

```
while(score >= 0)
```

to

```
while(score >= 0 && score <= 100 )
```

&& is a logical AND operator, which requires both the (score >= 0) and (score <= 100) operands to be true to execute the statements in the block.

Test Your Understanding 3.14

Logical operators such as &&, ||, and ! can only be used in the conditional expression in the repeating statement, such as 'while'.
A. True
B. False

Test Your Understanding 3.15

Logical operators allow the application to handle more complex conditional statements.
A. True
B. False

Test Your Understanding 3.16

What is the value of the following logical expression?
(5>3) && (3>5)
A. True
B. False

Test Your Understanding 3.17

What is the value of the following logical expression?
(5>3) || (3>5)
A. True
B. False

Test Your Understanding 3.18

What is the value of the following logical expression?
!(5>3)
A. True.
B. False.

Test Your Understanding 3.19

What is the correct way to test if x is 3 or 4?
A. x = 3 || 4
B. x == 3 || 4
C. x = 3 || x = 4
D. x == 3 || x == 4

Programming Challenge 3.6
Write an application that can display a horizontal bar chart.

The application should prompt the user to enter a whole number between 1 and 50. Then the application will display that number of asterisks on the console screen. For example, if the user enters 9, it will display *********.

The application should continue to prompt the user for a whole number and display that number of asterisks, only terminating when a zero, negative number, or a number larger than 50 is entered.

Programing Challenge 3.7
Write an application that will display whole numbers from 1 to 30 consecutively in 30 lines. If a number is divisible by 2, display "TT" instead of the number. If a number is divisible by 3, display "TTT" instead of the number. If a number is divisible by both 2 and 3, display "TTTTTT" instead of the number. The first 10 lines will look like this:
1
TT
TTT
TT
5
TTTTTT
7
TT
TTT
TT

3.4 Agile Roles

You learned in chapter one that the Agile Manifesto values individuals and interaction more than the process and tools. You also learned that agile blurs the lines between different roles in the traditional development team (ex. - programmers can also be involved in design, analysis, and testing). However, agile does have three distinct roles. This section will describe these three roles: product owner, scrum master, and team members.

3.4.1 Product Owner

As you learned in chapter one, one major issue of the Waterfall approach was the lack of user involvement. The product owner fills part of this gap. A product owner is typically a business manager who works on the development team. The product owner may not know much about programming or testing, but they play the critical role of gathering business requirements for the development team.

The product owner owns the software and can represent the customers who are paying for the project. The product owner must work with the scrum team on a daily basis. When a team member has a question about the requirements, he or she can just ask the product owner without having to leave the room. This enhances communication between the developer and the business.

The product owner's primary jobs are writing up the requirements (called user stories; will be discussed in Chapter 5) with the scrum master (discussed later in this chapter) and prioritizing the requirements with other business managers according to the business values the user story provides.

It is important to note that the product owner is not just a business user. The product owner is the champion or sponsor of the project and has the authority to make decisions for the project, particularly decisions regarding whether a feature is done and can be released (Pichler, 2010).

The product owner is usually a single person, not a committee, so the time it takes to reach an agreement is reduced.

The product owner plays a critical role in the success of the project. He or she directs the product vision and goals and decides what the business values are. There are six characteristics of a good product owner (Pham and Pham. 2012; the authors listed seven, but we think the last characteristic belongs to the scrum master):

1. Deep knowledge of the product being developed.

2. Good at meeting stakeholder's expectations, even with conflicting priorities.

3. Able to gather requirements that achieve the product vision and goals.

4. Be fully available to actively engage with the team at all times.

5. A good organizer who can handle issues on both business and technological sides.

6. A good communicator who can express the requirements from the business to the development team effectively and send frequent feedback to the development team.

Test Your Understanding 3.20

How many product owners are in a typical agile team?
A. 1
B. 2
C. 3
D. 4

Test Your Understanding 3.21

The product owner must be a good programmer at minimum.
A. True
B. False

Test Your Understanding 3.22

The product owner is critical to the success of the development team, but does not write a single line of code.
A. True
B. False

Test Your Understanding 3.23

Which of the following is a characteristic of a good product owner?

A. Leadership skills
B. A skilled programmer
C. Deep knowledge of the product being developed
D. Be available to actively engage with the team at least once a day

Test Your Understanding 3.24

Which of the following is a characteristic of a good product owner?
A. Good project manager
B. Deep knowledge of programming language being used
C. Good organizer who can handle business issues
D. Good communicator between the business and the team

3.4.2 Scrum Master

The scrum master has two major responsibilities. One is to ensure team productivity and the other is to monitor project progress by facilitating all scrum meetings and communicating between the team and the business (Resnick et al., 2011, Viscardi, 2013).

To ensure team productivity, the scrum master works as a facilitator and motivator of the development team (Jongerius, et al., 2014). He or she ensures that the team functions as smoothly as possible, whether that is making sure meetings are on time, or that a sick team member is accounted for. Scrum masters should try their best to keep team moral high and remove any obstacles. If the music from next door is too loud, or too many external meetings are requested from the company, the scrum master will be responsible for talking to the people next door, or communicating with the company manager. Because the scrum master manages the team by servicing them, they are often referred to as the "servant leader" (Liden et al., 2014).

To monitor the project's progress, the scrum master facilitates all meetings, such as daily scrum meetings, which function to uncover issues and make adjustments to overcome those issues. He or she makes sure that everyone knows what the goal is, is kept up to date on the progress of the project, and collaborates to achieve that goal. Additionally, the scrum master often decides team size. A scrum master may prefer fewer members if they believe additional members will not increase productivity.

The scrum master also acts as a liaison between the team and the clients. Even though the product owner can communicate directly with the development team, the scrum master is usually the first to learn of any major changes from the business side (ex. - major feature changes, budget cuts).

The scrum master also educates and coaches the team on agile (Measey and Radtac, 2015). This includes visualizing team goals and championing the implementation of new technical practices. The team buy-in to the agile approach is critical to success.

Finally, the scrum master makes sure that the team follows agile principles effectively (Cooke, 2010). This includes, but is not limited to, accounting for meeting attendance and ensuring that only the high priority items from the product backlog are selected for the sprint backlog.

Test Your Understanding 3.25

The scrum master is like a project manager for the team.
A. True
B. False

Test Your Understanding 3.26

Servant leader is a term used to describe the _____.
A. product owner
B. scrum master
C. team members
D. none of the above

Test Your Understanding 3.27

What are the two major responsibilities of a scrum master?
A. to ensure team productivity and manage the project
B. to ensure team productivity and monitor project progress
C. to monitor project progress and manage the project
D. to manage the project and help the team in any technical problems

Test Your Understanding 3.28

In an agile team, who serves as a communicator between the business and the development team?
A. scrum master
B. product owner
C. both scrum master and product owner
D. neither scrum master nor product owner

3.4.3 Team Members

Team members are people who actually develop software. How they work determines the quality, scope, budget and schedule of the project. The first step towards teamwork is ensuring trust and transparency between members. This is typically stated in the team working agreement (Payton, 2015).

The agreement should be created via a discussion between team members and the scrum master. The objective is to have a positive and productive experience. The agreement should be written and posted in an easy to see place. It will serve as reference throughout the project.

Team size is typically around five to nine people. This magic range may have originated from a classic publication by Miller (1956) describing limits to how much information human beings can keep in working memory. This range was accepted by the Scrum Guide (2016). Too many members may make collaboration difficult, while too few members can create gaps in skill sets necessary to deliver the software. Do note that there have been cases where three or four member teams are successful.

There are five characteristics that an agile team member should have (Cooke, 2012):

1. Multi-skilled: An agile team blurs the lines between traditional roles. Every member needs to be comfortable working in roles they are not used to.

2. Open-minded and flexible: This characteristic ensures that members are not only able to do work outside their expertise, but are willing to do it.

3. Highly communicative: Interactivity is one of the four values stated in the Agile Manifesto. Idea sharing, pair programming, and collaboration all require excellent communication skills.

4. Self-motivated: A self-motivated person can work both as a team player as well as an individual. Agile encourages individual members to decide how he/she wants to work, and what to work on beyond what is assigned by the manager.

5. Holistic thinker: A member in an agile team should be able to appreciate both the technical and business contexts of the product.

Agile methodology favors a set up where all team members are physically located in the same place, as explained in Chapter 2. Then is it possible for a virtual team to succeed? The answer is yes, as long as team dynamic and collaboration can be established (Crowder and Friess, 2015). Ideally, the team will meet at the beginning of the project and regularly during the project as budget permits.

Test Your Understanding 3.29

For a virtual agile team to succeed, the team must establish _____.
A. team dynamic
B. collaboration
C. both A and B
D none of above

Test Your Understanding 3.30

Agile team members have different responsibilities, e.g. analysis, coding.
A. True
B. False

Test Your Understanding 3.31

Which of the following is NOT a characteristic of an agile team member?
A. Multi-skilled
B. Highly communicative
C. Self-motivated
D. Atomistic thinker

Test Your Understanding 3.32

Which of the following is NOT an agile role?

A. Project manager
B. Product owner
C. Scrum master
D. Team members

Test Your Understanding 3.33

The normal size for an agile team is _____ people.
A. three to five
B. five to nine
C. nine to eleven
D. more than eleven

Test Your Understanding 3.34

The _____ is the person who makes sure that the team follows the agile principles effectively.
A. product owner
B. scrum master
C. team member
D. product owner and scrum master

3.5 Chapter Summary

In this chapter, you learned how to selectively execute a block of statements based on certain conditions. You also learned how to repeat a block of statements either a pre-defined number of times or as long as certain conditions are true. You can solve most problems with just these three constructions: sequence, conditional, and repetition. You will use these constructions for the rest of the book.

In the agile sections of this chapter, you learned the three roles of agile: product owner, scrum master, and team members. These distinct roles work in collaboration toward the project objectives.

3.6 References

Cooke, J. L. (2010). Agile Principles Unleashed : Proven Approaches for Achieving Real Productivity in Any Organisation. Ely: IT Governance Publishing. Cambridgeshire, UK

Cooke, J. L. , 2012, Everything You Want to Know About Agile: How to Get Agile Results in a Less-Than-Agile Organization. Ely: IT Governance Publishing. Cambridgeshire, UK

Crowder, J. A and Friess, S. 2015, Agile Project Management: Managing for Success, Springer.

Jongerius, P., Offermans, A., Vanhouche, A. Sanwikarja, P., and Geel, J.V. 2014, Get Agile: Scrum for UX, design and development, BIS Publishers, Amsterdam.

Liden, R. C., Wayne, S. J., Liao, C., and Meuser, J. D. 2014, Servant Leadership and Serving Culture: Influence on Individual and Unit Performance, Academy of Management Journal, Oct, 57:5, p 1434-1452.

Measey, P. and Radtac, 2015, Agile Foundations -- Principles, Practices and Frameworks, BCS, Swindon, UK.

Miller, G. A. 1956, The Magic Number Seven, Plus or Minus Two: Some Limits on Our Capacity for Processing Information, Psychological Review, 63, p. 81-97.

Payton, T. 2015, How to create agile team working agreement, Visited November 19, 2016, https://www.scrumalliance.org/community/articles/2015/march/how-to-create-agile-team-working-agreements

Pham, A. and Pham, P. 2012, Scrum in Action: Agile Software Project Management and Development, Course PTR, Boston, MA.

Pichler, Roman. 2010. Agile product management with Scrum: Creating products that customers love. Boston: Addison-Wesley.

Resnick, S., De la Maza, M., Bjork, A., 2011, Professional Scrum with Team Foundation Server 2010, Wrong Guides Series, Wrox, Indianapolis, IN.

Schwaber, K. and Sutherland, J. 2016, The Scrum Guide, available at www.scrumguides.org Visited November 19, 2016.

Viscardi, S. 2013, The Professional ScrumMaster's Handbook: A Collection of Tips, Tricks, and War Stories to Help THE Professional ScrumMaster Break the Chains of Traditional Organizatin and Management, Packt Publishing, Birmingham, U.K.

3.7 Solutions to Programming Challenges

Programming Challenge 3.1

```csharp
static void Main(string[] args)
{
    // prompt user for first integer
    Console.WriteLine("Enter first integer: ");
    // store the integer in a variable
    int firstInteger = int.Parse(Console.ReadLine());
    // prompt user for second integer
    Console.WriteLine("Enter second integer: ");
    // store the integer in a variable
    int secondInteger = int.Parse(Console.ReadLine());
    // display menu
    Console.WriteLine("Enter 1, 2, or 3");
    Console.WriteLine("1. Addition");
    Console.WriteLine("2. Multiplication");
    Console.WriteLine("3. Exit");
    int selection = int.Parse(Console.ReadLine());
    // if 1 is entered
    if (selection == 1)
    {
        Console.WriteLine(firstInteger + secondInteger);
    }
    else if (selection == 2)
    {
        Console.WriteLine(firstInteger * secondInteger);
    }
    // if 3 is entered, let the program terminate
    // no need to write any code
    // hold the console screen
    Console.ReadKey();
}
```

Programming Challenge 3.3

```csharp
static void Main(string[] args)
{
    // declare an int array of 12 elements
    int[] rainFall = new int[12];
    // using loop to prompt user for rain fall amount, one at a time
    for (int count = 0; count < rainFall.Length; count++)
    {
        Console.WriteLine("Enter a rainfall amount:");
        rainFall[count] = int.Parse(Console.ReadLine());
    }
    // Display the statistics
    Console.WriteLine("Average: {0}", rainFall.Average());
    Console.WriteLine("Highest: {0}", rainFall.Max());
```

```
        Console.WriteLine("Lowest:   {0}", rainFall.Min());
        Console.ReadKey();
    }
```

Programming Challenge 3.4
Add the following line right before Console.ReadKey();

```
        Console.WriteLine("Total:    {0}", rainFall.Sum());
```

Programming Challenge 3.5 (hint: add one line of code to display the class BMI average.)

```
    static void Main(string[] args)
    {
        // create an array that can hold 15 student's BMI
        double[] bmi = new double[15];
        // using a loop to prompt user for bmi, one at a time
        for(int count = 0; count < bmi.Length; count++)
        {
            Console.WriteLine("Enter a BMI:");
            bmi[count] = double.Parse(Console.ReadLine());
        }
        // variables to hold number of students in each weight status
        int numberOfUnderWeight = 0;
        int numberOfNormalWeight = 0;
        int numberOfOverWeight = 0;
        int numberOfObese = 0;
        // using a loop to compare each bmi to find the category
        for (int count =0; count < bmi.Length; count++)
        {
            if (bmi[count] < 18.5)
                numberOfUnderWeight++;
            else if (bmi[count] < 25)
                numberOfNormalWeight++;
            else if (bmi[count] < 30)
                numberOfOverWeight++;
            else
                numberOfObese++;
        }
        // display the result
        Console.WriteLine("Number of under weight:  {0}", numberOfUnderWeight);
        Console.WriteLine("Number of normal weight: {0}", numberOfNormalWeight);
        Console.WriteLine("Number of over weight:   {0}", numberOfOverWeight);
        Console.WriteLine("Number of obese:         {0}", numberOfObese);
        Console.ReadKey();
    }
```

Programming Challenge 3.6

```
    static void Main(string[] args)
    {
        // prompt user for a whole number
        Console.WriteLine("Enter a number between 1 and 50:");
```

```csharp
// store the number in a variable
int number = int.Parse(Console.ReadLine());
// use a loop to make sure the number is valid
while (number >= 1 && number <= 50)
{
    // use a nested loop to display the asterisks
    for (int i = 0; i < number; i++)
    {
        Console.Write("*");
    }
    Console.WriteLine();
    // prompt user for another number
    Console.WriteLine("Enter a number between 1 and 50:");
    number = int.Parse(Console.ReadLine());
}
Console.ReadKey();
}
```

3.8 Solutions to Test Your Understanding

3.1 A; 3.2 B; 3.3 B; 3.4 B; 3.5 A; 3.6 B; 3.7 A; 3.8 A; 3.9 A; 3.10 A; 3.11 D; 3.12 D; 3.13 D; 3.14 B; 3.15 A; 3.16 B; 3.17 A; 3.18 B; 3.19 D; 3.20 A; 3.21 B; 3.22 A; 3.23 C; 3.24 D; 3.25 B; 3.26 B; 3.27 B; 3.28 C; 3.29 C; 3.30 B; 3.31 D; 3.32 A; 3.33 B; 3.34 B;

Chapter 4: C# Methods and Agile Events

4.1 A Method is a Logical Group of Statements

When you give instructions to computers, you write statements by following C# syntax. Applications often have thousands of lines of statements, if not millions. You need a better way to organize these statements. One way is by grouping them into methods.

Statements that accomplish the same task can be grouped into a method. Suppose you would like every line of message displayed in the console to have a blank line before and after the text, with a line of asterisks to separate the messages. You can code this with or without utilizing a method, as we will demonstrate in the next two examples.

Example 4.1

Problem:
Write an application to display the line of text: "C# is fun." Insert a blank line before and after the text and add a line of asterisks after the blank line.

Solution:

Create a new project. Inside the default Main() method of the program class, add the statements so they resemble the following:

```
static void Main(string[] args)
{
    Console.WriteLine();
    Console.WriteLine("C# is fun.");
    Console.WriteLine();
    Console.WriteLine("*************************");
    Console.ReadKey();
}
```

Example 4.2

Problem:
Write an application to display the line of text: "C# is fun." Insert a blank line before and after the text and add a line of asterisks after the blank line. This time, use a method.

Solution:

You can either create a new project or modify Example 4.1 so that the Program.cs resembles Figure 4.1 below:

```
1     using System;
2
3     namespace Chapter4DisplayTextMethod
4     {
5         class Program
6         {
7             static void Main(string[] args)
8             {
9                 DisplayText();
10                Console.ReadKey();
11            }
12            // DisplayText method
13            static void DisplayText()
14            {
15                Console.WriteLine();
16                Console.WriteLine("C# is fun.");
17                Console.WriteLine();
18                Console.WriteLine("**********************");
19            }
20        }
21    }
22
```

Figure 4.1 Code for Example 4.2

Explanation:

Lines 13 to 19 define a method named DisplayText(). The keyword, static, is a modifier. It makes the DisplayText() method static. Not all methods have to be static; this method has to be static because it will be used in the Main() method, which is static. The rule is that a static method, such as the Main() method, can only call other static methods, such as the DisplayText() method.

On Line 13, void is a keyword for the return type. In this example, it does not return anything, so 'void' is used. DisplayText is the method name. You can name your own method anything you'd like. Just follow the same rules as for naming variables. Conventionally, the first letter of every word in a method name is capitalized (ex. - DisplayStudentName()).This style of function name is called Pascal case.

You cannot skip the ( ) after the method name. It is called the parameter list. A parameter list is used to input any values to be used in the method. In this example, the method does not need anything, so the parameter list is blank. However, the parameter list must still be there.

All statements between Lines 14 and 19 are part of the method body. The method body should be inside a pair of braces {}. These statements are executed to accomplish the common goal of the method.

Line 9 inside the Main() method calls the DisplayText() method, which displays the message. One common error for beginners is having a method but never calling the method. The statements inside a method will not be executed automatically except in the Main() method. The method call triggers the statements in the method to be executed. Figure 4.2 summarizes the different components of a method in C#.

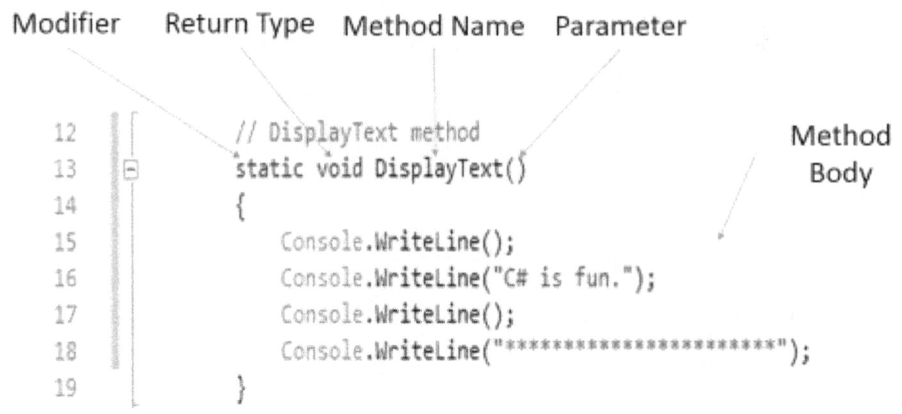

Modifier   Return Type   Method Name   Parameter

```
12          // DisplayText method                              Method
13          static void DisplayText()                          Body
14          {
15              Console.WriteLine();
16              Console.WriteLine("C# is fun.");
17              Console.WriteLine();
18              Console.WriteLine("************************");
19          }
```

Figure 4.2 Components of a method

Test Your Understanding 4.1
A method is a logical group of statements with a common goal.
A. True
B. False

Test Your Understanding 4.2
Which of the following is NOT a component of a method?
A. method variable
B. method modifier
C. method return type
D. method name

Test Your Understanding 4.3
Which of the following is NOT a component of a method?
A. method modifier
B. method return type
C. method goal
D. parameter list

Test Your Understanding 4.4
What is the parameter in a method?
A. a pair of parentheses
B. value(s) to be used in the method from outside of the method
C. the border of the method
D. an optional value of the method

Test Your Understanding 4.5

What happens if you write a method and do not call it?

A. an error

B. a compiler error

C. statements inside the method will not execute

D. statements inside the method can only execute once

4.2 A Method can have Parameters

You learned in the previous section that a method is a logical group of statements for a common objective. A method can also work on one or more values from outside the method. These values are called parameters of the method.

Example 4.3

Problem:

Modify the Example 4.2 DisplayText() method so that it can display different messages (not just "C# is fun") according to the parameter value passed in from outside.

Analysis:

The original method DisplayText() in Example 4.2 did not get any input (parameter is blank), so it can only display what is written in it. If you allow the method to receive some inputs (arguments), then it will be able to display the inputs. For example, if the user wants to display "Agile is more fun", you don't need to change the method. Just pass the message when calling the method. This is demonstrated in Line 10 of Figure 4.3.

Solution:

Update Example 4.2 so that the Program class looks like Figure 4.3.

```
1      using System;
2
3      namespace Chapter4DisplayTextWithParameter
4      {
5          class Program
6          {
7              static void Main(string[] args)
8              {
9                  // call the DisplayText method and passing a text.
10                 DisplayText("Agile is more fun.");
11                 Console.ReadKey();
12             }
13             // DisplayText method
14             static void DisplayText(string message)
15             {
16                 Console.WriteLine();
17                 Console.WriteLine(message);
18                 Console.WriteLine();
19                 Console.WriteLine("**********************");
20             }
21         }
22     }
23
```

Figure 4.3 Code for Example 4.3

Explanation:

Line 14 of Figure 4.3 is different from Line 13 of Figure 4.1. This time, the parameter is no longer blank. It has a string variable called a message. This means if you want to use/call this method, you have to provide a string value as an argument.

Line 17 in the method body of Figure 4.3 is also different from Line 16 of Figure 4.1. Instead of displaying "C# is fun." on the console screen, it will display any string value passed in by the caller.

Line 10 is calling the DisplayText() method. Note that it is different from the method call in the earlier example where you didn't pass an argument to the method. This time, you have to provide a string value, e.g. "Agile is more fun."

The value(s) a method expects are often called the parameter(s), and the value(s) passed in to the method are often called argument(s). In the example, "message" is a parameter and "Agile is more fun" is an argument.

Test Your Understanding 4.6

The variable that shows in the method header is often called a(n) _____.
A. parameter
B. argument
C. agile
D. C#

Test Your Understanding 4.7

The value that is passed to a method is often called a(n) _____.
A. parameter
B. argument
C. agile
D. C#

Test Your Understanding 4.8

A method may accept zero or more values to work on.
A. True
B. False

Programming Challenge 4.1
Write an application that asks the user for where he or she graduated, and then display a message that says that the school is a great school. For example, if the user enters "Oxford University", the display will be "Oxford University is a great school". The display should be accomplished by a method called DisplayText that accepts one argument and returns no value.

4.3 A Method can Return a Value

So far, your methods do not return anything, as represented by the "void" keyword in the method header. A method often returns a value after the method's work.

Example 4.4

Problem:
Write a method named Plus() that will accept two whole numbers and return the sum of the two values. Demonstrate the Plus() method by calling it from inside the Main() method.

Solution:

```
1        using System;
2
3        namespace Chapter4ReturnValue
4        {
5            class Program
6            {
7                static void Main(string[] args)
8                {
9                    // create two int variables with values
10                   int a = 3;
11                   int b = 5;
12                   // call the Plus() method and store the return value in total
13                   int total = Plus(a, b);
14                   // display the result
15                   Console.WriteLine("The sum of {0} and {1} is {2}", a, b, total);
16                   Console.ReadKey();
17               }
18               // Plus() method
19               static int Plus(int x, int y)
20               {
21                   int sum;
22                   sum = x + y;
23                   return sum;
24               }
25           }
26       }
```

Figure 4.4 Code for Example 4.4

Explanation:

Line 19 is the header line of the Plus() method. The return type for the Plus() method is not void; it is int. This indicates that the Plus() method will return an int value. The parameter list for this line contains two variables. This means the Plus() method will accept two int values. As a result, this method will accept two input values of int type and return one value of int type.

Line 23 includes a keyword "return", which returns a value that matches the return type declared in the Plus() method header.

Line 13 in the Main() method calls the Plus method. Note it passes two int values because Line 19 requires two int values. The values must match in number and type (int). The sequence also matters.

In line 15, the variables after the formatting string (a. b, total) will fill in the string's corresponding place holders ({0}, {1}, {2}) when displayed on the console screen.

Test Your Understanding 4.9
A method must have a "return" keyword inside the method body.
A. True
B. False

Test Your Understanding 4.10
A method returned value inside the method body must match the return type in the method header.
A. True
B. False

Test Your Understanding 4.11
A method may return one or many values or references by using multiple return statements.
A. True
B. False

Programming Challenge 4.2

Write a method named Multiply() that will accept two whole numbers and return the multiplication product of the two values. Demonstrate the Multiply() method by calling it from inside the Main() method.

4.4 A Method Can Return More Than One Value

A method can only return one value by using the return statement. If you want a method to return two or more values, you can use the "out" parameter modifier.

Example 4.5

Problem:
Write a method named Divide() that will accept two whole numbers and return the quotient and the remainder of these two values. Demonstrate the Divide() method by calling it from inside the Main() method.

Solution:
Start a new project called Chapter4OutModifier. Type the code as shown in Figure 4.5.

```
1        using System;
2
3        namespace Chapter4OutModifier
4        {
5            class Program
6            {
7                static void Main(string[] args)
8                {
9                    // create three int variables
10                   int a = 11;
11                   int b = 5;
12                   int remainder;
13                   // call the Divide() method and store the return value in quotient
14                   int quotient = Divide(a, b, out remainder);
15                   // display the result
16                   Console.WriteLine("{0} divided by {1} is {2} with remainder of {3}",
17                       a, b, quotient, remainder);
18                   Console.ReadKey();
19               }
20               // Divide() method
21               static int Divide(int x, int y, out int r)
22               {
23                   int q;
24                   q = x / y;
25                   r = x % y;
26                   return q;
27               }
28           }
29       }
30
```

Figure 4.5 Code for Example 4.5

Explanation:

Line 12 declares a variable called remainder that can hold the remainder value.

Line 14 passes more than just the dividend (a) and the divisor (b). It also passes the remainder. Note the remainder has an "out" keyword before the type.

Line 21 defines the Divide() method with 'out' as the parameter modifier.

Line 25 assigns a value to the variable r, which is the remainder.

The out modifier actually modifies the variable value passed into the method. To see the difference between 'out' and 'no out', add this line of code x = x *x; right before Line 26. It won't change the variable 'a' value that is passed into the method since the 'x' variable in Line 21 does not have the 'out' keyword.

Using the out parameter modifier allows you to return more than one value back from a method.

Test Your Understanding 4.12

The 'out' parameter modifier makes it possible for a method to return more than one value.
A. True
B. False

Programming Challenge 4.3

Write a method called SumAndDifference() that will accept two whole numbers and return the sum and the difference of the two values (ex. - if the two input whole numbers were 5 and 2, the sum would be 7 and the difference would be 3). Demonstrate the method by calling it from the Main() method.

Programming Challenge 4.4

Write a method called Square() that will accept a whole number between 1 and 20. The method will print a solid square of asterisks with that number of asterisks on each side. In the main method, prompt the user to enter a whole number between 1 and 20. Then call the method to display a solid square of asterisks. For example, if a user entered 3, the output would look like:
* * *
* * *
* * *

Example 4.6

Problem: Rock Paper Scissors
Develop a console application in C# to allow a user to play Rock-Paper-Scissors against the computer. On the console screen, a player can type Rock, Paper, or Scissors. At the same time, the computer will display one of the three words in random. Then the application will display who is the winner.

Additionally, the application will prompt the user if he or she wants to play again.

Solution:

This example has the most lines of code so far. Divide the code into method for better organization and comprehension. Build one part at a time. Save and test each part before moving on to the next step.

Step 1: Computer always wins

Start a new project called RockPaperScissors. Type in the code as shown in Figure 4.6 and Figure 4.7.

```
1      using System;
2
3      namespace RockPaperScissors
4      {
           0 references
5          class Program
6          {
               0 references
7              static void Main(string[] args)
8              {
9                  bool playAgain = true;
10                 while (playAgain)
11                 {
12                     string userShape = UserShape();
13                     string computerShape = ComputerShape();
14                     string winner = Winner(userShape, computerShape);
15                     Console.WriteLine("User shape: {0}\nComputer shape: {1}\n{2} won",
16                         userShape, computerShape, winner);
17                     Console.WriteLine("Play again? y/n");
18                     string choice = Console.ReadLine().ToUpper();
19                     if (choice == "Y" || choice == "YES")
20                         playAgain = true;
21                     else
22                     {
23                         Console.WriteLine("Thanks for playing.");
24                         playAgain = false;
25                     }
26                 }
27                 Console.ReadKey();
28             }
```

Figure 4.6 Code for Example 4.6 Part 1.

Explanation:

Line 9 declares a Boolean variable to control the loop that asks the user if he or she wants to play again. A Boolean variable can only hold two values: true or false. Such variables are good for controlling loops or condition statements.

Lines 10 to 26 are a loop that allows a user to play as many times as he or she desires.

Line 12 calls the UserShape() method, which is defined in Figure 4.7. It stores the returned value in a string variable called userShape.

Line 13 calls the ComputerShape() method, which is defined in Figure 4.7. It stores the returned value in a string variable called computerShape.

Line 14 calls the Winner() method, which is defined in Figure 4.7. It includes two arguments, userShape and computerShape, and returns a string. The returned value is stored in the string called winner.

Lines 15 and 16 display the results of user shape, computer shape, and the winner.

Lines 17 to 25 allow the user to control whether the loop should continue.

Line 18 uses the ToUpper() method of a string to convert user input to all upper case (so that user input will be case insensitive).

```
      1 reference
29    private static string Winner(string userShape, string computerShape)
30    {
31        string winner = "Nobody";
32        if (userShape == "ROCK" && computerShape == "PAPER")
33            winner = "Computer";
34        return winner;
35    }
      1 reference
36    private static string ComputerShape()
37    {
38        string str;
39        str = "PAPER";
40        return str;
41    }
      1 reference
42    private static string UserShape()
43    {
44        string str;
45        str = "ROCK";
46        return str;
47    }
48    }
49 }
```

Figure 4.7 Code for Example 4.6 Part 2.

Explanation:

Lines 29 to 35 define the Winner() method, which has two parameters: userShape and computerShap. It also returns the winner. It checks only one simple case. A more detailed check will be performed in Step 3.

Lines 36 to 41 define the ComputerShape() method, which always returns "PAPER" for testing purposes. The completed method will be in Step 4.

Lines 42 to 47 define the UserShape() method, which always returns "ROCK" for testing purposes. The completed method will be in Step 2.

Save and run the application. The user should only show ROCK, and the computer should only show PAPER, thus making the computer the guaranteed winner.

Step 2: Player can choose to draw or lose

Update the UserShape() method with the code from Figure 5.8.

```
        1 reference
42      private static string UserShape()
43      {
44          string str = "ROCK";
45          bool isCorrectSpelling = false;
46          while (!isCorrectSpelling)
47          {
48              Console.WriteLine("Enter Rock, Paper, or Scissors:");
49              str = Console.ReadLine().ToUpper();
50              if (str == "ROCK" || str == "PAPER" || str == "SCISSORS")
51                  isCorrectSpelling = true;
52          }
53          return str;
54      }
```

Figure 5.8 Code for the UserShape() method.

Explanation

Line 45 includes a Boolean variable to control the while loop (Lines 46 to 52). If the user did not spell ROCK, PAPER, or SCISSORS correctly, the loop would prompt for another input.

Line 49 uses the ToUpper() method of a string to make the user input case insensitive.

Save and run the application.

Even though the user can enter any one of the three shapes, the result will either be a loss or a tie: if the user enters ROCK, he or she will lose; if the user enters any other shape, it will be a tie. This is due to our currently incomplete winner checking method.

Step 3: Player can choose to win, lose, or draw

Update the Winner() method with the code from Figure 5.9.

```
                       1 reference
29        ⊟        private static string Winner(string userShape, string computerShape)
30                 {
31                     string winner = "Nobody";
32                     if (userShape == "ROCK" && computerShape == "PAPER"
33                         || userShape == "PAPER" && computerShape == "SCISSORS"
34                         || userShape == "SCISSORS" && computerShape == "ROCK")
35                         winner = "Computer";
36                     else if (userShape == "ROCK" && computerShape == "SCISSORS"
37                         || userShape == "PAPER" && computerShape == "ROCK"
38                         || userShape == "SCISSORS" && computerShape == "PAPER")
39                         winner = "Player";
40                     return winner;
41                 }
```

Figure 5.9 Code for the Winner() method.

Explanation

The method checks only if the computer wins or the player wins. Everything else counts as nobody winning (a draw).

Save and run the application. Since the computer still only shows PAPER, you can easily play to win. Try playing, and see if you can get the different results.

Step 4: It's a real game

Update the ComputerShape() method with the code from Figure 5.10.

```
1 reference
42    private static string ComputerShape()
43    {
44        string str = "PAPER";
45        Random random = new Random();
46        int randomNumber = random.Next(1, 4);
47        switch (randomNumber)
48        {
49            case 1:
50                str = "ROCK";
51                break;
52            case 2:
53                str = "PAPER";
54                break;
55            case 3:
56                str = "SCISSORS";
57                break;
58        }
59        return str;
60    }
```

Figure 5.10 Code for the ComuterShape() method.

Explanation

Line 45 instantiates a Random object called 'random' from the Random class.

Line 46 calls the Next() method of the Random class to generate a random number between 1 (included) and 4 (not included).

Lines 47 to 58 use the switch statement to convert the random number to text describing the shape. You can use an if statement to accomplish this as well.

Save and run the application. Test it multiple times to see if there are any errors.

Programming Challenge 4.5
Modify the Rock-Paper-Scissors game so that a player can choose to play 'best two out of three games' or 'best three out of five games'.

4.5 Agile Events

As you learned in Chapter 2, there are three roles, five events, and three artifacts in Scrum. You learned the three roles in Chapter 3. You will learn the five events in this chapter. Scrum founders want you to use prescribed events to create consistency and to avoid any extra meetings. There are five events defined in the 2017 Scrum Guide (Schwaber and Sutherland, 2017). All scrum events are time-boxed, meaning the duration of the events have been predetermined and agreed upon by all members of the scrum team.

Test Your Understanding 4.13
The purpose of having regular scrum event meetings is to avoid additional meetings.
A. True
B. False

Test Your Understanding 4.14

All scrum events are time-boxed, which means _____.
A. all events have the same length
B. all events have their own predetermined length
C. all event lengths are recorded
D. all events can take as much time as they require

4.5.1 The Sprint

In chapter one, we introduced the concept of sprints when we compared the similarities and differences between waterfall and agile approaches. A sprint is a container event that includes all tasks that are necessary to achieve a delivery. From our toy retailer example, outlined in Chapter 1, a sprint might include the events for the development of features that allow the owner to check inventory levels and add new arrivals. At the end of the sprint, the development team will deliver the components of the application that allow the owner to check inventory and update inventory when new shipments arrive. Such a delivery is called an increment.

A sprint starts with sprint planning. Then, on a daily basis, the team should have brief scrum meetings. And, of course, sprints involve the actual work of completing the delivery. At the end of the sprint, the team should have a sprint review and sprint retrospective. Later in the chapter, you will learn each of these events in more detail.

A sprint duration is typically two weeks, but can be as long as a month. The purpose of limiting the duration is to increase the predictability of the software. During this short sprint, the delivery scope is less likely to be changed, and the risk of abandoning the delivery is lower.

The sprint duration should be the same for all sprints in the project. The length is agreed upon at the beginning of the project between the product owner, scrum master, and the scrum team. On rare occasions, a sprint duration may be longer in order to complete a delivery (e.g. when the delivery cannot fit into a sprint).

A sprint can be cancelled if the goal of the delivery is no longer valid. In our toy retailer example, if you have a sprint working on a shopping cart software, and the owner decided to purchase the shopping cart software, then there's no longer a reason to continue the sprint. The product owner decides whether to cancel or not. When a sprint is cancelled, any completed items are reviewed and may be released if the product owner desires so.

There are basic rules to sprints. During the sprint, changes are not allowed to user stories already in the sprint. If the product owner wants to make any changes, he or she can update the product backlog (a concept that will be explained in the next chapter), which contains all the user stories. This allows the team to focus on the current task.

During the sprint, the development team is not allowed to lower the quality of the goal either. This is to protect the benefits of the customer. However, as the product owner and the development team learn more about the product, a sprint clarification of the scope is allowed.

Test Your Understanding 4.15
A sprint delivers a software increment.
A. True
B. False

Test Your Understanding 4.16
A sprint is typically time-boxed at two to four weeks.
A. True
B. False

Test Your Understanding 4.17
The length of a sprint is always determined by the user story. The longer the story, the longer the sprint.
A. True
B. False

Test Your Understanding 4.18

Which of the following is NOT a sprint event?
A. sprint planning
B. daily scrum meeting
C. sprint review
D. scrum master

Test Your Understanding 4.19
The product owner is the only person allowed to make changes to stories already in a sprint.
A. True
B. False

Test Your Understanding 4.20
An agile team can slightly lower the quality of the product in order to meet the sprint deadline.
A. True
B. False

Test Your Understanding 4.21
A product owner can make changes to the user stories in the product backlog.
A. True
B. False

4.5.2 Sprint Planning

A sprint starts with a plan meeting. The main purpose of the meeting is to pick stories from the product backlog that can be completed in one sprint (Sutherland, 2014). There are three agenda items to a sprint plan meeting:

1. Which user stories should be included in this sprint? This is determined by the priority list of the user stories in the product backlog and the projected capacity of the team for the sprint. To accomplish this task, all team members should have a thorough understanding of the user stories in the product backlog. Every story in the product backlog has a priority ranking (set by the product owner) and story points (estimated by the team members). The story points for a story indicates how much efforts is needed. The team picks stories by ranking them from high to low. How many stories they pick is based on how many story points the team can complete in one sprint. The total story points selected should not be greater than that the team can complete in one sprint. Deviating slightly in terms of priority ranking and total story points is allowed.

2. After the stories are picked, it is time to write the sprint goal. The sprint goal explains the reasons for the work and provides motivation for running the sprint. A sprint goal must be specific, measurable, and attainable (Pichler, 2012). In our toy retailer example, the sprint goal could be "Mr. Lincoln can update the inventory when a new shipment arrives".

3. The development team decides how to achieve the goal and successfully deliver the software increment in this order: first, the user stories will be broken down into more manageable individual tasks. Next, each member picks the tasks he or she is comfortable completing. Lastly, each member reports an estimate of when he or she will finish. This estimate is usually measured in hours.

Three items above are collectively called the sprint backlog.

A sprint planning meeting is suggested to last 8 hours for a month-long sprint. Shorter sprints should correspond with shorter time-boxes.

Test Your Understanding 4.22

Which of the following is NOT an agenda item on a sprint planning meeting?
A. take attendance
B. pick stories from product backlog
C. write sprint goal
D. decide how to achieve the goal

Test Your Understanding 4.23

Suppose there are five stories in the product backlog:
Story 1: 20 points
Story 2: 40 points
Story 3: 40 points
Story 4: 13 points
Story 5: 20 points
If the team can complete 70 story points per sprint (their 'velocity'), and the priority is the same as the story number (meaning 1 is of highest priority, and 5 the lowest), which stories will probably be picked by the team?
A. Story 1, Story 3, and Story 5
B. Story 1, Story 2, and Story 4
C. Story 2, Story 4, and Story 5
D. Story 1, Story 3, and Story 4

4.5.3 Daily Scrum

Daily scrum is a meeting amongst the development team, time-boxed at 15 minutes. To avoid long meetings, members are required to stand up. Every member answers the following three questions.

1. What did I do yesterday?

2. What will I do today?

3. Do I see any impediments for me or the team?

Daily scrum meetings are not simple status updates. The daily scrum is a time to make commitments. If a member states he or she will complete the "Add new inventory" feature today, you should expect to see that done by tomorrow's meeting.

Compared to the status update meeting, which is typically held once a week or once a month, daily scrum has the advantage of identifying problems early (Hoogendoorn, 2014). Members may delay reporting problems or issues due to laziness or shyness if they only meet once a month. With daily scrum, slow progress is immediately visible.

The meeting also helps members know what others are doing. It can show who needs help. It also provides transparency.

The scrum master should help resolve any issues raised by a member. If a member does not know how to make something work, the scrum master helps.

Test Your Understanding 4.24

Daily scrum meetings should have members standing to avoid prolonging the meeting.
A. True
B. False

Test Your Understanding 4.25

Which of the following questions is NOT asked in the daily scrum meeting?
A. What did I do yesterday?
B. What will I do today?
C. What do I plan to do tomorrow?
D. Do I see any impediments for me or the team?

4.5.4 Sprint Review Meeting

At the end of the sprint, the team meets to inspect the increment, usually accompanied by a live software demo to show to the business users. The meeting will also update the product backlog according to feedback.

The meeting is time-boxed at four hours for a month long sprint. The meeting is informal, and any stakeholder can attend. The key value is to get feedback from the business users. To enforce the informality, some teams forbid the use of PowerPoint slides.

The key purpose is to compare the completed increment with the sprint goal set up from the sprint planning meeting, and to see how close the goal is to being achieved.

The review can be a bit daunting, since it is one of few events where multiple stakeholders are directly involved. Stakeholders may ask questions the team aren't prepared for. Features may not work as planned. However, team members should remember that this is not a status check. The purpose of the review is to elicit feedback and nurture collaboration.

There are four keys to the success of a sprint review (Lacey, 2016).

1. Take time to plan. Planning can increase the team's confidence. Take time to set up the software so that customers can interact with the product.

2. Document decisions. People tend to forget things. Keeping track of customer statements in print makes everyone accountable.

3. Ask for acceptance. Customers may or may not accept the product on the spot at the review meeting. It never hurts to ask, particularly for what can be improved. It is important that the team meet the "definition of done" in the first place.

4. Be brave. The review meeting can be intimidating, since the customer may not accept the increment. Members may panic. The team should try their best to communicate with the customers and work closely with the product owner to reach their goal.

Test Your Understanding 4.26

The sprint review meeting is a time when the team can see what they did well and what needs improvement from the past sprint.
A. True
B. False

Test Your Understanding 4.27

Which of the following is NOT a key to success in a sprint review meeting?
A. Take time to plan
B. Document decisions
C. Ask for acceptance
D. Make it a formal meeting with customers

Test Your Understanding 4.28

Which of the following is NOT a purpose of the sprint review?
A. Customers can check the status of the project.
B. The team can check how close they are to the sprint goal.
C. The team elicits feedback from the customers.
D. The team and the customers get to collaborate.

4.5.5 Sprint Retrospective

Sprint retrospective is a three-hour meeting for a one-month long sprint. It is held after the sprint review meeting and before the new sprint. All members, including the scrum master and the product owner, should attend the meeting. It has three purposes:

1. To examine how well the last sprint went.

2. To list what went well and what did not go well.

3. To plan for improvement.

There are many ways to achieve the three purposes (Cohn, 2010). One way is to let every member in the team voice what should be implemented in the next sprint, what should be continued in the next sprint, and what should be stopped. After a list is made, the team votes. Based on the results and possibly further discussion, a plan for the next sprint is created.

Retrospectives are often omitted by scrum teams that believe the meetings are optional and don't directly add value to the product (Lacey, 2016). This omission is often the beginning of a failed scrum practice. Recall the three foundations of scrum you learned in Chapter 2: transparency, inspection, and adaptation. All other events discussed in this section focus on the product delivery. This is the only event that can support all three foundations. This meeting helps team members know how to work more efficiently and productively. This is also the only time the team learns about new techniques in the field that they can utilize.

There are four keys to the success of a sprint retrospective (Lacey, 2016).

1. Show them the way: The retrospective schedule should be brief enough to avoid schedule conflicts. Right before the meeting, a reminder should be sent out that includes the meeting agenda, the benefits of the meeting, and how to prepare for the meeting.

2. Build a good environment: One major problem with the retrospective meeting is the endless discussion on one issue and inability to reach an agreement. You can either remove chairs and/or use a timer for each agenda item to limit the discussion. In addition, make necessary artifacts available so that the team can inspect and adapt. These items include "burn-down" charts (which indicate how many stories are left in the backlog; agile metrics will be discussed in Chapter 6) and the team's vision for the product and sprint (sprint artifacts will be discussed in detail in the next chapter).

Even though members should trust each other and are allowed to work with a lot of freedom, some ground rules will help. These rules should be made available to all participants before the meeting. Example rules include being respectful, putting away laptops/phones, and not interrupting while others speak.

3. Hold them when you need them: Retrospectives are not just held at the end of a sprint. It can be held anytime a big issue arises, like if there is a major defect, or a change in team membership. It can also be held after a major release, or when the customers demand one. This is analogous to a time out in a basketball game.

4. Set high priority: You should not hold a retrospective only when there's a problem for the team. It is good for supporting scrum foundations and team self-organization. Many beginner agile teams realize this too late.

Test Your Understanding 4.29

Which of the following is NOT a purpose of sprint retrospectives?
A. Examining how well the last sprint went.
B. Listing what went well and what did not go well.
C. Planning for improvement.
D. To demo the software to the customers.

Test Your Understanding 4.30

Which of the following is NOT a key to the success of a sprint retrospective?
A. Show them the way.
B. Product owner should not be present.
C. Build a good environment.
D. Hold them when you need them.

Test Your Understanding 4.31

When should a team hold a sprint retrospective?
A. After the sprint review.
B. Any time a big issue arises.
C. At the end of the sprint, plus any time a big issue happens.
D. When a new user story is added to the product backlog.

4.6 Chapter Summary

In this chapter, you learned how to organize logically related statements into a method. A method can have parameters that receive arguments from the caller. A method can also return a value. A method makes your code better organized. Better-organized code makes maintenance much easier, and thus saves money for the business.

You also learned the five events for scrum. They are the sprint, sprint plan meeting, daily scrum, sprint review meeting, and sprint retrospective. These meetings make the scrum practice more consistent, and prevent additional unnecessary meetings.

4.7 References

Cohn, M. (2010), Succeeding with Agile: Software Development Using Scrum, Addison-Wesley Professional PTG.

Hoogendoorn, S., (2014), This Is Agile, Beyond the Basics, Beyond the Hype, Beyond Scrum, Dymaxicon, Sausalito, CA.

Lacey, M. (2016), The Scrum Field Guide, 2nd Edition, Addison-Wesley, Boston.

Pichler, R., (2012), Effective Sprint Goals, Available at

http://www.romanpichler.com/blog/effective-sprint-goals/ Visited November 20, 2016.

Schwaber, K. and Sutherland, J. (2017), The Scrum Guide, available at www.scrumguides.org Visited November 20, 2018.

Sutherland, J. (2014), Scrum the Art of Doing Twice the Work in Half the Time, Crown Business, New York.

4.8 Solutions to Selected Programming Challenges
Programming Challenge 4.1

```csharp
class Program
{
    static void Main(string[] args)
    {
        // prompt user for input
        Console.WriteLine("Enter a school name:");
        // store user input in a variable
        string schoolName = Console.ReadLine();
        // call the DisplayText method by passing the school name
        DisplayText(schoolName);
        Console.ReadKey();
```

```
    }
    // DisplayText() method
    static void DisplayText(string message)
    {
        Console.WriteLine();
        Console.WriteLine(message + " is a great school.");
        Console.WriteLine();
        Console.WriteLine("***********************");
    }
}
```

Programming Challenge 4.2

```
class Program
{
    static void Main(string[] args)
    {
        // create two variables
        int a = 11;
        int b = 5;
        // call the Multiply() method and store return value in product
        int product = Multiply(a, b);
        // display the product
        Console.WriteLine("The product of {0} and {1} is {2}", a, b, product);
        Console.ReadKey();
    }
    // Multiple() method
    static int Multiply(int x, int y)
    {
        int p;
        p = x * y;
        return p;
    }
}
```

Programming Challenge 4.3

```
class Program
{
    static void Main(string[] args)
    {
        // create three int variables
        int a = 11;
        int b = 5;
        int diff;
        // call the SumAndDifference() method and store return value in total
        int total = SumAndDifference(a, b, out diff);
        // display the result
        Console.WriteLine("The sum of {0} and {1} is {2}", a, b, total);
        Console.WriteLine("The difference of {0} and {1} is {2}", a, b, diff);
        Console.ReadKey();
    }
```

```
// Divide() method
static int SumAndDifference(int x, int y, out int d)
{
    int s;
    s = x + y;
    d = x - y;
    return s;
}
}
```

4.9 Solutions to Test Your Understanding

4.1 A; 4.2 A; 4.3 C; 4.4 B; 4.5 C; 4.6 A; 4.7 B; 4.8 A; 4.9 B; 4.10 A; 4.11 B; 4.12 A; 4.13 A; 4.14 B; 4.15 A; 4.16 A; 4.17 B; 4.18 D; 4.19 B; 4.20 B; 4.21 A; 4.22 A; 4.23 B; 4.24 A; 4.25 C; 4.26 B; 4.27 D; 4.28 A; 4.29 D; 4.30 B; 4.31 C;

Chapter 5: C# Classes and Agile Artifacts

5.1 A Class is a Logical Group of Methods and Fields

In the last chapter, you learned how to group a block of statements with a common goal into a method. In this chapter, you will learn how to group a set of related methods into a class. Because methods usually need data to work on, a class will also contain the related data. In Object Oriented Programming (OOP) terminology, data is termed 'fields'.

The concept of a class is not new to you. You have used classes since Chapter One; the class name was Program, and your first program classe contained a Main() method. In the last chapter, you added more methods to the Program class. In this chapter, you will learn how to create your own custom class by following the Object-Oriented Programming approach.

A class is a conceptual category, like students, employees, cars, or houses. A class is not an object; an object is a specific instance that belongs to a class. So, if you had the class 'students', 'Alice' may be an object of that class. Or, as another example, a class could be the blueprints to a certain model of house, and the house built from that is the object of that class. When you program the object-oriented way, you create a class. When you need to use an object, you use the class to instantiate an object.

A class keeps track of a certain status. For example, all students have a name and GPA. Therefore, the student class includes name and GPA as statuses. As another example, all cars have a make and color. The car class would have make and color as statuses. In OOP, the statuses of a class are called 'fields'.

A class also has behaviors. Students can take a course, or convert a numeric grade to a letter grade. A car can speed up or down, or change tires. In OOP, these behaviors are called 'methods'.

In short, a class is a conceptual category. A class can have fields to keep track of statuses and methods to carry out actions. In most cases, you will create an object to use the methods.

Test Your Understanding 5.1
A class is a logical group of methods and fields.
A. True
B. False

Test Your Understanding 5.2
In OOP, classes and objects are the same thing.
A. True
B. False

Test Your Understanding 5.3
In OOP, a class is like a blueprint, and an object is like a house built out of that blueprint.
A. True
B. False

Test Your Understanding 5.4
John Doe is a student. In OOP terminology, which of the following statements is correct?
A. John Doe is a class
B. John Doe is an object
C. Student is an object
D. Both John Doe and students are objects

Test Your Understanding 5.5
A class can have _____ to keep track of statuses and _____ to carry out actions.
A. objects, fields
B. fields, methods
C. objects, methods
D. methods, objects

Example 5.1

Problem:

A student has a name and a numerical grade/score. The numerical score can be converted to a letter grade. Create a class called Student with those fields (name and numeric score) and method (change numeric score to letter grade). Then demonstrate the class by instantiating the two student objects shown below.

Name: Alice, numeric score: 97
Name: Bob, numeric score: 87

Finally, print the two students' names and letter grades on the console screen.

The formula for converting a numeric score to a letter grade is 90-100 A; 80-89 B; 70-79 C; 60-69 D; 0-59 F.

Analysis:

You can easily program this problem with just the default Program class and the Main() method, with all your statements inside the Main() method. However, you should learn how to code in OOP so you can handle more difficult problems as they come along and build more robust applications.

The student class has two fields: studentName and studentScore. These fields will store individual names and numeric scores. The student class also has the method GetLetterGrade(), which will return a letter grade based on the studentScore field value.

Solution:

By following this solution, you will learn how to solve the problem in OOP.

In the problem, you can see that student is a class that has name and score fields, and has a method that converts a numeric score to a letter grade.

Create a new project called Chapter5Class1. In the "Solution Explorer" window, right click on the Chapter5Class1 Project (not the solution). In the pop-up context menu, point to "Add" then "Class", as shown in the Figure 5.1.

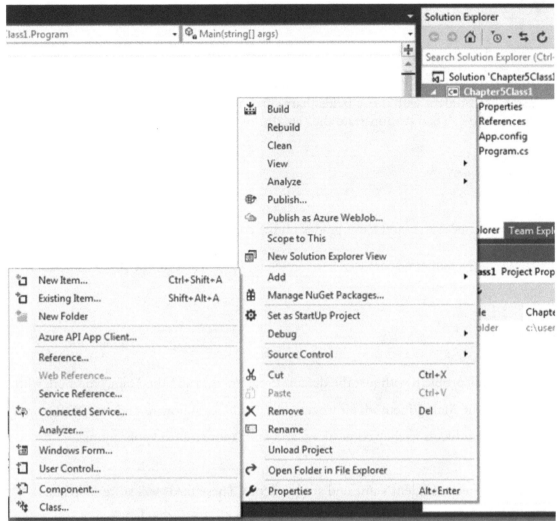

Figure 5.1 Create a class in a project

The "Add new item" dialog will pop up as shown in Figure 5.2. Type in the new name 'Student.cs' then click on the "Add" button. This will create a new class called Student in the project, as shown in Figure 5.3.

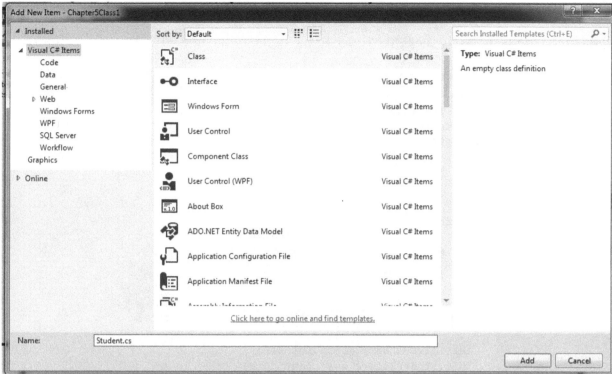

Figure 5.2 Add New Item Dialog window.

```
Student.cs  ⊣ ×  Program.cs
C# Chapter5Class1                          ▾   Chapter5Class1.Student
    1    ⊟using System;
    2     using System.Collections.Generic;
    3     using System.Linq;
    4     using System.Text;
    5     using System.Threading.Tasks;
    6
    7    ⊟namespace Chapter5Class1
    8     {
    9    ⊟    class Student
   10         {
   11         }
   12    }
```

Figure 5.3 Class template created by Visual Studio.

You will add all components of the Student class inside the class braces, { and }, between Lines 10 and 11 of Figure 5.3. Move the cursor to Line 10 after the beginning brace {. Push enter a few times and type in the code as shown in Figure 5.4 (The figure does not show any using directives at the top because they are not used). To remove unnecessary usings, you can right click on the using directive and select "Remove and Sort usings".

```
1    namespace Chapter5Class1
2    {
3        class Student
4        {
5            // fields
6            private string studentName;
7            private int studentScore;
8            // properties
9            public string StudentName
10           {
11               get { return studentName; }
12               set { studentName = value; }
13           }
14           public int StudentScore
15           {
16               get { return studentScore; }
17               set { studentScore = value; }
18           }
19           // constructors
20           public Student(string studentName, int studentScore)
21           {
22               this.studentName = studentName;
23               this.studentScore = studentScore;
24           }
25           // methods
26           public char GetLetterGrade()
27           {
28               char letterGrade = '\0';
29               if (StudentScore >= 90)
30                   letterGrade = 'A';
31               else if (StudentScore >= 80)
32                   letterGrade = 'B';
33               else if (StudentScore >= 70)
34                   letterGrade = 'C';
35               else if (StudentScore >= 60)
36                   letterGrade = 'D';
37               else
38                   letterGrade = 'F';
39               return letterGrade;
40           }
41           public override string ToString()
42           {
43               string str;
44               str = string.Format("Name: {0} Letter Grade: {1}",
45                   StudentName, GetLetterGrade());
46               return str;
47           }
48       }
49   }
```

Figure 5.4 Completed Student class

Explanation of Student class (Figure 5.4):

Lines 6 and 7 declare two private variables called fields: one to store student name, and the other to store student score. The first one should be a string data type, and the second one should be an int data type. The private modifier allows this variable to be used only inside this class. In OOP terminology, this is called encapsulation, which prevents outside objects from accessing the implementation details of a class.

Lines 9 to 13 define a property. A property provides access to a field from outside of the class, so a property is typically public and related to a specific field. One property for one field. It allows the retrieval of the field value from the field or the storage of a value to the field. The "value" in the code is a keyword. It represents the value assigned to the property. For example: In code outside of this class, you cannot assign a value like this studentName = "Lynn" because studentName is private. However, you can do StudentName = "Lynn" because StudentName (note the upper case first letter) is a public property. Inside the class, it is a good practice to avoid using a field directly.
The student class has two fields. There are two corresponding properties. Note, by convention, a field name begins with a lower-case letter while a property name begins with a capital letter.

Lines 20 to 24 define a constructor. A constructor of a class is a special method that is called every time a new object is created. Usually, you use a constructor to initialize the field values. You might have noticed the use of the "this" keyword, which points to the object itself. Since you have two studentName variables, one in the constructor parameter, the other in the field, the keyword "this" makes the two different. The this.studentName is the one in the field, and studentName refers to the one in the parameter. The assignment assigns the value from the parameter to the value in the field.

A constructor does not have a return type (not even the "void" keyword). A constructor must have the same name as the class, including the case. In this example, both the constructor and the class are called Student.

Lines 26 to 40 are the GetLetterGrade() method, which checks studentScore and returns a letter grade for the student.

Lines 41 to 47 are the ToString() method, which returns a string based on the field values. You can modify it so that it returns different values or returns the same values in a different format. Every class has a ToString() method by default inherited from the "object" class. C# makes all classes automatically inherited from the "object" class. The keyword "override" simply means that this class won't use the default ToString() method implementation and will use this new one. ToString() is very convenient, and you should get used to having one for every class you create. Line 45, StudentName is a property, not a field. It is a good practice to use properties instead of fields.

In summary, a class typically has zero or many fields. Each field has a corresponding property. A class also has one or many constructors. Additionally, a class has zero or many methods for class behavior. All classes come with a ToString() method, which you should override to have a meaningful outcome when an object of the class is printed.

Test Your Understanding 5.6
By convention, a field name begins with a(n) _____ case letter while a property name begins with a(n) _____ case letter.
A. lower, upper
B. upper, lower
C. lower, lower
D. upper, upper

Test Your Understanding 5.7
A(n) _____ of a class allows the retrieval of the field value or the storage of a value to the field.
A. property
B. constructor
C. object
D. toString method

Test Your Understanding 5.8
A _____ of a class is a special method that is called every time a new object is created.
A. field
B. property
C. constructor
D. toString method

Test Your Understanding 5.9
In the following code snippet, what is the purpose of using the keyword "this"?
private string studentName;
private int studentScore;
public Student(studentName, studentScore)
{
      this.studentName = studentName;
      this.studentScore = studentScore;
}
A. this.studentName refers to the studentName in the field.
B. studentName refers to the studentName in the field.
C. this.studentName refers to the variable with the same name inside the constructor.
D. this.studentName is the same as studentName.

Test Your Understanding 5.10
Which of the following is NOT a component of a class?
A. fields
B. properties
C. methods
D. repeating statements

Next, go to the "Solution Explorer" window and double click on the "Program.cs" file to display it in the code window. Type in the statements as shown in Figure 5.5 (just the code inside the Main() method).

```
1        using System;
2
3        namespace Chapter5Class1
4        {
5            class Program
6            {
7                static void Main(string[] args)
8                {
9                    // create two students
10                   Student student1 = new Student("Alice", 97);
11                   Student student2 = new Student("Bob", 87);
12                   // display the data
13                   Console.WriteLine(student1);
14                   Console.WriteLine(student2);
15                   Console.ReadKey();
16               }
17           }
18       }
```

Figure 5.5 The Main() method demonstrates the Student class.
Explanation of the Main() method

Line 10 creates a student object, called student1, by calling the constructor of the Student class and passing two arguments, "Alice" for studentName and 97 for her score. A Student type variable called student1 is declared and assigned the reference to the newly created Student object.

Line 11 creates another student object called student2.

Line 13 prints the object student1. It will automatically call the ToString() method of the Student class. For learning purposes, you are encouraged to make some changes to the ToString() method of the Student class. You can see how the console display changes when you run the program.

Test Your Understanding 5.11

Suppose s1 is an object of the Student class. What will the following statement do?
Console.WriteLine(s1);

A. s1 will be displayed on the console screen.
B. the ToString() method of the Student class will be called.
C. the constructor of the Student class will be called if defined.
D. a compiler error will result if the ToString() method of the Student class is not defined.

Test Your Understanding 5.12

When creating a new object of a class, a constructor of the class is called.
A. True.
B. False.

Test Your Understanding 5.13
When creating a new object of a class, the object's name is always "new".
A. True.
B. False.

Test Your Understanding 5.14
You cannot live in a blueprint. You have to build a house to live in it. Similarly, for most classes, you cannot use it directly, you have to create an instance of the class before calling its methods.
A. True

B. False

Programming Challenge 5.1

At Tiny College, every student takes three exams: two midterms and one final. Each midterm counts as 30%, and the final exam counts as 40% of the semester grade. Each exam has a maximum of 100 points. Your tasks: start a new project, and add a new class named CollegeStudent. The CollegeStudent class should not be in the same file as the Program class. This class has four fields: studentName, midTerm1, midTerm2, and finalExam. The class also has a method called CalculateSemesterGrade() that will calculate the semester grade based on the three exams. Add appropriate properties, constructors, and ToString() methods to the CollegeStudent class.

Demonstrate the CollegeStudent class in the Main() method of the Program class by prompting the user to enter a student name and three scores. Then create a CollegeStudent object with the user data and display the object in the console screen.

Example 5.2

Problem:

In a company, an employee has an employee ID, employee name, and date promoted. Write a class that includes the fields described.

The employee class should have a method called Promote(). This method will display the message "It's time for a promotion." on the console screen if the employee's last promotion date is more than three months ago.

Demonstrate the employee class by creating two employees with one having been promoted more than three months ago, and the other less than three months ago. Display each employee's data on the console screen.

Solution:

Create a new project called Chapter5Employee. Add a new class called Employee to the project. The Employee class should resemble Figure 5.6

```csharp
1   using System;
2   namespace Chapter5Employee
3   {
4       class Employee
5       {
6           // fields
7           private string employeeId;
8           private string employeeName;
9           private DateTime datePromoted;
10          // properties
11          public string EmployeeId
12          {
13              get { return employeeId; }
14              set { employeeId = value; }
15          }
16          public string EmployeeName
17          {
18              get { return employeeName; }
19              set { employeeName = value; }
20          }
21          public DateTime DatePromoted
22          {
23              get { return datePromoted; }
24              set { datePromoted = value; }
25          }
26          // constructor
27          public Employee(string employeeId, string employeeName,
28              DateTime datePromoted)
29          {
30              this.employeeId = employeeId;
31              this.employeeName = employeeName;
32              this.datePromoted = datePromoted;
33          }
34          // methods
35          public string Promote()
36          {
37              string message ="";
38              if (DatePromoted.AddMonths(3) < DateTime.Now)
39                  message = "It's time for promotion";
40              return message;
41          }
42          public override string ToString()
43          {
44              string str;
45              str = string.Format("{0, -10}{1, -10}{2, 20}",
46                  EmployeeId, EmployeeName, Promote());
47              return str;
48          }
49      }
50  }
```

Figure 5.6 The Employee class

Explanation:

The Employee class is very similar to the Student class. It also has fields, properties, constructors, and methods.

Line 9 uses a data type called DateTime that can hold date and time values. It holds the date the employee was promoted.

Line 38 adds three months to the date the employee was promoted, and if that is less than today's date, then the employee should be promoted.

Lines 27 and 28 were cut into two lines due to this book's width limitations.

Lines 45 and 46 were cut into two lines due to this book's width limitations.

Line 45's format string includes three place holders, which correspond to the three following values. In each place holder, the second number indicates how many characters are needed in the place holder, and the negative sign indicates the left alignment. These place holders are good for displaying tables.

To demonstrate the Employee class, go to the Main() method of the Program class and add statements so they resemble the Figure 5.7

```
1       using System;
2
3       namespace Chapter5Employee
4       {
5           class Program
6           {
7               static void Main(string[] args)
8               {
9                   // create two employees
10                  Employee employee1 = new Employee("111", "Alice",
11                      DateTime.Parse("11/11/2015"));
12                  // you should change the following date to a more recent
13                  // date so that Bob won't see the promotion message
14                  Employee employee2 = new Employee("222", "Bob",
15                      DateTime.Parse("9/4/2016"));
16                  // display the messages
17                  Console.WriteLine(employee1);
18                  Console.WriteLine(employee2);
19                  Console.ReadKey();
20              }
21          }
22      }
```

Figure 5.7 The Employee demo

Programming Challenge 5.2

In a company, every employee has an employee ID, employee name, salary, and date promoted. Write a class that includes the above fields and the following method:

A method called Promote() will increase the employee's current salary by 10% if the employee was last promoted more than three months ago.

Add necessary properties, constructors, and the ToString() method to the class.

Demonstrate the Employee class with two employees, one promoted more than three months ago and the other less than three months ago. Have both employees start with the same salary. Display the employees' data before and after the promotion to see the differences in salaries.

Example 5.3

Problem: Tic Tac Toe

Develop a console application of the Tic Tac Toe game. The Tic Tac Toe board includes nine squares in three rows by three columns. The game starts with all empty squares marked with an "E". Two players take turns using the same keyboard. Whoever claims three consecutive squares first wins. The first player is "X". The second player is "O". A player claims a square by marking the square with either "X" or "O".

A player declares a square by entering a row number (with the top row as 0, middle row as 1, and bottom row as 2) followed by a column number (with the left column as 0, middle column as 1, and right column as 2).

If a player declares a square that is already declared, the game will display "invalid move" and the player should enter another choice.

The game is over when one player wins or when all squares have been declared.

Solution:

Step 1: Display the board.

Start a new project called TicTacToe. Add a new class called Board to the project. Type the code as shown in Figure 5.8.

The Board class has only one field called allCells, which is a two dimensional array. This corresponds to the 3 by 3 game board.

The Board class has a ToString() method that will display the board with the content from allCells. A sample output will look like this:

```
E | X | E
E | O | E
E | E | E
```

```
1    namespace TicTacToe
2    {
         10 references
3        public enum CellValue { E, X, O}
         5 references
4        class Board
5        {
6            // field
7            private CellValue[ , ] allCells;
8            // property
             30 references
9            public CellValue[ , ] AllCells
10           {
11               get { return allCells; }
12               set { allCells = value; }
13           }
14           // constructor
             1 reference
15           public Board()
16           {
17               allCells = new CellValue[3, 3];
18           }
19           // methods
             0 references
20           public override string ToString()
21           {
22               string str;
23               str = AllCells[0, 0] + " | " + AllCells[0, 1] + " | " + AllCells[0, 2] +
24                       "\n----------\n" +
25                     AllCells[1, 0] + " | " + AllCells[1, 1] + " | " + AllCells[1, 2] +
26                       "\n----------\n" +
27                     AllCells[2, 0] + " | " + AllCells[2, 1] + " | " + AllCells[2, 2];
28               return str;
29           }
30       }
31   }
```

Figure 5.8 Code for the Board class.

Explanation:

Line 3 creates an enum type called CellValue, with possible values of E, X, and O.

Enumeration is a programmer defined type. It works like a constant variable, which you learned earlier can be more meaningful than a numeric literal. Enumeration prevents errors by not allowing programmers to type in anything other than what is defined.

Declaring an enumeration is similar to declaring a class. Just replace the "class" keyword with the "enum" keyword. The content of an enum is much simpler. Just include all allowed values.

Line 7 declares a two dimensional array of CellValue type called allCells.

Line 17 creates a two dimensional array of CellValue type. The size of the array is 3 by 3, meaning it has three rows and three columns. The rows count from 0 to 2. The same is true for columns. The memory address of this new array is assigned to the allCells array variable declared in Line 7. The default value of this array is E, because that's the first one on the CellValue enum type.

In Line 23 AllCells[0, 0] holds the value of row 0 (the first row) and column 0 (the first column). Similarly AllCells[0, 1] holds the value of row 0 (the first row) and column 1 (the second column).

In Line 24, \n is a new line symbol.

Next, in the default Main() method of the Program class, type in the code as shown in Figure 5.9.

```
1        using System;
2
3      namespace TicTacToe
4        {
                 0 references
5            class Program
6            {
                     0 references
7                static void Main(string[] args)
8                {
9                    Console.Title = "Tic Tac Toe";
10                   Board board = new Board();
11                   Console.WriteLine(board);
12
13                   Console.ReadKey();
14               }
15           }
16       }
```
Figure 5.9 Code for the Main() method.

Save and run the program. You should see a console output as shown in Figure 5.10.

Figure 5.10 Output at the end of Step 1.

Step 2: Play forever.

We are going to change the letter E to X or O based on which the player plays. After the first player (X) chooses the row and column numbers, that position will be replaced with X. Next, the second player (O) chooses a position to put O. The two players take turns to play forever. After all squares are declared, no valid play is possible.

Add a Player class to the project. Type the code shown in Figure 5.11.

```
1     namespace TicTacToe
2     {
          3 references
3         class Player
4         {
5             // fields
6             private CellValue playerName;
7             private int selectedRow;
8             private int selectedColumn;
              1 reference
9             public CellValue PlayerName
10            {
11                get { return playerName; }
12                set { playerName = value; }
13            }
              1 reference
14            public int SelectedRow
15            {
16                get { return selectedRow; }
17                set { selectedRow = value; }
18            }
              0 references
19            public int Column
20            {
21                get { return selectedColumn; }
22                set { selectedColumn = value; }
23            }
              1 reference
24            public Player(int selectedRow, int selectedColumn,
25                CellValue playerName)
26            {
27                this.selectedRow = selectedRow;
28                this.selectedColumn = selectedColumn;
29                this.playerName = playerName;
30            }
              1 reference
31            public void PlayerMove(Board board)
32            {
33                board.AllCells[SelectedRow, selectedColumn]
34                    = PlayerName;
35            }
36        }
37    }
```

Figure 5.11 Code for the Player class.

Explanation:
Lines 6 to 8 declare three fields of the Player class.

Lines 9 to 23 are the corresponding three properties of the Player class.

Lines 24 to 30 are for the constructor.

Lines 31 to 35 define the PlayerMove() method, which will update the two dimensional array for the specific player.

Next, add the block of code shown in Figure 5.12 inside the Main() method right before the Console.ReadKey() line.

```
13          CellValue playerName = CellValue.X;
14          int row;
15          int column;
16          bool playerWins = false;
17          bool stalemate = false;
18          while (!(playerWins || stalemate))
19          {
20              do
21              {
22                  Console.WriteLine("Player " + playerName + " moves");
23                  Console.WriteLine("Enter row number (0, 1, 2): ");
24                  row = int.Parse(Console.ReadLine());
25                  Console.WriteLine("Enter column number (0, 1, 2): ");
26                  column = int.Parse(Console.ReadLine());
27                  if (board.AllCells[row, column] != CellValue.E)
28                      Console.WriteLine("Invalid move.");
29              } while (board.AllCells[row, column] != CellValue.E);
30
31              Player player = new Player(row, column, playerName);
32              player.PlayerMove(board);
33              Console.WriteLine(board);
34
35              playerName = (playerName == CellValue.X) ?
36                  CellValue.O : CellValue.X;
37          }
```

Figure 5.12 Additional code for the Main() method.

Explanation:

Line 13 initializes the first player (player X).
Lines 14 and 15 declare two variables to hold the row and column numbers entered by a player.
Lines 16 and 17 declare and initialize two variables to check if the game is over. The game is over when one player wins or all squares on the board are declared.
Lines 18 to 37 are a while loop that will run until the game is over. Because we don't know how to check if a player wins or if all squares on the board are declared, this loop will run forever.

Lines 20 to 29 is another loop nested inside the first loop that will run until the player enters a valid row and column number. A valid row and column number is a square that has the E value (empty).

Line 31 instantiates a player object with the row and column chosen by the player and the player name.

Line 32 calls the PlayerMove() method to update the array value.

Line 33 displays the board with the new content.

Lines 35 and 36 change the player name. The ternary expression is the same as the following:

```
if (playerName == CellValue.X)
      playerName = CellValue.O;
else
      playerName = CellValue.X;
```

Save and run the program to see the X and Os replacing Es.

Step 3: Game over

The only part left is to check if a player has won, or if all squares on the board have been declared (not E).

Add the IsPlayerWin() method as shown in Figure 5.13 to inside the Player class:

```csharp
                        0 references
37    public bool IsPlayerWin(Board board)
38    {
39        bool wins = false;
40        if (board.AllCells[0, 0] != CellValue.E &&
41            board.AllCells[0, 0] == board.AllCells[1, 1] &&
42            board.AllCells[1, 1] == board.AllCells[2, 2])
43        {
44            wins = true;
45        }
46        if (board.AllCells[0, 2] != CellValue.E &&
47            board.AllCells[0, 2] == board.AllCells[1, 1] &
48            board.AllCells[1, 1] == board.AllCells[2, 0])
49        {
50            wins = true;
51        }
52        for (int r = 0; r < 3; r++)
53        {
54            if (board.AllCells[r, 0] != CellValue.E &&
55                board.AllCells[r, 0] == board.AllCells[r, 1] &&
56                board.AllCells[r, 1] == board.AllCells[r, 2])
57            {
58                wins = true;
59            }
60        }
61        for (int c = 0; c < 3; c++)
62        {
63            if (board.AllCells[0, c] != CellValue.E &&
64                board.AllCells[0, c] == board.AllCells[1, c] &&
65                board.AllCells[1, c] == board.AllCells[2, c])
66            {
67                wins = true;
68            }
69        }
70        return wins;
71    }
```

Figure 5.13 Code for IsPlayerWin method.

Explanation:

There are four situations in which a player wins: 1) the diagonal, from top left to bottom right are the same letter; 2) the diagonal, from top right to bottom left are the same letter; 3) any of the three rows are the same letter; 4) any of the three columns are the same letter. The IsPlayerWin() does exactly that.

Next, add the HasNoMoreE() method, as shown in Figure 5.14, inside the Board class. I suggest that you place the method right before the ToString() method.

```
     1 reference
20   public bool HasNoMoreE()
21   {
22       bool noMoreE = true;
23       for (int r = 0; r < 3; r++)
24       {
25           for (int c = 0; c < 3; c++)
26           {
27               if (allCells[r, c] == CellValue.E)
28                   noMoreE = false;
29           }
30       }
31       return noMoreE;
32   }
```

Figure 5.14 Code for HasNoMoreE() method.

Finally, add the code, as shown in Figure 5.15, inside the Main() method towards the end of the method right before the following line:

```
playerName = (playerName == CellValue.X)?
```

```
35           playerWins = player.IsPlayerWin(board);
36           stalemate = board.HasNoMoreE();
37           if (playerWins)
38               Console.WriteLine("Player " + playerName + " wins.");
39           if (stalemate)
40               Console.WriteLine("Stalemate!");
```

Figure 5.15 Code for checking if a player won, or if all squares on the board have been declared.

Save and run the application to see how your Tic Tac Toe game works.

5.2 Agile Artifacts

As you learned in Chapter 2, there are three roles, five events, and three artifacts in scrum. You learned the agile roles and events in the previous two chapters. In this chapter, you will learn the three artifacts. The agile artifacts include product backlog, sprint backlog, and increments.

5.2.1 Product Backlog and User Story

The product backlog contains all software requirements in the form of user stories. The product backlog starts with rough software requirements. Over time, when more about the software is known and more increments are completed, the product backlog evolves.

Product Backlog
User Story 1 (most valuable and detailed)
User Story 2 (next valuable and detailed)
....
Epic (less detailed)
....
Theme (least detailed)

Figure 5.16 Product backlog with different priority and granularity levels.

User stories in the product backlog are organized with those of higher priority at the top and those of lower priority at the bottom (Figure 5.16). Priority is based on how much value the completed user story will add to the business. The product owner decides which user stories are the most valuable based on the value analysis.

Test Your Understanding 5.15
Product backlog contains user stories.
A. True
B. False

Test Your Understanding 5.16
User stories are software requirements.
A. True
B. False

Test Your Understanding 5.17

User stories with higher priority should be _____ of the product backlog.
A. at the top
B. in the middle
C. at the bottom
D. anywhere

Test Your Understanding 5.18

User stories at the top of the product backlog are in _____ details.
A. normal
B. more
C. less
D. least

To determine business values, first determine the area the completed user story will affect (Marchewka, 2015). The following are areas affected:

1. Customer. These values are related to customers. For example, if the software functions or features can reduce product price, then the business value is in the customer area.

2. Strategic. If the completed user story can create new markets or increase the market share of the company, then the value is in the strategic area.

3. Financial. If the software can increase the return on investment or reduce the cost, then the value is in the financial area.

4. Operational. If the software can increase the efficiency and effectiveness of the company operation, the value is in the operational area.

5. Social. If the software can benefit society, such as dissemination of knowledge, or reduction of pollution, the value is in the social area.

Next, develop an appropriate metric to measure the business value. Not all values can be easily quantified, though business values in the financial area are relatively easy to quantify.

Test Your Understanding 5.19

Which of the following is NOT a business value area?
A. customer
B. financial
C. social
D. technical

Test Your Understanding 5.20

If the completed feature of the user story can create new market for the company, the business value is in _____ area.
A. customer
B. financial
C. strategic
D. technical

Test Your Understanding 5.21
If the completed feature of the user story can reduce product price, the business value is in _____ area.
A. customer
B. social
C. strategic
D. technical

Another prioritization method is called MoSCow, outlined in the Dynamic Systems Development Method (DSDM) (Craddock et al., 2012), which is one of many agile approaches. MoSCow includes four priority levels:

1. Must haves: Requirements in this category must be implemented, otherwise the solution won't work or will be useless. These are the minimum components the team must deliver.

2. Should haves: Requirements in this category are important, but can be omitted if the schedule or budget won't permit.

3. Could haves: These requirements enhance the solution, but can be left out or are not critical.

4. Want to haves: These requirements are nice to have and can be included in later development. They are not included in the initial delivery.

Test Your Understanding 5.22

In MoSCow, which category includes requirements that are important, but can be omitted if the schedule or budget won't permit?
A. Must haves
B. Should haves
C. Could haves
D. Want to haves

Test Your Understanding 5.23
In MoSCow, which category includes requirements that are nice to have and can be included in the next development?
A. Must haves
B. Should haves
C. Could haves
D. Want to haves

Test Your Understanding 5.24

In MoSCow, which category includes the requirements that can enhance the solution, but can be left out or are not critical?
A. Must haves
B. Should haves
C. Could haves
D. Want to haves

Test Your Understanding 5.25

In MoSCow, which category includes requirements that must be implemented?

A. Must haves

B. Should haves
C. Could haves
D. Want to haves

As shown in Figure 5.16, not all user stories in the product backlog are in the same granularity (Patton, 2014). For those at the top of the list, greater detail is needed. Those at the bottom of the list may not even count as stories. They may instead be referred to as 'epics' or 'themes'. An epic is a user story that is too big to be designed, coded, or tested within a single sprint. A theme is a very general story or a big idea, sometimes containing the whole release or even multiple releases. Most requirements start out as themes or epics, since the first idea customers have for their software tend to be abstract. As the project progresses, stories will become more detailed to fit the work.

Test Your Understanding 5.26
User stories in product backlog have different granularity; stories with higher priority should have less details.
A. True
B. False

Test Your Understanding 5.27
Items inside the product backlog have different granularity; the most general and abstract item is a
_____.
A. general story
B. general item
C. abstract story
D. theme

Test Your Understanding 5.28
List items in the product backlog from least to most detailed.
A. user story, epic, theme
B. theme, epic, user story
C. epic, user story, theme
D. epic, theme. User story

You have seen the term "user story" many times, but what exactly is a user story? A user story includes a statement of the requirements and any acceptance criteria. A user story takes this format:

As a <type of user>, I want <some goal>, so that <some reason>

In our toy retailer example, a possible user story can be:

As a manager, I want to check the inventory level at any time so that I know when to place a replenishment.

A user story is written on an index card, implying it shouldn't be too long or complicated.

Acceptance criteria is written on the back of the user story (Cohn, 2004). The criteria includes assumptions made by the customers. In the retailer example, the manager may state that he wants to be able to check the inventory by product id, product name, and partial product name, and be able to view all products on one screen.

The criteria can also be used to determine if a story is fully implemented. From the same example, the manager may simply want all inventory information to be displayed on one screen and be able to print it off onto paper.

Test Your Understanding 5.29

Which of the following is NOT a component of a user story?
A. user
B. goal
C. platform
D. reason

Test Your Understanding 5.30
A user story should be written on an index card so that it is short and simple.
A. True
B. False

To write a good user story, you must follow the INVEST acronym (Cohn, 2010):

Independent: The user story must be able to stand alone. Ideally, user stories can be delivered in any order.

Negotiable: A user story is a conversation, not a specification. Collaboration and discussion about the best way to solve the business problem should happen between the product owner and the development team.

Valuable: A user story should provide business values to the company, as you learned earlier in this chapter.

Estimable: A user story must be detailed enough that a team can estimate the amount of effort needed to complete it.

Small: A story should be small enough to fit into a single sprint.

Testable: If a story is not testable, it is too vague.

Test Your Understanding 5.31

A user story is a conversation, not a specification. This is _____ in the INVEST acronym.
A. independent
B. negotiable
C. valuable
D. estimable

Test Your Understanding 5.32

A user story should not be vague. This is _____ in INVEST acronym.
A. independent
B. negotiable
C. small
D. testable

User stories in the product backlog must be estimated. If not all stories are estimated, at least those stories at the top should be estimated. Estimation is about predicting how much effort will be required to complete the story by the development team. It is measured by story points and determined by the development team. Many development teams estimate effort by using the planning poker game (Rubin, 2013):

Each team member has a stack of cards with the numbers ½, 1, 2, 3, 5, 8, 13, 20, 40, and 100. A story is then picked. The team reads the story and discusses it. Then, independently, team members place a card face down indicating how much effort they think the story will be. Values correspond to difficulty level. All cards are flipped over at the same time. The members with the smallest and largest values should explain their reasoning. The game is repeated until all numbers are relatively similar. Then, the team can select a number for the story.

Story points reflect the team's estimate for how much effort is needed to complete the story. It is a relative number. In other words, the story points for one team cannot be compared to the story points of another team.

Test Your Understanding 5.33

When estimating a user story with the planning poker game, the average of all members' card face values is used as the story's points.
A. True
B. False

Test Your Understanding 5.34

If Team A estimates 40 points, and Team B estimates 20 points for the same user story, one can conclude that Team B can complete the story in about half the time of Team A.
A. True
B. False

Before closing our discussion about the product backlog, lets consider the characteristics of a good product backlog, according to the DEEP principle (Cohn, 2010).

Detailed appropriately: Higher priority stories contain more details than lower priority stories.

Estimated: User stories in the product backlog should be estimable by the development team. This indicates the team can understand the stories. At the very least, stories at the top should be estimable.

Emergent: Stories in the product backlog are constantly evolving. When more about the marketplace is known, or technology advancement takes place, the product backlog should be updated. The product backlog is also updated between the sprints.

Prioritized: All stories should be prioritized based on the business value a story provides.

Test Your Understanding 5.35

Which of the following is NOT a characteristic of a good product backlog?
A. Detailed appropriately
B. Length appropriately
C. Estimate
D. Prioritized

Test Your Understanding 5.36

Stories in the product backlog are constantly evolving. This is a property of _____.
A. detailed appropriately
B. estimate
C. emergent
D. prioritized

5.2.2 Sprint Backlog

The sprint backlog contains items from the product backlog selected by the development team for the current sprint. It also includes any items added in the sprint planning meeting, such as the sprint goal. It is a forecast by the development team about what features will be included in the next increment, and the work needed to complete the features. The stories from the product backlog are often picked based on the team velocity (the number of story points the team can complete in one sprint).

The stories in the sprint backlog are broken down into sprint tasks, which are small enough to be assigned to one member as a day's work or less. Every sprint task is then estimated for number of hours needed to complete it. User stories in the product backlog are estimated for effort in story points, while tasks in the sprint backlog are estimated by hours. As a result, each story in the sprint backlog also has a time estimate. Note that the relationship between story points and time estimates are not linear. In other words, if a 20 points story takes 200 hours, it does not mean that a 40 points story will take 400 hours. Story points are relative numbers while task estimates are absolute. Table 5.1 shows a comparison between product backlog and sprint backlog

Items	Product Backlog	Sprint Backlog
Scope	Project	Sprint
Detail	Less	More
Measurement	Story point	Hour
Ownership	Product owner	Team
Update Frequency	Weekly	Daily

Table 5.1 Comparison between Product Backlog and Sprint Backlog

Test Your Understanding 5.37
Stories in the product backlog are estimated by story points while the tasks in the sprint backlog are estimated by hours.
A. True
B. False

5.2.3 Increment

The increment is the piece of software containing all currently completed and tested items. All increments must be completed to be 'done' and accepted by the product owner. Thus, the increment gets larger and larger as more sprints are completed. The increment of the last sprint of the project is the whole, completed software the customer asked for.

Test Your Understanding 5.38

An increment is all the items completed in one sprint.
A. True
B. False

Test Your Understanding 5.39

The increment of the last sprint is _____.
A. a milestone
B. a closure
C. the final sprint
D. the software the customer wants

5.3 Chapter Summary

In this chapter, you learned that a class is a logical group of methods and the data that these methods work on. When you think of a class, you think of its status and behavior. The status is the fields, and the behavior is the methods. Most classes will include fields, properties, constructors, normal methods, and ToString() methods.

You also learned the three artifacts of scrum: product backlog, sprint backlog, and increment. The product backlog contains all user stories, epics, and themes. The sprint backlog are stories picked from the product backlog by the team to be in the current sprint backlog, plus additional items agreed upon by the team during sprint planning. The increment is the accumulated parts of software after each sprint.

5.4 References

Cohn, M. (2004). User Stories Applied for Agile Software Development, Addison-Wesley. Boston.

Cohn, M. (2006). Agile estimating and planning. Prentice Hall. Upper Saddle River, NJ.

Cohn, M. (2010). Succeeding with Agile: Software development using Scrum. Addison-Wesley. Boston, MA.

Craddock, A., Roberts, B., Richards, K. Godwin, J., and Tudor, D. (2012), The DSDM Agile Project Framework for Scrum. DSDM consortium.

Marchewka, J. T. (2015), *Information Technology Project Management*, 5th Edition. Wiley.

Patton, J. (2014), User Story Mapping Discover the whole story, Build the Right Product. O'Reilly. Sebastopol, CA.

Rubin, K.S. (2013). Essential Scrum A Practical Guide to the Most Popular Agile Process, Addison-Wesley. Boston.

5.5 Solutions to Selected Programming Challenges

Programming Challenge 5.1

```
namespace ProgrammingChallenge51
{
    class CollegeStudent
    {
        // fields
        private string studentName;
        private int midTerm1;
        private int midTerm2;
        private int finalExam;
        // properties
        public string StudentName
        {
            get { return studentName; }
            set { studentName = value; }
        }
        public int MidTerm1
        {
            get { return midTerm1; }
            set { midTerm1 = value; }
        }
        public int MidTerm2
        {
            get { return midTerm2; }
            set { midTerm2 = value; }
```

```
        }
        public int FinalExam
        {
            get { return finalExam; }
            set { finalExam = value; }
        }
        // constructor
        public CollegeStudent(string studentName, int midTerm1, int midTerm2, int
finalExam)
        {
            this.studentName = studentName;
            this.midTerm1 = midTerm1;
            this.midTerm2 = midTerm2;
            this.finalExam = finalExam;
        }
        // methods
        public double SemesterGrade()
        {
            double grade;
            grade = 0.3 * MidTerm1 + 0.3 * MidTerm2 + 0.4 * FinalExam;
            return grade;
        }
        public override string ToString()
        {
            string str;
            str = string.Format("Student name: {0} Semester grade: {1}", StudentName,
SemesterGrade());
            return str;
        }

    }
}
```

In the Main() method of the Program class, use the following code.

```
class Program
{
    static void Main(string[] args)
    {
        // prompt user for a name and three scores
        Console.WriteLine("Enter a name:");
        string name = Console.ReadLine();
        Console.WriteLine("Enter midterm one score:");
        int mid1 = int.Parse(Console.ReadLine());
        Console.WriteLine("Enter midterm two score:");
        int mid2 = int.Parse(Console.ReadLine());
        Console.WriteLine("Enter final exam score:");
        int finalExam = int.Parse(Console.ReadLine());
        // create a student
        CollegeStudent cs1 = new CollegeStudent(name, mid1, mid2, finalExam);
        // display the data
        Console.WriteLine(cs1);
        Console.ReadKey();
    }
```

```
    }
```

Programming Challenge 5.2
Create a project called Chapter5Employee2, add a class called Employee.

```csharp
using System;
namespace Chapter5Employee2
{
    class Employee
    {
        // fields
        private string employeeId;
        private string employeeName;
        private double salary;
        private DateTime datePromoted;
        // properties
        public string EmployeeId
        {
            get { return employeeId; }
            set { employeeId = value; }
        }
        public string EmployeeName
        {
            get { return employeeName; }
            set { employeeName = value; }
        }
        public double Salary
        {
            get { return salary; }
            set { salary = value; }
        }
        public DateTime DatePromoted
        {
            get { return datePromoted; }
            set { datePromoted = value; }
        }
        // constructor
        public Employee(string employeeId, string employeeName,
            double salary, DateTime datePromoted)
        {
            this.employeeId = employeeId;
            this.employeeName = employeeName;
            this.salary = salary;
            this.datePromoted = datePromoted;
        }
        // methods
        public void Promote()
        {
            if (DatePromoted.AddMonths(3) < DateTime.Now)
            {
                salary += 0.1*salary;
            }
        }
        public override string ToString()
```

```
        {
            string str;
            str = string.Format("{0, -10}{1, -10}{2, 20}",
                EmployeeId, EmployeeName, Salary);
            return str;
        }
    }
}
```

Add code to the Main() method of the default Program.cs

```
    class Program
    {
        static void Main(string[] args)
        {
            // create two employees
            Employee employee1 = new Employee("111", "Alice", 78000.00,
DateTime.Parse("11/11/2015"));
            Employee employee2 = new Employee("222", "Bob", 78000.00,
DateTime.Parse("9/4/2016"));
            // display before promotion
            Console.WriteLine(employee1);
            Console.WriteLine(employee2);
            // promotion
            employee1.Promote();
            employee2.Promote();
            // display after the promotion
            Console.WriteLine("After the promotion...");
            Console.WriteLine(employee1);
            Console.WriteLine(employee2);
            Console.ReadKey();
        }
    }
```

5.6 Solutions to Test Your Understanding

5.1 A; 5.2 B; 5.3 A; 5.4 B; 5.5 B; 5.6 A; 5.7 A; 5.8 C; 5.9 A; 5.10 D; 5.11 B; 5.12 A; 5.13 B; 5.14 A; 5.15 A; 5.16 A; 5.17 A; 5.18 B; 5.19D; 5.20 C; 5.21 A; 5.22 B; 5.23 D; 5.24 C; 5.25 A; 5.26 B; 5.27 D; 5.28 B; 5.29 C; 5.30 A; 5.31 B; 5.32 D; 5.33 B; 5.34 B; 5.35 B; 5.36 C; 5.37 A; 5.38 B.5.39 D.

Chapter 6: C# Inheritance and Agile Metrics

6.1 Inheritance

In the last chapter, you learned how to create your own custom classes and how to instantiate a class to use its methods. What if the two classes you need to create are very similar? You can create two classes anyway. However, since there are many duplicated fields and methods, there is a better way to do it. Put all those common fields and methods from those two classes in a third class called 'super type' and let the two classes, known as sub type, to inherit all elements from the super type.

Instead of creating two classes, you end up with writing three classes. Since all common members are now in the super class, the two sub classes are now simpler. This also enhances the maintenance. If you need to update one common member while using the two classes approach, you would have to update in two places. If you use the three classes approach, you only have to update in one location.

Example 6.1

Problem:

At Tiny College, both undergraduate and graduate students have a student ID, a student name, and a numeric grade score between 0 and 100. However, undergraduates have letter grades (A, B, C, D, and F) with pluses and minuses, while graduates only have a letter. Create three classes: one super class called Student and two sub classes called Undergraduate and Graduate respectively.

Demonstrate the classes you created with four students, two undergraduates and two graduates in the Main() method.

Analysis:

In this example, you don't see many problems with the two class approach. However, when there are many fields and methods, you would see a lot of duplications. Duplication not only creates extra typing for the programmers, it also causes nightmares when maintaining the code. For example, when Tiny College wants to keep more student records, it decides to separate a student's name into first and last. To achieve this, you would have to recode in all related classes. It is almost guaranteed that something will be omitted. Companies often wind up paying consulting firms to fix these costly, accumulated problems.

A better approach is to create a super class called Student that contains all common elements of both the undergraduate class and graduate class and to let both sub classes inherit from the super class. A Unified Modeling Language (UML) class diagram is displayed in Figure 6.1.

A class diagram uses a rectangle box to represent a class, with all fields, properties, and methods inside the box. It uses the empty arrow head to show the inheritance relationship. The arrow points to the super class from the sub class. The inheritance relationship is often called an "is-a" relationship, because a sub type "is-a" super type.

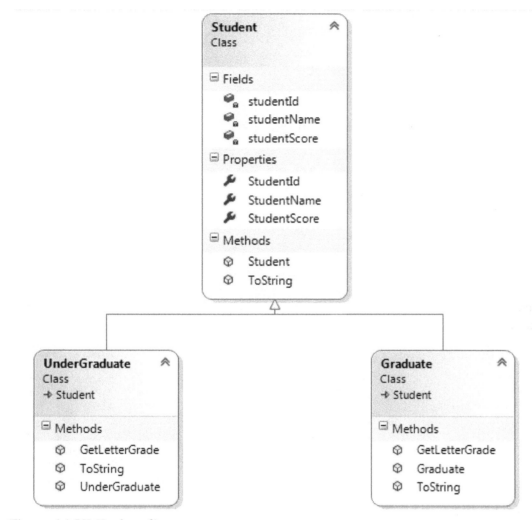

Figure 6.1 UML class diagram

As you can see from the diagram, neither Undergraduate nor Graduate classes need to repeat the common fields and properties. They just need those unique member elements. When a change is needed for student name, only the Student class needs to be updated. This avoids many potential errors.

Test Your Understanding 6.1

A super class contains all the common attributes and fields of the sub classes so that the sub classes don't need to include those members.

A. True
B. False

Test Your Understanding 6.2

The relationship between the super type and sub type in an inheritance is often called an _____
relationship.
A. super-sub
B. belongs to
C. has-a
D. is-a

Test Your Understanding 6.3

A diagram with rectangles to represent classes with fields, properties, and methods inside the box and
arrows showing the relationships is a(n) _____ class diagram.
A. UML
B. CML
C. UCL
D. UMC

Solution:

Step 1. Add the Student class:

Create a new project called Chapter6Student. Right click on the project in the "Solution Explorer"

window, and add a new class called "Student". In the Student Class, nothing new is introduced. Just

type the code as shown below:


```
namespace Chapter6Student
{
    public class Student
    {
        // fields
        private string studentId;
        private string studentName;
        private int studentScore;
        // properties
        public string StudentId
        {
```

```
        get { return studentId; }
        set { studentId = value; }
    }
    public string StudentName
    {
        get { return studentName; }
        set { studentName = value; }
    }
    public int StudentScore
    {
        get { return studentScore; }
        set { studentScore = value; }
    }
    // constructor
    public Student(string studentId, string studentName, int studentScore)
    {
        this.studentId = studentId;
        this.studentName = studentName;
        this.studentScore = studentScore;
    }
    public override string ToString()
    {
        string str;
        str = string.Format("Name: {0} Socre: {1}", StudentName, StudentScore);
        return str;
    }
}
}
```

Step 2. Add the Undergraduate class:

Next, right click on the project Chapter6Student in the "Solution Explorer" window again to add a new class called "Undergraduate.cs". Add the code as shown in Figure 6.2.

```
1   namespace Chapter6Student
2   {
3       public class UnderGraduate:Student
4       {
5           // constructor
6           public UnderGraduate (string studentId, string studentName,
7               int studentScore)
8               :base(studentId, studentName, studentScore)
9           {
10          }
11          // method
12          public string GetLetterGrade()
13          {
14              string letterGrade;
15              if (StudentScore >= 94)
16                  letterGrade = "A";
17              else if (StudentScore >= 90)
18                  letterGrade = "A-";
19              else if (StudentScore >= 87)
20                  letterGrade = "B+";
21              else if (StudentScore >= 84)
22                  letterGrade = "B";
23              else if (StudentScore >= 80)
24                  letterGrade = "B-";
25              else if (StudentScore >= 77)
26                  letterGrade = "C+";
27              else if (StudentScore >= 74)
28                  letterGrade = "C";
29              else if (StudentScore >= 70)
30                  letterGrade = "C-";
31              else if (StudentScore >= 67)
32                  letterGrade = "D+";
33              else if (StudentScore >= 64)
34                  letterGrade = "D";
35              else if (StudentScore >= 60)
36                  letterGrade = "D-";
37              else
38                  letterGrade = "F";
39              return letterGrade;
40          }
41          public override string ToString()
42          {
43              string str;
44              str = base.ToString() + string.Format("Letter grade: {0}",
45                  GetLetterGrade());
46              return str;
47          }
48      }
49  }
```

Figure 6.2 Code for Undergraduate class

Line 3: in addition to the normal class declaration, you added ":Student". This indicates that the current class inherits from the Student class. So, if class A inherits from class B, you use A:B in the class header.

Lines 6 to 10 define the constructor, but only Line 8 is new. This indicates the three arguments are passed to the super class constructor. In other words, the current constructor will not do anything to those three parameters. The super class constructor will handle it. The super class is also called the base class. It calls the super class constructor by passing arguments for the fields in the super class.

Line 44: The base.ToString() will call the ToString() method in the base class and adds content there.

Test Your Understanding 6.4
If Class A inherits from Class B, you don't need to do anything on Class B.
A. True
B. False

Test Your Understanding 6.5
If Class A inherits from Class B, you should add :B in the Class A header to indicate Class A inherits from Class B.
A. True
B. False

Test Your Understanding 6.6
Constructors in a sub class often need to call the super class constructor by using :base().
A. True
B. False

Step 3. Add the Graduate class:

Next, right click on the project Chapter6Student in the "Solution Explorer" window again to add a new class called "Graduate.cs". Add the code as shown below:

```
namespace Chapter6Student
{
    public class Graduate:Student
```

```csharp
{
    // constructor
    public Graduate(string studentId, string studentName,
        int studentScore)
        :base(studentId, studentName, studentScore)
    {
    }
    // methods
    public string GetLetterGrade()
    {
        string letterGrade;
        if (StudentScore >= 90)
            letterGrade = "A";
        else if (StudentScore >= 80)
            letterGrade = "B";
        else if (StudentScore >= 70)
            letterGrade = "C";
        else if (StudentScore >= 60)
            letterGrade = "D";
        else
            letterGrade = "F";
        return letterGrade;
    }
    public override string ToString()
    {
        string str;
        str = base.ToString() + string.Format(" Letter grade: {0}",
            GetLetterGrade());
        return str;
    }
}
}
```

Step 4. Demonstrate the classes in the Main() method.

Finally, in the "Solution Explorer" window, double click on "Program.cs" to write code in the Main() method to test the classes. Type in code that resemble Figure 6.3.

```
1      using System;
2      using System.Collections.Generic;
3
4      namespace Chapter6Student
5      {
6          class Program
7          {
8              static void Main(string[] args)
9              {
10                 List<Student> allStudents = new List<Student>();
11                 UnderGraduate ud1 = new UnderGraduate("111", "Alice",
12                     98);
13                 allStudents.Add(ud1);
14                 UnderGraduate ud2 = new UnderGraduate("222", "Bob",
15                     88);
16                 allStudents.Add(ud2);
17                 Graduate g1 = new Graduate("333", "Chuck", 76);
18                 allStudents.Add(g1);
19                 Graduate g2 = new Graduate("444", "Dan", 56);
20                 allStudents.Add(g2);
21                 foreach(Student s in allStudents)
22                 {
23                     Console.WriteLine(s);
24                 }
25                 Console.ReadKey();
26             }
27         }
28     }
```

Figure 6.3 Code for example 6.1 Main() method

Line 10 introduces a new concept, the List. A List is almost the same as an array, but a List is more convenient to use. A List has more methods and can expand as needed. This line declares a new List called allStudents that can hold any Student. The class name in the bracket <Student> indicates the List will hold only the Student type. Because both undergraduate and graduate inherits from Student, we say the relationship is an "is a" relationship. In other words, an undergraduate is a student, and a graduate is a student too.

Using Student to represent both undergraduate and graduate is called polymorphism in object oriented programming. Polymorphism means "multiple forms". In this example, allStudents can have "two forms", an undergraduate or a graduate.

Line 13 uses the Add method of a List to add the new object ud1 created in Lines 11 and 12 (due to the width of the print screen, we added the line break. You don't have to for your own code).

Lines 21 to 24 are a foreach loop that pulls out every element in the allStudents List one at a time, and then displays them on the console screen (Line 23).

Test Your Understanding 6.7

The statement, List<Student> allStudents = new List<Student>(); will create a list called allStudents that can only hold references to a student type, not any other types.
A. True
B. False

Test Your Understanding 6.8

If the Graduate class inherits from the Student class, then, anywhere in the code, when a Student object is expected, a Graduate object can be used. This is called _____.
A. encapsulation
B. polymorphism
C. inheritance
D. representation

Test Your Understanding 6.9
A List in C# is similar to an array that can be used to hold a group of values. However, a List is more convenient because _____.
A. it has more methods, and it runs faster
B. it can expand as needed, and it runs faster
C. it has more methods, and it can expand as needed
D. none of the above

Test Your Understanding 6.10
To add an element to a List, you can use the _____ method of the List class.
A. Add()
B. Include()
C. Element()
D. AddElement()

Programming Challenge 6.1

The Tiny Company has two types of employees: full time and part time. Both types have an employee ID and employee name. Full time employees have a salary, and part time employees have an hourly wage and hours worked.

A full time employee gets paid weekly by dividing the salary by 52 while a part time employee gets paid by the product of hourly wage and hours worked.

Specifically, you will create an Employee class with the common elements (employee ID, employee name, ToString() method). Then create a Fulltime employee class with salary field and the GetWeeklyPaid() method. Similarly, create a Parttime employee class with hourly wage and hours worked fields and the GetWeeklyPaid() method. Add appropriate properties, constructors, and ToString() methods. Each class should be in its own cs file.

Finally, demonstrate the classes in the Main() method of the Program class with data made up for two full time employees and two part time employees in a List. Display the employee's payment data in a foreach loop.

Example 6.2

Problem:

The Tiny Mart keeps track of two types of customers. A member customer pays everything at 5% discount. A VIP customer pays everything at 10% discount. A member customer pays an annual fee of $10.00. A VIP customer membership is not bought. A VIP customer must register so that the purchase record can be kept. Once a VIP customer spends more than $1,000.00, he or she automatically receives 10% discount. For simplicity, we don't allow a membership customer to automatically become a VIP customer. Instead, the application will suggest that the member customer registers as a VIP customer. If a VIP customer order makes the $1000 mark, that order will receive the discount immediately. For example, if on day one a VIP customer spends $100, there will be no discount. In Day 2, if the same customer spends $900, they will receive a $9 discount (because 100 plus 900 is 1000 and thus qualifies for the VIP discount).

Demonstrate the classes by writing code in the Main() method of the program with the following activities:

Create a VIP customer, c1 with id = "111", name = "Alice", and make a first purchase of $500, followed by displaying purchasing data. Next, Alice makes a purchase of $1000, followed by displaying purchasing data. Finally, Alice makes a purchase of $100, followed by displaying purchasing data.

Additionally, create a membership customer, c2 with id = "222", name = "Bob", with a first purchase of $500, followed by displaying purchasing data. Next, Bob makes a purchase of $1000, followed by displaying purchasing data.

When you run the program, you should see Bob receive a discount while Alice does not for the first purchase.

Analysis:

Both types of customers have customer ID and name. You can also include constant variables for member discount and VIP discount. This will make changing the discount rate easier in the future. Both types of customers need to keep track of current purchase and accumulated amount. Also, a common method, MakePurchase(),will add the current purchase amount to the accumulated amount and update the current purchase amount. Because the discount rates are different, and you want the two sub classes to have their own MakePurchase() methods, you will make this method in the super class virtual, which allows the sub classes to override it.

Test Your Understanding 6.11
In C#, a virtual method in the super class can be overridden by a method in the sub class if a different implementation is used in a sub class.
A. True
B. False

Test Your Understanding 6.12
In C#, a virtual method in the super class must be overridden by a method in the sub class.
A. True
B. False

Test Your Understanding 6.13
In C#, any method in the super class can be overridden by a sub class if a different implementation is used in the sub class.
A. True
B. False

Solution:

Step 1. Add the Base Type -- Customer class.

Create a new project called Chapter6Customer. Add a new class called Customer to the project. The code for Customer class/base class/super class is displayed below. Note the keyword "virtual" in the MakePurchase() method indicates the method can be overridden by the methods in its sub classes if necessary.

```csharp
namespace Chapter6Customer
{
    class Customer
    {
        // fields
        public const decimal VIPDiscountRate = 0.10m;
        public const decimal memberDiscountRate = 0.05m;
        private string customerId;
        private string customerName;
        private decimal accumulatedPurchase;
        private decimal currentPurchaseAmount;
        // properties
        public string CustomerId
        {
            get { return customerId; }
            set { customerId = value; }
        }
        public string CustomerName
        {
            get { return customerName; }
            set { customerName = value; }
        }
        public decimal CurrentPurchaseAmount
        {
            get { return currentPurchaseAmount; }
            set { currentPurchaseAmount = value; }
        }
        public decimal AccumulatedPurchase
        {
            get { return accumulatedPurchase; }
            set { accumulatedPurchase = value; }
        }
        // constructor
        public Customer(string customerId, string customerName)
        {
            this.customerId = customerId;
            this.customerName = customerName;
            accumulatedPurchase = 0.0m;
        }
        // methods
        public virtual void MakePurchase(decimal purchaseAmount)
        {
```

```
            if (purchaseAmount > 0)
            {
                AccumulatedPurchase += purchaseAmount;
            }
        }
        // ToString() method
        public override string ToString()
        {
            string str;
            str = string.Format("{0}: Total Purchase this year {1:C}", CustomerName,
AccumulatedPurchase);
            return str;
        }
    }
}
```

Step 2: Add a Sub Type -- the VIPCustomer class.

Add another class called VIPCustomer to the project. The code for VIP customer class/sub class is displayed below. Note the use of :Customer, which indicates the VIPCustomer class is inherited from the Customer class. Also note the keyword "override" in the MakePurchase() method. This keyword allows the MakePurchase() method to behave differently than its parent's method with the same name, same parameters (this is called method signature), and same return type.

```
namespace Chapter6Customer
{
    class VIPCustomer: Customer
    {
        // constructor
        public VIPCustomer(string customerId, string customerName)
            :base(customerId, customerName)
        {
        }
        // override MakePurchase() method
        public override void MakePurchase(decimal purchaseAmount)
        {

            if (purchaseAmount > 0m && AccumulatedPurchase > 1000m)
            {
                CurrentPurchaseAmount = purchaseAmount;
                base.MakePurchase(purchaseAmount * (1 - VIPDiscountRate));
            } else if (purchaseAmount > 0m)
            {
                CurrentPurchaseAmount = purchaseAmount;
                base.MakePurchase(purchaseAmount);
            }
        }
        // override ToString() method
        public override string ToString()
```

```
    {
        string str;
        str = base.ToString();
        if (AccumulatedPurchase >= 1000m)
            str += string.Format(" You saved {0:C} as an VIP.",
CurrentPurchaseAmount*VIPDiscountRate);
        return str;
    }

    }
}
```

Step 3: Add Another Sub Type -- MemberCustomer class.

Next, add a new class called MemberCustomer to the project. The Member customer class is another sub class and is very similar to the VIPCustomer class. The code is displayed below:

```
namespace Chapter6Customer
{
    class MemberCustomer: Customer
    {
        // constructor
        public MemberCustomer(string employeeId, string employeeName)
            :base(employeeId, employeeName)
        {
        }
        // override MakePurchase() method
        public override void MakePurchase(decimal purchaseAmount)
        {
            if (purchaseAmount > 0.0m)
            {
                CurrentPurchaseAmount = purchaseAmount;
                base.MakePurchase(purchaseAmount*(1.0m - memberDiscountRate));
            }

        }
        //ToString() method
        public override string ToString()
        {
            string str;
            str = base.ToString() + string.Format(" You saved {0:C} as a member.",
CurrentPurchaseAmount * memberDiscountRate);
            if (AccumulatedPurchase > 1000m)
                str += string.Format("\nYou are qualified as a VIP customer. Please talk to
a manager.");
            return str;
        }
    }
}
```

Step 4: Demonstrate the classes in the Main() method.

Finally, the statements in the Main() method of the Programming class should look like the following:

```csharp
using System;

namespace Chapter6Customer
{
    class Program
    {
        static void Main(string[] args)
        {
            // create a regular customer
            VIPCustomer c1 = new VIPCustomer("111", "Alice");
            c1.MakePurchase(500);
            Console.WriteLine(c1);
            c1.MakePurchase(1000);
            Console.WriteLine(c1);
            c1.MakePurchase(100);
            Console.WriteLine(c1);
            Console.WriteLine();
            MemberCustomer c2 = new MemberCustomer("222", "Bob");
            c2.MakePurchase(500);
            Console.WriteLine(c2);
            c2.MakePurchase(1000);
            Console.WriteLine(c2);
            Console.ReadKey();
        }
    }
}
```

Test Your Understanding 6.14
When a method in the sub class overrides a method in the super class, the two methods must have the same signature.
A. True
B. False

Test Your Understanding 6.15
A method's name and parameter lists are often called a method's _____.
A. header
B. Main
C. signature
D. method body

Programming Challenge 6.2
The Tiny Bank provides two types of accounts. A checking account has an account number, customer ID, and balance. It can write a check, which will deduct the writing amount from the balance. It can make a deposit to increase the balance. A savings account has an account number, customer ID, interest rate, and balance. It can make a deposit the same as a checking account. It can also earn interest, which will be added to the balance. The interest is calculated as Interest amount = balance * (interest rate).

Decide what characteristics are common for both checking and savings accounts, and include these characteristics as members in the base class called BankAccount. Define subclasses for checking and savings by adding unique characteristics to its corresponding class. Each class must be in its own cs file.

Finally, use the Main() method in the default Program class to test your design with the following data:

Checking account number:11111; customer ID: 123, opening balance: $200.00; Write a check of $50.00; Make a deposit of $100.00. Display the balance after every activity.

Savings account number: 22222; customer ID: 789, opening balance: $1000.00, interest rate 0.05; Make a deposit of $2000.00; Calculate the interest; Add interest to the account. Display the balance after every activity.

6.2 Abstract Method and Abstract Class

In Example 6.1, you may notice that both Graduate and Undergraduate sub classes have a GetLetterGrade() method that is not in the super class. Why is a common method is not in the super class? This is because they have different implementations. However, a better design is to put the GetLetterGrade() method in the super class as an abstract method.

We have to make the GetLetterGrade() method in the super class as abstract because we don't have any implementations for that method. The implementation depends on whether a student is a graduate or undergraduate. An abstract method has only a method header without a method body, not even the pair of curly braces. The abstract method terminated with a semicolon.

Open Chatper6Student project of Example 6.1. Inside the Student class, add the following abstract method right before the ToString() method:

```
public abstract string GetLetterGrade();
```

You will notice that the method name has a red squiggly line. If you point your mouse over it, you will see why.

```
GetLetterGrade();
```

ⓥ string Student.GetLetterGrade()

'Student.GetLetterGrade()' is abstract but it is contained in non-abstract class 'Student'

The error message tells you that you must make the class abstract because you now have an abstract method. Therefore, add the keyword "abstract" right before the "class Student" in the class header, like this:

```
abstract class Student
```

Note that an abstract class cannot be instantiated, or cannot have objects. In other words, Tiny College can have graduate or undergraduate students, but cannot have any categorized as simply 'students'.

The Student class is now free of errors. However, both the UnderGraduate and Graduate classes have errors. This is because when a sub class inherits from an abstract super class, all abstract methods in the super class must be overridden or kept abstract. Go to both classes and add the "override" keyword to the GetLetterGrade() methods in both UnderGraduate and Graduate classes:

```
public override string GetLetterGrade()
```

The benefit of adding an abstract method in the super class without implementation is that you can be sure that all sub classes have that method with its own implementation. In our example, you can be sure that all sub classes from the Student class have a GetLetterGrade() method. No programmers can "forget" to add that method in a sub class.

Test Your Understanding 6.16
If a class in C# has an abstract method, the class must _____.
A. have a corresponding overloaded method
B. have a corresponding overridden method
C. have no other method(s)
D. be abstract

Test Your Understanding 6.17
A benefit of adding an abstract method in the super class without implementation is _____.
A. for the backward compatibility
B. flexibility
C. that you can be sure that all sub classes have that method with its own implementation.
D. code brevity

Test Your Understanding 6.18
Unlike a concrete class, an abstract class cannot _____.
A. be instantiated
B. be updated
C. have fields
D. have non abstract methods

Test Your Understanding 6.19
When a sub class inherits from an abstract super class, all abstract methods in the super class must be

_____.
A. overridden
B. overloaded
C. overridden or kept abstract.
D. overloaded or kept abstract

Programming Challenge 6.3
Make a copy of Program Challenge 6.1 project folder. Open the new Programming Challenge 6.1 in
Visual Studio. With Employee class in code view, add GetWeeklyPaid() abstract method to the class.
Make all necessary changes so that the program can still run as expected.

6.3 Interface

Interface is similar to an abstract class, but it plays a very different role. A superclass defines common

behavior for related subclasses. For example, a super class called Student can be used for all types of

student to inherit, but not for faculty. An interface, on the other hand, can be used to define common

behaviors for any classes (including unrelated classes; for example, both students and faculty can set

up an email account). Additionally, a class can only inherit from one class, but can implement many

interfaces.

An interface is like a contract that if a class implements this interface, it meets all the requirements of

the interface. In everyday life, suppose you want to buy a plug for an outlet of a new house. You

would need to find out about the pins, voltages, etc. Or, if you know the type follows the US

Department of Commerce International Trade Administration (ITA) standard, you can buy the same

type of plug and be sure they will match. You can think of the type by ITA as an interface. Even

though ITA does not make any outlets or plugs, if a plug and an outlet meet the ITA's type standard,

you can be sure they will match.

Interfaces define a specific set of functionality without having to provide any details. Any class that implements the interface has to provide the details and make the methods work. Different classes implementing the same interface can have different implementations of the same functionality. For example, both credit cards and debit cards have a "make a purchase" functionality, but credit card purchases increase balance while debit card purchases decrease balance.

Example 6.3

Problem:

Continue Example 6.1 for Tiny College. Create an interface called IRegistration with two properties: parttimeMaxHours and fulltimeMaxHours , and two methods: checkPrerequisite() and addClass().

Next, create a new class called ParttimeStudent that inherits from Graduate and implements IRegistration interface.

Finally, demonstrate the ParttimeStudent in the Main() method.

Solution:

Open the Chapter6Student project in Visual Studio. In the "Solution Explorer" window, right click on the "Chapter6Student" project. Select "Add", then select "New Item". In the middle panel of the popup "Add new item" window, select "Interface", then type in "IRegistration.cs" in the "Name" field at the bottom. Refer to Figure 6.4 for details.

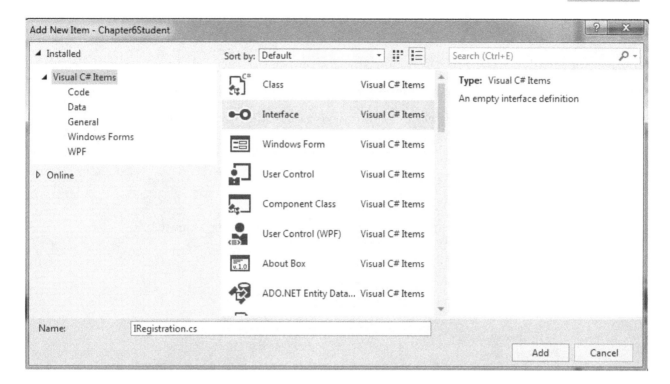

Figure 6.4 Add New Item window

Click on the "Add" button to have a blank interface.

Use the code from Figure 6.5 for the IRegistration interface.

```
1      using System;
2
3    □namespace Chapter6Student
4      {
            1 reference
5    □     interface IRegistration
6          {
               1 reference
7              int ParttimeMaxHours { get; set; }
               1 reference
8              int FulltimeMaxHours { get; set; }
               2 references
9              Boolean CheckPrerequisite();
               2 references
10             string AddClass();
11         }
12     }
```

Figure 6.5 Code for IRegistration interface.

Explanation:

You may notice that there is no access modifier for any property or method in an interface. Also, a method does not have a body as an abstract method does. All members of an interface are public and abstract by default. Additionally, interfaces cannot have data fields. By convention, all interface names begin with the capital letter "I".

Next, add a class called ParttimeStudent to the project. Use the code from Figure 6.6.

```
1    namespace Chapter6Student
2    {
         7 references
3        class ParttimeStudent : Graduate, IRegistration
4        {
5            // constructor
             2 references
6            public ParttimeStudent(string studentId, string studentName,
7                int studentScore)
8                : base(studentId, studentName, studentScore)
9            {
10           }

             1 reference
12           public int ParttimeMaxHours { get; set; } = 6;
             1 reference
13           public int FulltimeMaxHours { get; set; } = 18;
             2 references
14           public string AddClass()
15           {
16               if (CheckPrerequisite())
17                   return "Class added.";
18               else
19                   return "Cannot add class at this time.";
20           }
             2 references
21           public bool CheckPrerequisite()
22           {
23               if(GetLetterGrade() == "A")
24                   return true;
25               return false;
26           }
27       }
28   }
```

Figure 6.6 Code for the ParttimeStudent class.

Explanation:

Line 3 indicates that the ParttimeStudent class inherits from the Graduate class and implements the IRegistration interface.

Line 12 sets the default value for ParttimeMaxHours property at 6.

Finally, update the Main() method of the Program class by adding (updating) to the following code.

```
ParttimeStudent p1 = new ParttimeStudent("555", "Franklin", 88);
ParttimeStudent p2 = new ParttimeStudent("666", "Gray", 99);
allStudents.Add(p1);
allStudents.Add(p2);
foreach(Student s in allStudents)
{
    Console.WriteLine(s);
    if(s is ParttimeStudent)
        Console.WriteLine(((ParttimeStudent)s).AddClass());
}
```

In the code "is ParttimeStudent", check if the object is a ParttimeStudent type. If yes, then include the AddClass() method.

(ParttimeStudent)s down casts the objects to ParttimeStudent from a Student type so that you can use the AddClass() method.

Test Your Understanding 6.20
Interface is similar to an abstract class, but it plays a very different role.
A. True
B. False

Test Your Understanding 6.21

An interface is like a _____ . If a class implements this interface, it meets all the requirements of the interface.
A. method
B. contract
C. window
D. field

Test Your Understanding 6.22
All members of an interface are _____ by default.
A. public and abstract
B. private and abstract
C. public and static
D. private and static

Test Your Understanding 6.23
In C#, an interface cannot have _____.
A. data fields
B. properties
C. methods
D. both properties and methods in the same interface

Test Your Understanding 6.24
Which of the following statements about interface naming is correct?
A. all interface names must begin with a lower case "i"
B. all interface names must begin with the upper case "I"
C. by convention, all interface names begin with a lower case "i"
D. by convention, all interface names begin with the upper case "I"

Programming Challenge 6.4

Open Programming Challenge 6.3 in Visual Studio. Create an interface called IMinimumWage with a property for state minimum hourly wage and a method called MetMinimum that returns true if the wage meets the minimum.

Next, create a new class called CommissionEmployee that inherits from ParttimeEmployee and implements an IMinimumWage interface. A commission employee has a name, weekly sales amount, commission rate, and weekly hours worked. A commission employee is paid by weekly sales amount multiplied by the commission rate.

Finally, demonstrate the CommissionEmployee class by creating two commission employees in the Main() method: one that meets the minimum wage and one that does not.

6.4 Agile Metrics

Metrics are good communication tools that allow both stakeholders and team members to know where they are and how well they are doing (Broadus, 2013). Such communication is a success factor for agile project management (Tilk, 2016). In this section, we introduce three metrics. They are the Kanban board, burn down chart, and information radiator.

6.4.1 Kanban Board

You learned the concept of Kanban in chapter two. Every user story is written on one card, and each card is posted under one category to indicate the current status of that user story. A card will be rearranged after the status changes. This Kanban provides a visual representation of the software development status.

Agile teams often use a white board or simply the wall with sticky notes. The board is separated into five regions as shown in Figure 6.7

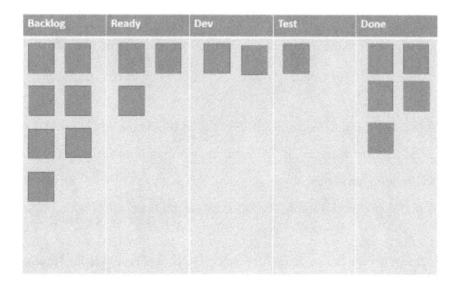

Figure 6.7 A Sample Kanban Board

Backlog category: The product owner is in charge of this category. A user story is written on a sticky note and posted in the order of priority. Each story also contains a story point estimated by the development team. Depending on the size of the project, the list can be long and the product owner may update the category as needed, usually between the sprints.

Ready category: Stories in this category are in the hands of the development team. The stories are picked from the backlog category and are for the current sprint. Because each story usually should be broken down into multiple tasks, a sticky note from this column and any notes to the right of the same row will represent the different tasks of the same story. Estimation of the story is also changed from story points to time units, such as hours. There can be multiple tasks (sticky notes) on each row to represent the tasks for that story.

Development category: The development team is working on these tasks.

Test category: The development team is testing on these tasks to make sure the code is working as expected.

Done category: The tasks in this column are considered ready to be delivered to a customer. When all tasks of a user story are in this column, the sticky note that represents the user story is moved to this column.

Each column identifies a key hand-off or milestone for the tasks as a story is moved from one column to the next. Holding daily scrum meetings in front of the Kanban board makes the meeting more effective and also facilitates information sharing among the team members (Dinsmore and Cabanis-Brewin, 2014). Each member can easily see what the rest of the team are working on.

The Kanban board allows for quick feedback on potential issues. For example, if two members are working on the same column of the same row, they can discuss with each other to avoid interrupting each other's work. Also, the member working on the next column can estimate what task will come next and thus plan ahead.

In addition to providing a visual presentation of the project work flow, the major idea is to limit the number of stories that are a work-in-process (WIP), especially in the development and test columns (Ordysinski, 2013) so that bottlenecks can be identified. If more than a minimum number of WIPs are in a column, other members should take the opportunity to step up and assist.

Test Your Understanding 6.25
A sticky note on a Kanban board usually represents a user story.
A. True
B. False

Test Your Understanding 6.26
Which of the following is NOT an agile metric?
A. Kanban board
B. Burn-down chart
C. information radiator
D. user stories

Test Your Understanding 6.27

Metrics are good _____ that allow both stakeholders and team members to know where they are and how well they are doing.
A. status checks
B. measurements
C. reporting tools
D. communication tools

Test Your Understanding 6.28
Except the Backlog column, each row in a Kanban board represents a user story.
A. True
B. False

Test Your Understanding 6.29
Which of the following is NOT a benefit of using Kanban?
A. visual representation of the status
B. identifying any bottlenecks
C. code transparency
D. communication metrics

Test Your Understanding 6.30

A user story is often estimated in hours, and a task of a user story is often estimated by story points.
A. True
B. False

6.4.2 Burn-Down Charts

A burn-down chart has two axes. The horizontal axis displays the number of days in the sprint, with larger numbers on the left and smaller numbers on the right. The vertical axis displays the number of hours left. Some teams display the number of hours left for the whole project, while some teams just display it for one sprint. This book follows the latter.

Let us explain how to draw a burn-down chart with an example. Suppose a team has 3 members, and each member works 8 hours a day, 5 days a week, and a sprint is time-boxed at 2 weeks. The team has 10 days marked on the horizontal axis and 240 hours (3x8x5x2 = 240) on the vertical axis. When there are 10 days left, there are 240 hours' worth of tasks left. When there are 9 days left, there are 216 hours' worth of tasks left. When there are 8 days left, there are 192 hours' worth of tasks left. Continuing with this trend, when there is 1 day left, there are 24 hours' worth of tasks left. When there are zero days left, there are zero hours' worth of tasks left. This is called a perfect burn down line or a planned burn down line. This line represents the ideal situation and is used for comparison purposes. Figure 6.8 displays the planned burn down chart.

Figure 6.8 Planned Burn Down Chart

On the same chart, let's draw another line to reflect the team's actual burn down. Suppose after the first day of work, the team completes 30 hours' worth of tasks. Mark the chart with (9, 210). Then there are two points on the chart. In the beginning of the sprint, there are always 240 hours' worth of tasks left (10, 240), and on 9 days left, there are 210 hours' worth of tasks left. Figure 6.9 shows the result after one day's work.

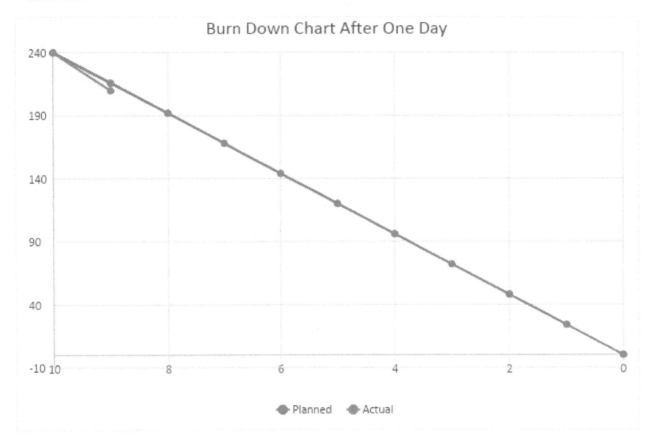

Figure 6.9 The burn down chart after one day's work.

Lets continue to draw the burn down chart for the team. Suppose on the second day (8 days left), the team completes another 35 hours' worth of tasks. Now there are only 175 (210-35) hours left. The new point is (8, 175). Figure 6.10 displays the burn down chart after two days' work.

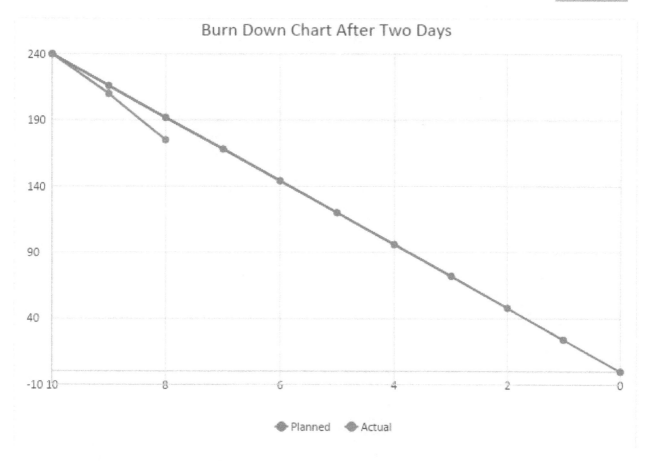

Figure 6.10 The burn down chart after two days' work.

Suppose, on the third day (7 days left), the team completes only 20 hours' worth of tasks. Now there are only 155 (175-20) hours left. The new point is (7, 155). Figure 6.11 displays the burn down chart after three days' work by the team.

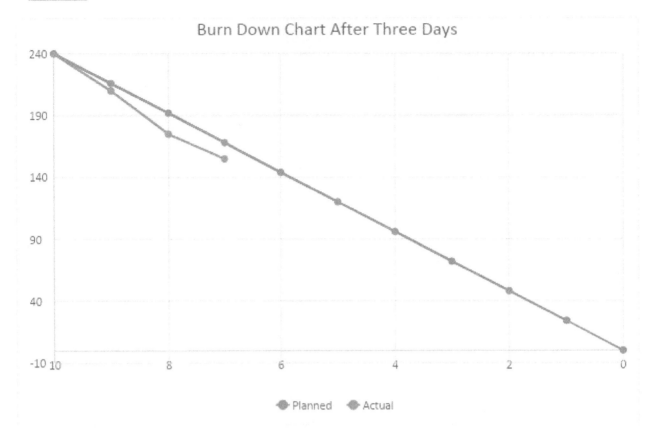

Figure 6.11 The burn down chart after three days' work.

You should have no difficulty completing the chart as the team completes more work until the end of the sprint.

A word of warning: it is possible for the actual line to go up when something went wrong (Vanderjack, 2015). For example, a task might've been underestimated. In general, if the "actual" line is under the "planned" line, the team is ahead of schedule, as shown in the figures. However, if the "actual" line is above the "planned" line for several days, the team must determine if they are able to finish the planned amount of work within the sprint.

Test Your Understanding 6.31
In a burn down chart, the horizontal axis represents number of hours left, and the vertical axis represents the number of days left in the sprint.
A. True
B. False

Test Your Understanding 6.32
The perfect burn down line is a straight line from top left to bottom right.
A. True
B. False

Test Your Understanding 6.33
To draw the burn down chart, at the end of each day, the team finds a point that represents how many days are left and how many hours' worth of work are left and connect that point to the existing trend.
A. True
B. False

Test Your Understanding 6.34
If the team burn down chart is above the planned burn down line, this indicates that the team will complete the sprint as scheduled.
A. True
B. False

6.4.3 Information Radiators

One major communication limitation is that the result is not readily available (Koch, 2005). For example, the result of face-to-face communication is stored in our memory, which may not last long. Written documents filed away in a cabinet may never be seen again. Even files in a computer may not be easily found (do you remember the file name for your last homework assignment?). Even if a file in computer is easy to find, you may not open it every day. "Information radiator" in agile was invented to solve this problem.

Information radiator is a low tech metric used in agile software development. It keeps all useful information posted around the team's physical workspace so that they will see it on a regular basis. It is persistent and will be there at all times. It is up to date and reflects the team's current status. It is easy to locate when a member needs it. It is simple to use, since one just raises their head to see the team's progress. In short, the information radiator provides a simple and effective way for any stakeholder to understand the exact status of the development project.

The radiator also helps reinforce important philosophies and principles among the team members. Like TV commercials that are on screen all the time, the radiator can affect team subconscious with information that promotes team moral. Teams can decide what to post and how often to update the posts.

Test Your Understanding 6.35
Information posted around a team's physical working space is called a(n) _____.
A. valuable data
B. team domain
C. information posted
D. information radiator

Test Your Understanding 6.36
An information radiator can help enhance team moral.
A. True
B. False

Test Your Understanding 6.37
Information radiators were invented to solve a major limitation of communication. What was the limitation?
A. Not everyone in an agile team spoke English
B. Not everyone had a computer open at all time
C. The result of communication was not readily available
D. The result of communication was not signed by a manager

6.5 Chapter Summary

In this chapter, you learn that if two or more classes have common members (fields and methods), a super class can be created to include those common members and allow other classes to inherit the super class and add their own unique members. This is not just to save typing time. It is one of the most important aspects of object oriented programming.

In class inheritance, if different sub classes have different implementation of the same method, then you can use abstract classes. An abstract method can be used in the super class. An abstract method has a method header only without a body part.

Similar to an abstract class, an interface can be used to define behaviors for a group of classes as long as they all implement the interface. All interface members are public and abstract by default.

You also learned the common communication techniques used in agile. They are the Kanban board, burn down chart, and information radiator. These are just some techniques for you to start with. In the real world, you may modify and enhance them for your own team.

6.6 References:

Broadus III, W. A. (2013). Stakeholder Needs and Expectations: Planning Your Agile Project and Program Metrics. Defense AT & L. Vol.42, Issue 6, Nov/Dec, p 50-54.

Dinsmore, P. C., & Cabanis-Brewin, J. (2014). The AMA Handbook of Project Management. New York: AMACOM.

Koch, A. S. (2005). Agile Software Development : Evaluating the Methods for Your Organization. Boston, MA: Artech House, Inc.

Ordysinski, T. (2013). Kanban Based Information Management in Organization, Studies & Proceedings Polish Association for Knowledge Management, 63, p. 76-85.

Tilk, D. (2016). Five Steps to Agile Project Success, Internal Auditor. Apr. Vol. 73 Issue 2, p57-61.

Vanderjack, B. (2015). The Agile Edge : Managing Projects Effectively Using Agile Scrum. New York: Business Expert Press.

6.7 Solutions to Programming Challenges

Programming Challenge 6.1

```
namespace Chapter6Employee
{
    class Employee
    {
        // fields
        private string employeeId;
        private string employeeName;
        // properties
        public string EmployeeId
        {
            get { return employeeId; }
            set { employeeId = value; }
        }
        public string EmployeeName
        {
            get { return employeeName; }
```

```
        set { employeeName = value; }
    }
    // constructor
    public Employee(string employeeId, string employeeName)
    {
        this.employeeId = employeeId;
        this.employeeName = employeeName;
    }
    // ToString() method
    public override string ToString()
    {
        string str;
        str = string.Format("ID: {0} Name: {1}", EmployeeId, EmployeeName);
        return str;
    }
  }
}
```

The Full Time employee class

```
namespace Chapter6Employee
{
    class FullTimeEmployee: Employee
    {
        // field
        private decimal annualSalary;
        // property
        public decimal AnnualSalary
        {
            get { return annualSalary; }
            set { annualSalary = value; }
        }
        // constructor
        public FullTimeEmployee(string employeeId, string employeeName, decimal
annualSalary)
            :base(employeeId, employeeName)
        {
            this.annualSalary = annualSalary;
        }
        // GetWeeklyPaid() method
        public decimal GetWeeklyPaid()
        {
            decimal payAmount;
            payAmount = AnnualSalary / 52;
            return payAmount;
        }
        // ToString() method
        public override string ToString()
        {
            string str;
            str = base.ToString() + string.Format(" Pay amount: {0:C}", GetWeeklyPaid());
            return str;
        }
    }
```

```
}
```

The Part time employee class

```
namespace Chapter6Employee
{
    class PartTimeEmployee: Employee
    {
        // fields
        private decimal hourlyWage;
        private decimal hoursWorked;
        // properties
        public decimal HourlyWage
        {
            get { return hourlyWage; }
            set { hourlyWage = value; }
        }
        public decimal HoursWorked
        {
            get { return hoursWorked; }
            set { hoursWorked = value; }
        }
        // constructor
        public PartTimeEmployee(string employeeId, string employeeName,
            decimal hourlyWage, decimal hoursWorked)
            :base(employeeId, employeeName)
        {
            this.hourlyWage = hourlyWage;
            this.hoursWorked = hoursWorked;
        }
        // GetWeeklyPaid method
        public decimal GetWeeklyPaid()
        {
            decimal payAmount;
            payAmount = HoursWorked * HourlyWage;
            return payAmount;
        }
        //ToString() method
        public override string ToString()
        {
            string str;
            str = base.ToString() + string.Format(" Pay amount: {0:C}", GetWeeklyPaid());
            return str;
        }
    }
}
```

Demo code in the Main() method

```
using System;
using System.Collections.Generic;

namespace Chapter6Employee
```

```csharp
{
    class Program
    {
        static void Main(string[] args)
        {
            // create a List for all employees
            List<Employee> allEmployees = new List<Employee>();
            // create two full time employees
            FullTimeEmployee fe1 = new FullTimeEmployee("111", "Alice", 67888.00m);
            FullTimeEmployee fe2 = new FullTimeEmployee("222", "Bob", 67555.00m);
            // create two part time employees
            PartTimeEmployee pe1 = new PartTimeEmployee("333", "Chuck", 22.12m, 20m);
            PartTimeEmployee pe2 = new PartTimeEmployee("444", "Dan", 23.33m, 18.45m);
            // add employees to the List
            allEmployees.Add(fe1);
            allEmployees.Add(fe2);
            allEmployees.Add(pe1);
            allEmployees.Add(pe2);
            // display data
            foreach(Employee emp in allEmployees)
            {
                Console.WriteLine(emp);
            }
            Console.ReadKey();
        }
    }
}
```

Programming Challenge 6.2

The BankAccount class

```csharp
class BankAccount
{
    // fields
    private int accountNumber;
    private int customerId;
    private decimal balance;
    // constructor
    public BankAccount(int accountNumber, int customerId, decimal balance)
    {
        this.accountNumber = accountNumber;
        this.customerId = customerId;
        this.balance = balance;
    }
    // Properties
    public int AccountNumber
    {
        get { return accountNumber; }
        set { accountNumber = value; }
    }
    public int CustomerId
    {
```

```
            get { return customerId;  }
            set { customerId = value; }
        }
        public decimal Balance
        {
            get { return balance; }
            set { balance = value; }
        }
        // method
        public void Deposit(decimal depositAmount)
        {
            balance += depositAmount;
        }
    }
```

The CheckingAccount class

```
    class CheckingAccount: BankAccount
    {
        // no fields
        // constructor
        public CheckingAccount(int accountNumber, int customerId, decimal balance): base
(accountNumber, customerId, balance)
        {

        }
        // no property
        // method
        public void WriteCheck(decimal checkAmount)
        {
            Balance -= checkAmount;
        }
    }
```

The SavingsAccount class

```
    class SavingsAccount: BankAccount
    {
        // field
        private decimal interestRate;
        // constructor
        public SavingsAccount(int accountNumber, int customerId, decimal balance, decimal
interestRate)
            :base(accountNumber, customerId, balance)
        {
            this.interestRate = interestRate;
        }
        // property
        public  decimal InterestRate
        {
            get { return interestRate; }
            set { interestRate = value; }
        }
```

```
    // method
    public void CalculateInterest()
    {
        decimal interest = Balance * interestRate;
        Balance += interest;
    }
}
```

The Main() method in the Programming class

```
class Program
{
    static void Main(string[] args)
    {
        // Checking
        Console.WriteLine("My checking account balance after each transaction");
        CheckingAccount checking1 = new CheckingAccount(1111111, 123, 200.00m);
        Console.WriteLine("{0}{1:C}", "My beginning balance: ", checking1.Balance);
        checking1.WriteCheck(50.00m);
        Console.WriteLine("{0}{1:C}", "After I wrote a check of $50, my balance is: ",
checking1.Balance);
        checking1.Deposit(100.00m);
        Console.WriteLine("{0}{1:C}", "Finally, I made a deposit of $100, my balance
is: ", checking1.Balance);
        // saving
        Console.WriteLine();
        Console.WriteLine("My saving account balance after each transaction");
        SavingsAccount saving1 = new SavingsAccount(2222222, 987, 1000.00m, 0.05m);
        Console.WriteLine("{0}{1:C}", "My beginning balance: ", saving1.Balance);
        saving1.Deposit(2000.00m);
        Console.WriteLine("{0}{1:C}", "I made a $2000 deposit, my balance is ",
saving1.Balance);
        saving1.CalculateInterest();
        Console.WriteLine("{0}{1:C}", "After adding the interest, my balace is ",
saving1.Balance);
        Console.WriteLine();
    }
}
```

6.8 Solutions to Test Your Understanding:

6.1 A; 6.2 D; 6.3 A; 6.4 A; 6.5 A; 6.6 A; 6.7 A; 6.8 B; 6.9 C; 6.10 A; 6.11 A; 6.12 B; 6.13 B; 6.14 A; 6.15 C; 6.16 D; 6.17 C; 6.18 A; 6.19 C; 6.20 A; 6.21 B; 6.22 A; 6.23 A; 6.24 D; 6.25 B; 6.26 D; 6.27 D; 6.28A; 6.29 C; 6.30 B; 6.31 B; 6.32 A; 6.33 A; 6.34 B; 6.35 D; 6.36 A; 6.37 C;

Chapter 7: C# Exception Handling and Agile Quality Assurance

Chapter Learning Outcomes

7.1 Recognizing the need for exception handling

7.2 Exemplifying exception handling in a program

7.3 Recalling the characteristics of software quality

7.4 Interpreting quality philosophies and principles and their relationships with pair programming

7.5 Exemplifying the Test Driven Development

7.1 What Is C# Exception?

So far, you focused on learning how to make the code run. It is time for you to learn that having an application that solves business problems is only half of the story. The other half, or perhaps more than half, is quality software.

Before you learn what an exception is, let's see an example:

Example 7.1

Problem:
Write an application that calculates the retail price based on the wholesale price plus mark ups. The program prompts the user for the wholesale price and management markup percentage, then displays the retail price.
For example, if the wholesale price is $10.00 and the markup percentage is 45%, then the retail price will be $14.50

Solution:

Create a new project called Chapter7RetailPrice. Type the code inside the Main() method of the Program class. Your completed code should resemble the following.

```csharp
using System;

namespace Chapter7RetailPrice
{
    class Program
    {
        static void Main(string[] args)
        {
            //Prompt user for wholesale price and markup percentage
            Console.WriteLine("Enter Wholesale Price:");
            double wholeSalePrice = double.Parse(Console.ReadLine());
            Console.WriteLine("Enter Markup Percentage:");
            double markupPercentage = double.Parse(Console.ReadLine());
            // calculate retail price
            double retailPrice = wholeSalePrice * (1 + markupPercentage/100);
            // display result
            Console.WriteLine("Retail Price: {0:C}", retailPrice);
            Console.ReadKey();
        }
    }
}
```

Explanation:

These statements solve the problem. If a user enters 10 as the whole sale price and 45 for the markup percentage, the console will display $14.50 as the retail price. That's correct. However, if the user enters "ten" for the wholesale price, the program will halt and display the following exception:

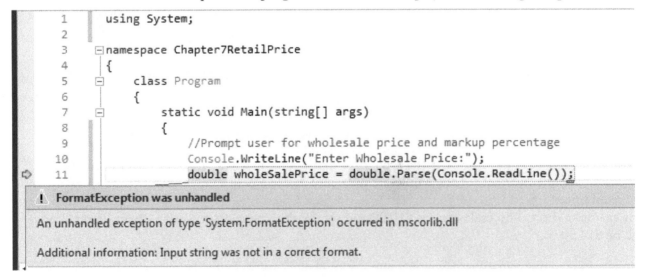

Figure 7.1 An exception for Example 7.1

This is an example of a run time error. A FormatException was thrown. You cannot convert "ten" to a double value. It's an error that C# caught (Common Language Runtime (CLR) to be exact), so an exception is thrown. An exception is C#'s response to any programming bug, invalid user input, or external issues (such as a connection to a nonexistent file). An exception is often a built-in class.

The above exception was thrown because of invalid user input. Usually, this type of exception can be fixed by the programmer. You can use C# flow control to make sure that the user enters the correct format. You can use an 'if' statement to accomplish this.

Example 7.2

Problem:

Use the 'if' statement to handle the exceptions in Example 7.1. If the user enters a non-numeric value for the wholesale price or percentage, display an error message.

Solution:

Modify your Chapter7RetailPrice project so the Main() method looks like Figure 7.2.

```
1     using System;
2
3     namespace Chapter7RetailPrice
4     {
5         class Program
6         {
7             static void Main(string[] args)
8             {
9                 // declare variables to hold user values
10                double wholeSalePrice;
11                double markupPercentage;
12                //Prompt user for wholesale price and markup percentage
13                Console.WriteLine("Enter Wholesale Price:");
14                if(!(double.TryParse(Console.ReadLine(), out wholeSalePrice)))
15                {
16                    Console.WriteLine("Whilesale price must be numeric");
17                }
18                else
19                {
20                    Console.WriteLine("Enter markup percentage:");
21                    if(!(double.TryParse(Console.ReadLine(), out markupPercentage)))
22                    {
23                        Console.WriteLine("Markup must be numeric");
24                    }
25                    else
26                    {
27                        // data are good
28                        // calculate retail price
29                        double retailPrice = wholeSalePrice * (1 + markupPercentage/100);
30                        // display result
31                        Console.WriteLine("Retail Price: {0:C}", retailPrice);
32                    }
33                }
34                Console.ReadKey();
35            }
36        }
37    }
38
```

Figure 7.2 Code for Example 7.

Explanation:

Line 14 uses the TryParse() method to convert the first argument (what the user enters) to the second argument (the wholeSalePrice variable). If the conversion succeeds, the TryParse() method will return true. Otherwise, it will return false. The ! operator is NOT in logic, so if the conversion failed, the condition in the if statement is true (thanks to !). It will then display to the user the feedback, "Wholesale price must be numeric."

You can think of the TryParse() method as doing two things: 1. Converting the first argument to the second argument; 2. Returning true if the conversion is successful, or false if otherwise.

Note that the TryParse() method uses the modifier out for the second parameter. This is because a method can only return one value or reference without using the out parameter modifier (see chapter 4 for more details). You want this method to return two values, one Boolean value and one wholesale price.

Lines 18 to 33 are executed if the conversion in Line 14 is a success. An almost identical validation for the markup percentage is nested inside the else block.

Line 21 also uses the out keyword. This allows the variables declared in Line 11 to be modified if the conversion is successful.

Test Your Understanding 7.1
An exception is C#'s response to a programming error.
A. True
B. False

Test Your Understanding 7.2
An exception is the same as a programming bug.
A. True
B. False

Test Your Understanding 7.3
If an invalid user input is not handled in the code, it can cause an exception.
A. True
B. False

Test Your Understanding 7.4
Which of the following is a C# built-in exception class? This exception will throw when the user enters 'ten' when the application expects the number '10'.
A. UserInputException
B. FormatException
C. RuntimeErrorException
D. Number10Exception

Test Your Understanding 7.5

What are the two things the TryParse() method does?
A. Returning two values to the caller.
B. Accepting one value and returning a bool value.
C. Accepting two values and returning a bool value.
D. Passing a value from the first parameter to the second and returning a bool value.

Programming Challenge 7.1
Modify the program in Example 7.2 so that it won't accept a negative number for the wholesale price nor for the markup percentage.

Example 7.3

Problem:

Example 7.2 fixed the exception issues with the if statements and TryParse() method. However, the user does not get a chance to enter a correct value. Rewrite the program so that the application keeps prompting the user for a value until a value in the correct format is entered.

Analysis:

This program will prompt the user to enter a numeric value for the wholesale price. If a value with an incorrect format is entered, it will prompt again. This is a loop, repeating the prompt until a value in the correct format is entered. Since you don't know how many times the user will enter a value in the wrong format, a while loop fits the purpose well. In short, when the user enters a value in the wrong format, a feedback message is shown and the prompt for entering the data is displayed again until the user enters the data in correct format.

Solution:

Create a new project called Chapter7RetailPrice3 or modify the existing Chapter7RetailPrice project in Chapter 6 Example 2. The Main() method should resemble the following:

```csharp
using System;

namespace Chapter7RetailPrice3
{
    class Program
    {
        static void Main(string[] args)
        {
```

```csharp
            // declare variables to hold user values
            double wholeSalePrice;
            double markupPercentage;
            //Prompt user for wholesale price and markup percentage
            Console.WriteLine("Enter Wholesale Price:");
            while (!(double.TryParse(Console.ReadLine(), out wholeSalePrice))
                || (wholeSalePrice < 0))
            {
                Console.WriteLine("Whilesale price must be numeric and positive.");
            }
            // wholeSalePrice is valid
            Console.WriteLine("Enter markup percentage:");
            while(!(double.TryParse(Console.ReadLine(), out markupPercentage))
                    || markupPercentage < 0)
            {
                Console.WriteLine("Markup must be numeric and positive.");
            }
            // markup percentage is valid
            // calculate retail price
                double retailPrice = wholeSalePrice * (1 + markupPercentage / 100);
            // display result
                Console.WriteLine("Retail Price: {0:C}", retailPrice);
            Console.ReadKey();
        }
    }
}
```

Explanation:

Each while loop in the Main() method does only two things: 1) Give feedback to the user, and 2) Receive new input from the user.

The condition for the loop is that the value entered cannot be converted to a double type number 'or' (the || symbol in the code) nor a negative number. As long as one of these two conditions is true, the input is invalid and the loop continues.

Test Your Understanding 7.6
A while loop with the TryParse() method is good for validating user input.
A. True
B. False

Programming Challenge 7.2
Write an application that lets the user enter a student name and an integer score between 0 and 100. Then the application displays the student name and the letter grade by using the formula: 90 or above A; between 80 and 89 B; between 70 and 79 C; between 60 and 69 D; below 60 F.
If the user enters an invalid score, prompt the user to enter again until a valid score is entered.

7.2 Exception Handling with Try ... Catch Statement

Example 7.4

Problem:

Write an application that asks the user to enter two whole numbers then divides the first number by the second number and displays the quotient.

Analysis:

You can use the same technique in the previous example so that only valid data is accepted. This example uses a different approach. Use the C# built in Exception classes to catch different types of exceptions. Note that in the real world, you should write more robust code to remove the bugs and validate user input. The Exception classes should be used to handle external errors that are rare and unexpected.

Solution 1:

This first solution will not include any exception handling.

Create a project called Chapter7Division. Type the code inside the Main() method so they are similar to the following:

```csharp
using System;

namespace Chapter7Division
{
    class Program
    {
        static void Main(string[] args)
        {
            // prompt use for dividend
            Console.WriteLine("Enter dividend:");
            int dividend = int.Parse(Console.ReadLine());
            // prompt user for divisor
            Console.WriteLine("Enter divisor:");
            int divisor = int.Parse(Console.ReadLine());
            // calculate the quotient
            int quotient = dividend / divisor;
            // display the result
            Console.WriteLine("{0} divided by {1} is {2}", dividend, divisor, quotient);
            Console.ReadKey();
        }
    }
}
```

Explanation:

This program will run if the user enters all valid input. For example, if you enter 10 for dividend and enter 3 for divisor, you will get the correct quotient.

Now try this:

Run the program by entering 5.4 as the dividend. You will see "FormatException"

Next, run the program by entering 5 as the dividend and 0 as the divisor. You will see "DivideByZeroException".

Finally, run the program by entering 2345678901. You will see "OverflowException." This is because the largest int allowed is 2,147,483,647, and you just entered a whole number larger than that.

C# programming has many built in Exception classes. Figure 7.3 shows a small part of the tree in the UML class diagram. All built in exceptions are inherited from the "SystemException" class, which in turn is inherited from the Exception class. All custom build exception classes should inherit from the "ApplicationException" class, which in turn is inherited from the Exception class. The arrows in Figure 7.3 point from a sub class to the super class.

There are many more built in exception classes under the "SystemException" class. For a complete list, visit https://msdn.microsoft.com/en-us/library/z4c5tckx%28v=vs.110%29.aspx.

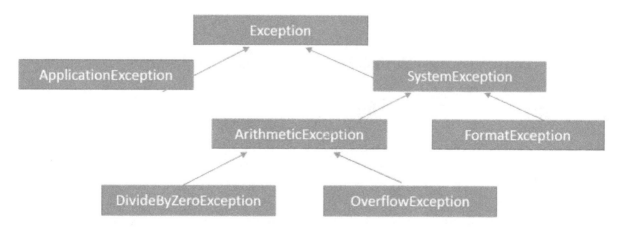

Figure 7.3 Sample built-in exception classes.

Test Your Understanding 7.7

If you want to write a custom exception class, it should be inherited from the _____ class.

A. Exception

B. ApplicationException

C. SystemException

D. CustomException

Test Your Understanding 7.8

In the UML class diagram, an arrow points from ClassA to ClassB, indicating _____.

A. ClassA is a super class

B. ClassB is a super class

C. neither ClassA nor ClassB is a super class

D. both ClassA and ClassB are super classes

Test Your Understanding 7.9

Which of the following is NOT a built-in exception class in C#?

A. Exception

B. ApplicationException

C. SystemException

D. BuiltInException

Test Your Understanding 7.10

If a user enters 2345678901 when an int data type value is expected by the program, what type of exception will it throw?

A. ApplicationException

B. FormatException

C. OverflowException

D. DivideByZeroException

Solution 2:

The second solution to the problem is to use the Try ... Catch statement to handle the exceptions. The following code shows the solution for Example 7.4 written with the Try ... Catch statement:

```
using System;

namespace Chapter7Division
{
    class Program
    {
        static void Main(string[] args)
        {
            try
            {
```

```csharp
        // prompt use for dividend
        Console.WriteLine("Enter dividend:");
        int dividend = int.Parse(Console.ReadLine());
        // prompt user for divisor
        Console.WriteLine("Enter divisor:");
        int divisor = int.Parse(Console.ReadLine());
        // calculate the quotient
        int quotient = dividend / divisor;
        // display the result
        Console.WriteLine("{0} divided by {1} is {2}", dividend, divisor, quotient);
        }
        catch (DivideByZeroException ex)
        {
            Console.WriteLine(ex.Message);
        }
        catch(OverflowException ex)
        {
            Console.WriteLine(ex.Message);
        }
        catch(ArithmeticException ex)
        {
            Console.WriteLine(ex.Message);
        }
        catch(FormatException ex)
        {
            Console.WriteLine(ex.Message);
        }
        catch(SystemException ex)
        {
            Console.WriteLine(ex.Message);
        }
        catch(Exception ex)
        {
            Console.WriteLine(ex.Message);
        }

        finally
        {
        Console.ReadKey();
        }
        }
    }
}
```

Explanation:

You put all the statements that may throw an exception inside the try block. When an exception is thrown, the execution will jump to one of the catch blocks and end up in the finally block.

You may notice how the sequence of catch blocks is organized. All catch blocks should be organized from specific to general, with more specific exceptions first and more general exceptions later.

By examining the class diagram in Figure 7.3, you can see a super class is more general and a sub class is more specific. This is because when one exception is caught, the program will leave the Try... Catch statement (and go to the finally block if it exists). If you put the most general exception class first, it will catch any exception and leave the statement and make the rest of the catch blocks useless.

After the execution of either the try or catch block, the finally block will follow. The finally block is optional.

Test Your Understanding 7.11
When using the try … catch statement to handle the exception, only one catch block will be executed at most, even if you put multiple catch blocks in the application.
A. True
B. False

Test Your Understanding 7.12
When using the try … catch … finally statement, the finally block will always be executed whether an exception is thrown or not.
A. True
B. False

Test Your Understanding 7.13
When using the try … catch statement to handle the exception, in the catch blocks, you should put more general exception classes before the more specific exception classes.
A. True
B. False

Programming Challenge 7.3
Write an application that can calculate a trip's gas usage in miles per gallon. The application prompts the user for the number of miles of a trip and how many gallons of gas was used for the trip. Then the application should display the miles per gallon. Use the try ... catch ... finally to handle the exceptions.

7.3 Software Quality

Quality is in the eyes of the beholder. Different people see the same software with differing levels of quality. Even the same person may see the same software at different times with differing quality. Furthermore, the definition of software quality may be different among experts. We believe that quality is about fulfilling requirements (Marchewka, 2015).

To understand quality, you need to know the eight characteristics of software quality defined by ISO/IEC 25010 (2011):

1. Functional suitability: A high quality application should meet the stated and implied needs of the users.

2. Performance efficiency: A high quality application should not require too many resources.

3. Compatibility: A high quality application should be able to exchange information with other applications easily.

4. Usability: A high quality application can be used by specified users for specific goals.

5. Reliability: A high quality application should perform specified functions under specified conditions for a long time without problems.

6. Security: A high quality application should provide protections for its information and data.

7. Maintainability: A high quality application should allow effective and efficient modifications when needed.

8. Portability: A high quality application can be easily transferred from one environment to another.

Test Your Understanding 7.14

There is more than one definition of quality. Which of the following is the definition from this book?
A. Quality is in the eyes of the beholder.
B. There is no definition for quality.
C. Quality is about fulfilling requirements.
D. Quality is something that will last forever.

Test Your Understanding 7.15

'A high quality application should meet the stated and implied needs of the users' describes which characteristic of software quality according to ISO/IEC 25010?
A. Functional suitability
B. Performance efficiency
C. Compatibility
D. Usability

Test Your Understanding 7.16

A high quality application should not require too many resources describes which characteristic of software quality by ISO/IEC 25010?
A. Functional suitability
B. Performance efficiency
C. Compatibility
D. Usability

Test Your Understanding 7.17

'A high quality application can be used by specified users for specified goals' describes which characteristic of software quality by ISO/IEC 25010?
A. Functional suitability
B. Performance efficiency
C. Compatibility
D. Usability

Test Your Understanding 7.18

'A high quality application should allow modifications when needed in an effective and efficient way' describes which characteristic of software quality by ISO/IEC 25010?
A. Reliability
B. Security
C. Maintainability
D. Portability

Test Your Understanding 7.19

'A high quality application should perform specified functions under specified conditions for a long time without problems' describes which characteristic of software quality by ISO/IEC 25010?
A. Reliability

B. Security
C. Maintainability
D. Portability

Test Your Understanding 7.20

Which of the following is NOT a characteristic of software quality defined by ISO/IEC 25010?
A. Functional suitability
B. Performance efficiency
C. Compatibility
D. Developer reputation

Test Your Understanding 7.21

Which of the following is NOT a characteristic of software quality defined by ISO/IEC 25010?
A. Usability
B. Reliability
C. Reusability
D. Security

7.4 Quality Philosophies and Principles

Software quality depends a lot on the development team. There are four general philosophies and principles that can guide a team through its journey in software development (Marchewka, 2015).

1. Focus on customer satisfaction: Software development is not to show off how smart the team is. It is to satisfy the customers' requirements. Only when this philosophy is a part of the team norm can the agile principles be implemented. Another reason for meeting customer and stakeholder requirements is because the customer is the ultimate judge of the quality (Ginac, 1998).

2. Prevention, Not Inspection: The cost of quality depends on its four components —prevention, inspection, internal failure, and external failure. The most efficient way to reduce the quality cost is through prevention (Lewis, 2008). The business rule of ten can be applied here. When a quality issue is identified by a team member, the cost may be $1. When the same issue is noticed by a customer, the cost can be $10.

3. Quality Is Everyone's Responsibility: Quality is not free. It requires time and effort. Team members should be responsible and empowered for ensuring quality and encouraged to take pride in their work. Every member should commit to the quality (McKay, 2007; Jyothi and Rao, 2012).

4. Fact-Based Management: Numbers, pictures, and charts should be used for ease of understanding and quick references. Data collected can be used for evaluating and improving the process (Kloppenborg and Petrick. 2002).

Test Your Understanding 7.22

'The goal of software development is to satisfy the customers' requirements' describes which quality philosophy?
A. Fact-Based Management
B. Focus on customer satisfaction
C. Prevention, not inspection
D. Quality is everyone's responsibility

Test Your Understanding 7.23

'Team members should be responsible and empowered for ensuring quality and encouraged to take pride in their work' describes which quality philosophy?
A. Fact-Based Management
B. Focus on customer satisfaction
C. Prevention, not inspection
D. Quality is everyone's responsibility

Test Your Understanding 7.24

Which of the following is NOT a quality philosophy discussed in the book?
A. Quality is not tangible
B. Focus on customer satisfaction
C. Prevention, not inspection
D. Quality is everyone's responsibility

7.5 Pair Programming

As you learned in Chapter 1, a non-agile team typically has a very clear line between the roles of developer and quality assurance (QA). This can be a problem.

Let's use an example. A developer is working on feature A and a QA may be working on something else. After the developer completes feature A and moves on to Feature B, the QA will start to test on feature A and may find some bugs. Now the developer has to stop working on feature B, reset up the environment for working on feature A, and fix the bugs of feature A. This will repeat for every feature, making the process inefficient and of low quality.

The pair programming approach will start with both the developer and the QA working on the test case before the developer starts coding. This will help the developer better understand the case and write better code. Once the developer starts to code, the QA can follow with the testing. This kind of teamwork ensures higher quality with less time spent on setting up the environment.

In short, agile requires a cross functional team which means the developer understands how the QA works, and the QA knows the programming. They should both know the analysis and design. By physically sitting together and working together, they can test the code as it is written. This increases the quality of software.

Pair programming involves two team members working on one computer with just one keyboard and mouse. The member who works at the keyboard with the mouse is called the "driver", and the other member who is also actively participating in the current work is called the "navigator". The two members take turns controlling the keyboard and mouse.

Pair programming allows team members with different expertise to code together, take turn controlling the keyboard, and learning from each other (Beck and Andres, 2005). There can be different flavors of pair programming. For example, peer review or peer code review is similar to pair programming.

Researchers have identified many benefits of pair programming (Hannay, 2009; Vanhanen and Mantyla, 2013). Improved quality is at the top of the list. Pair programming can result in higher quality product due to team effort. Also, "programming out loud" helps programmers think more clearly about the requirements.

When a development team is not physically located in one place, communication and collaboration may be more difficult and can negatively impact the performance of the pair programming. There are positive reports that benefits are still possible in the virtual team, even in the asynchronous mode (Zin, 2006). Carefully selected communication tools that are comfortable to use for all participants and sufficient training of team members will minimize the failure of pair programming in a distributed environment (Canfora et al, 2006).

Test Your Understanding 7.25
Pair programming works with two team members working together on one computer with two sets of keyboard and mouse.
A. True
B. False

Test Your Understanding 7.26
In pair programming, the member who works at the keyboard with the mouse is called the _____.
A. navigator
B. warrior
C. active coder
D. driver

Test Your Understanding 7.27
In pair programming, the member who is away from the keyboard and the mouse is called the

_____.
A. navigator
B. warrior
C. active coder
D. driver

Test Your Understanding 7.28

Pair programming helps programmers think more clearly about the requirements.
A. True
B. False

Test Your Understanding 7.29

Pair programming allows team members to learn from each other.
A. True
B. False

Test Your Understanding 7.30

The only concern of pair programming is the efficiency with two members working on one task.
A. True
B. False

7.6 Test Driven Development (TDD):

In traditional testing, the developers first write the code and testers test it afterwards. TDD requires that developers first write automated test cases and then write only the code necessary to make the test cases pass with no issues. This encourages the developers to think through the requirements before writing the code, encourages only the code that is needed is written, and ensures that each piece of the code has gone through an initial quality check before formal testing.

Example 7.5

Problem:

Write a test case so that if a student's test score is 90, then the student letter grade is A.

Solution:

Start a new project called Chapter7TDD. In the "Solution Explorer" window, right click on the Solution (not project, as you did so far to add a class to the project), then add new project as shown in Figure 7.4.

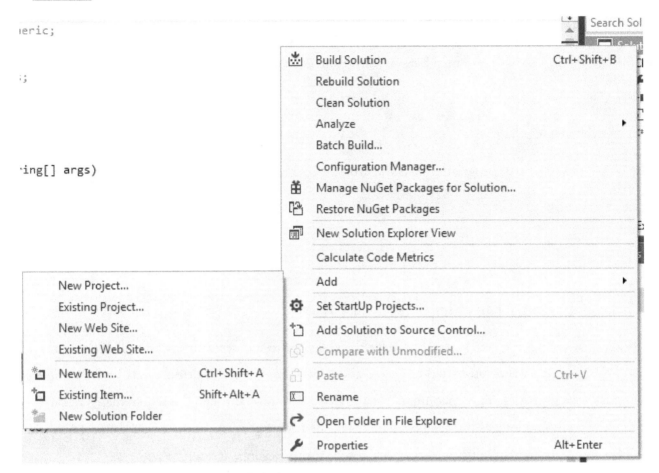

Figure 7.4 Add a new project to the Solution.

In the "Add New Project" dialog box, select "Visual C#", then "Test", then "UnitTestProject". Use the default name, "UnitTest1.cs" as shown in Figure 7.5.

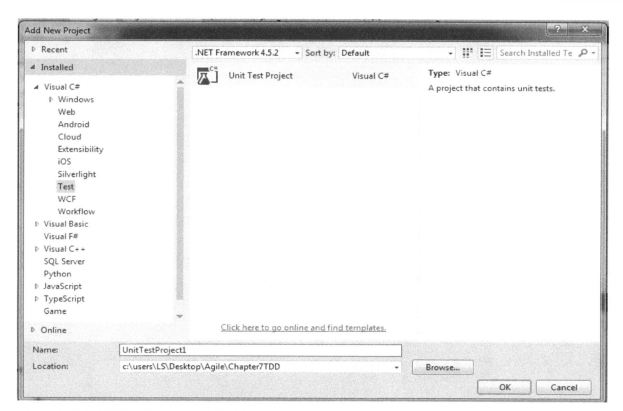

Figure 7.5 Add New Project of UnitTest Dialog box

After clicking on the "OK" button, the new code window will have the "UnitTest1.cs" open as shown in Figure 7.6.

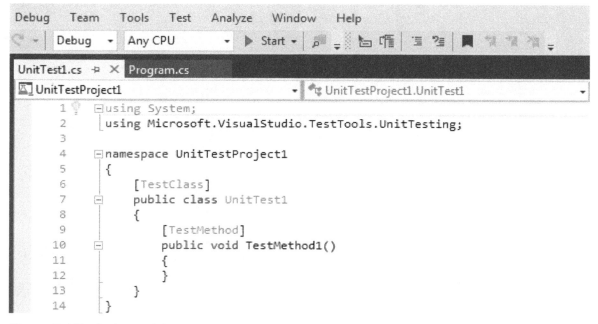

Figure 7.6 Default UnitTest1.cs file code

Now add statements inside the "TestMethod1()" method so they look like Figure 7.7.

```
1    using System;
2     using Microsoft.VisualStudio.TestTools.UnitTesting;
3
4    namespace UnitTestProject1
5    {
6        [TestClass]
7        public class UnitTest1
8        {
9            [TestMethod]
10           public void TestMethod1()
11           {
12               // create an object to test
13               Student s = new Student();
14               // define a test input and output value
15               int score = 90;
16               char expectedResult = 'A';
17               // run the method under test
18               char actualResult = s.GetLetterGrade(score);
19               // verify the result
20               Assert.AreEqual(expectedResult, actualResult);
21           }
22       }
23   }
```

Figure 7.7 The Code window with the statements in the method

Explanation:

Line 13 includes a red squiggle underscore, which is ok, because a class called Student has not been created yet.

Next, you will generate the Student class and the corresponding method from the test.

Place the cursor on the red squiggle beneath Student on Line 13 of Figure 7.8, Note the yellow light bulb. Click on the dropdown. On the shortcut menu, choose "Generate New Type".

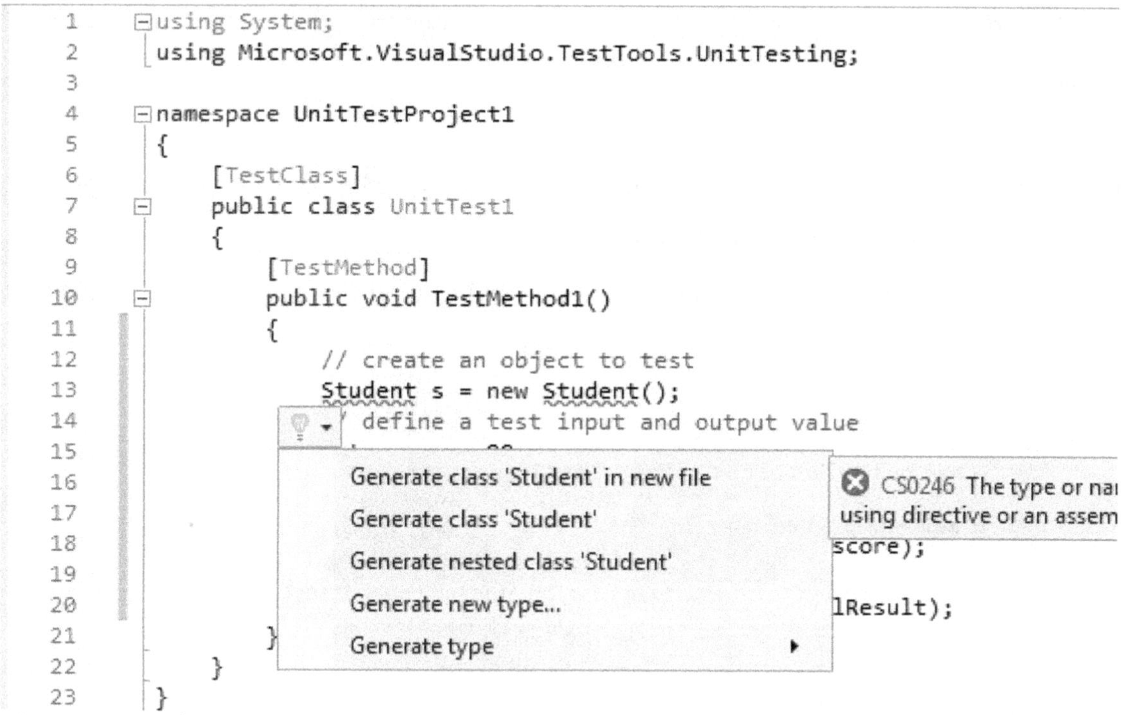

```
1    using System;
2    using Microsoft.VisualStudio.TestTools.UnitTesting;
3
4    namespace UnitTestProject1
5    {
6        [TestClass]
7        public class UnitTest1
8        {
9            [TestMethod]
10           public void TestMethod1()
11           {
12               // create an object to test
13               Student s = new Student();
14               // define a test input and output value
```

Generate class 'Student' in new file
Generate class 'Student'
Generate nested class 'Student'
Generate new type...
Generate type   ▶

CS0246 The type or nai
using directive or an assem
score);

lResult);

```
15
16
17
18
19
20
21
22           }
23    }
```

Figure 7.8 Code with shortcut menu

The "Generate Type" dialog box will popup. Set Project to the "Chapter7TDD" project. Select the "create new file" radio button, then click on "OK", as shown in Figure 7.9.

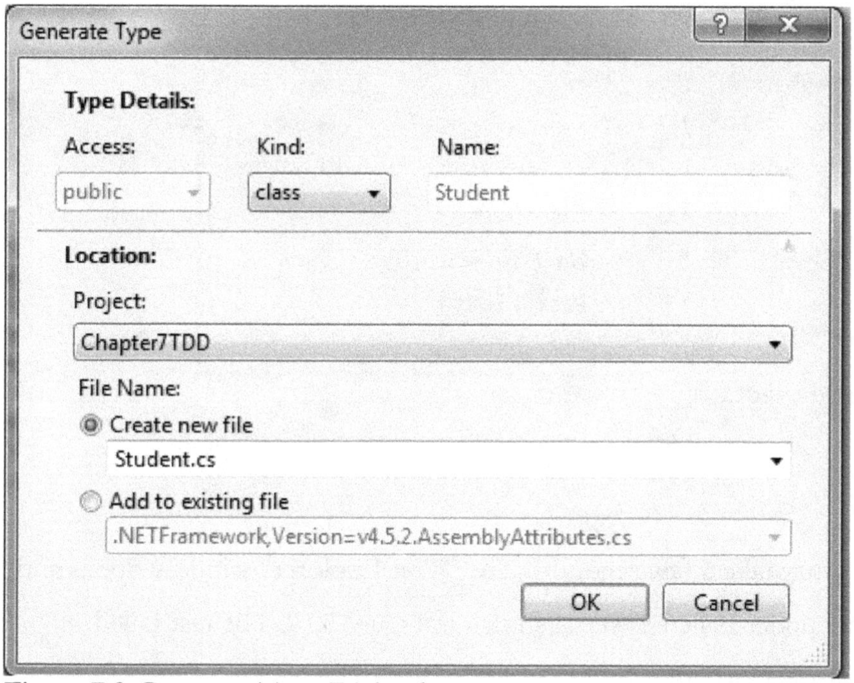

Generate Type

Type Details:

Access: Kind: Name:

public   ▼   class   ▼   Student

Location:

Project:

Chapter7TDD   ▼

File Name:

◉ Create new file

Student.cs   ▼

◯ Add to existing file

.NETFramework,Version=v4.5.2.AssemblyAttributes.cs   ▼

OK   Cancel

Figure 7.9 Generate Type Dialog box

You should see the red squiggle under Student disappear. The GetLetterGrade() method in Line 18 now has a red squiggle underscore.

Next, place the cursor on GetLetterGrade(). The light bulb will appear (alternatively, you can right click on the method and select "Quick Action" in the context menu). Click the dropdown on the light bulb. On the shortcut menu, choose the "Generate method" stub (Figure 7.10). You should see the red squiggle disappeared.

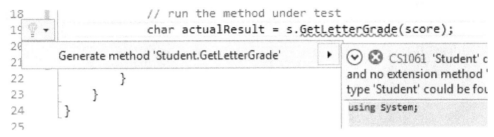

Figure 7.10 Light bulb with Generate method

It's time for running the unit test.

On the Test menu, choose "Run" then "All Tests" as shown in Figure 7.11.

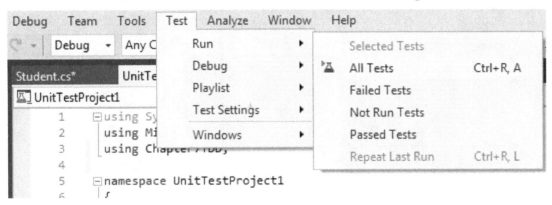

Figure 7.11 Run test menu

The solution builds and runs. (This may take a few seconds). The "Test Explorer" window opens and displays the results. The test appears under Failed Tests as shown in Figure 7.12. The test failed because you don't have the code for the GetLetterGrade() yet.

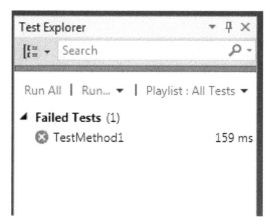

Figure 7.12 Text Explorer window

You just completed a test case. It's time to develop the code.

Open the "Student.cs" in the code window, and add the statements similar to those in Figure 7.13.

```
1      using System;
2
3     namespace Chapter7TDD
4       {
5           public class Student
6           {
7               public char GetLetterGrade(int score)
8               {
9                   char letterGrade = 'F';
10                  if (score == 90)
11                  {
12                      letterGrade = 'A';
13                  }
14                  return letterGrade;
15              }
16          }
17      }
```

Figure 7.13 The Student class with the GetLetterGrade() method

Save and run the test again. You should see the success in the "Test Explorer" window, as shown in Figure 7.14.

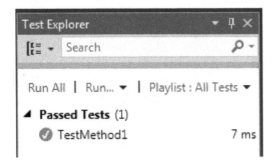

Figure 7.14 Test passed.

You may notice one problem in the example so far. What if the score is 91? Will it still be an A? No. Something is wrong with the test case. Let's add a new TestMethod() with the code shown as Figure 7.15.

```
1    using System;
2    using Microsoft.VisualStudio.TestTools.UnitTesting;
3    using Chapter7TDD;
4
5    namespace UnitTestProject1
6    {
7        [TestClass]
8        public class UnitTest1
9        {
10           [TestMethod]
11           public void TestMethod1()...
23           [TestMethod]
24           public void TestMethod2()
25           {
26               // create an object to test
27               Student s = new Student();
28               // define a test input and output value
29               for (int score = 90; score <= 100; score++)
30               {
31                   char expectedResult = 'A';
32                   // run the method under test
33                   char actualResult = s.GetLetterGrade(score);
34                   // verify the result
35                   Assert.AreEqual(expectedResult, actualResult);
36               }
37           }
38       }
39   }
40
```

Figure 7.15 A new TestMethod is added

Explanation:

While TestMethod1() tests for just one case: when the score is 90, TestMethod2() tests for all possible scores between 90 and 100 with a for loop.

Now run the test. TestMethod1 will pass, but TestMethod2 will fail, as shown in Figure 7.16

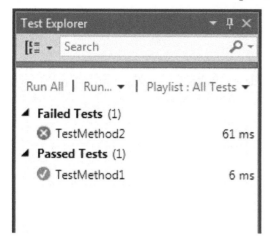

Figure 7.16 Test Explorer window with TestMethod1 passed, but TestMethod2 failed.

Go back to the Student class. Change the equal sign in line 10 (Figure 7.13) to a greater than or equal to sign.

Save and run all tests again. You should see both TestMethods passed, as shown in Figure 7.17

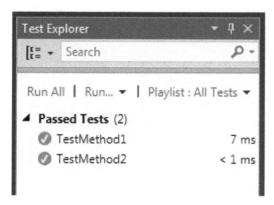

Figure 7.17 Test Explorer window indicates both testmethods passed

Test Your Understanding 7.31
In agile, the developers must first write the code. Testers test it afterwards.

A. True
B. False

Test Your Understanding 7.32

In test driven development, you write test case before you write software code.
A. True
B. False

Test Your Understanding 7.33
In test driven development, you only write enough software code to make it pass the test.
A. True
B. False

7.7 Chapter Summary

In this chapter, you learned exception handling in C#. One way to handle the exception is to write more robust code, such as using the 'if' statement. Another way is to use the Try ... Catch statement with the built in exception classes.

You also learned software quality and how agile enhances the quality of the software developed. You learned how pair programing works and how it enhances the software quality. Finally, you got hands on experience with test-driven-development (TDD).

7.8 References

Beck, K. and Andres, C. (2005), Extreme Programming Explained: Embrace Change, 2nd Edition, Addison-Wesley.

Canfora, G., Cimitile, A., Di Lucca, G. A., Visaggio, C. A. (2006). How Distribution Affects the Success of Pair Programming. INTERNATIONAL JOURNAL OF SOFTWARE ENGINEERING & KNOWLEDGE ENGINEERING. April Vol. 16 Issue 2, p293-313

Ginac, F. P. (1998), Customer Oriented Software Qual- ity Assurance. Upper Saddle River, NJ: Prentice Hall.

Hannay, J. E., Dyba, T., Arisholm, E., and Sjoberg, D. I. K. (2009). The Effectiveness of Pair Programming: A Meta Analysis. *Information and Software Technology*. 51(7). July, p. 1110-1122.

ISO/IEC 25010:2011(en), Systems and software engineering — Systems and software Quality Requirements and Evaluation (SQuaRE) — System and software quality models. Available at: https://www.iso.org/obp/ui/#iso:std:iso-iec:25010:ed-1:v1:en visited November 22, 2016.

Jyothi, V.E. and Rao, K. N. (2012). Effective Implementation of Agile Practices - Incoordination with Lean Kanban, International Journal on Computer Science and Engineering, 4(1), p. 87-91.

Kloppenborg, T. J. and J. A. Petrick. (2002), Managing Project Quality. Vienna, VA: Management Concepts.

Lewis, W. E. (2008), Software Testing and Continuous Quality Improvement. 3rd Edition, Boca Raton, FL: Auer- bach.

Marchewka, J. T. (2015), *Information Technology Project Management*, 5th Edition. Wiley.

McKay, J. (2007), "Quality Just Doesn't Happen." CIO Magazine. May 24.

Vanhanen, J. and Mantyla, M. V. (2013). A Systematic Mapping Study of Empirical Studies on the Use of Pair Programming in Industry, International Journal of Software Engineering and Knowledge Engineering, Vol. 23, Issue 9, p. 1221-1267.

Zin, A. M. Idris, S., and Subramaniam, N. K. (2006). Implementing Virtual Pair Programming in E-Learning Environment, JOURNAL OF INFORMATION SYSTEMS EDUCATION. Summer, Vol. 17 Issue 2, p113-117.

7.9 Solutions to Selected Programming Challenges

Programming Challenge 7.1

```
using System;

namespace Chapter7RetailPrice
{
    class Program
    {
        static void Main(string[] args)
        {
            // declare variables to hold user values
            double wholeSalePrice;
            double markupPercentage;
            //Prompt user for wholesale price and markup percentage
            Console.WriteLine("Enter Wholesale Price:");
            if(!(double.TryParse(Console.ReadLine(), out wholeSalePrice))
```

```
                ||(wholeSalePrice <0))
        {
            Console.WriteLine("Whilesale price must be numeric and positive.");
        }
        else
        {
            Console.WriteLine("Enter markup percentage:");
            if(!(double.TryParse(Console.ReadLine(), out markupPercentage))
                || markupPercentage <0)
            {
                Console.WriteLine("Markup must be numeric and positive.");
            }
            else
            {
                // data are good
                // calculate retail price
                double retailPrice = wholeSalePrice * (1 + markupPercentage/100);
                // display result
                Console.WriteLine("Retail Price: {0:C}", retailPrice);
            }
        }
        Console.ReadKey();
    }
  }
}
```

Programming Challenge 7.2

```
using System;

namespace Chapter7StudentGrade
{
    class Program
    {
        static void Main(string[] args)
        {
            // declare variables to hold user values
            string studentName;
            double studentScore;
            //Prompt user for name and score
            Console.WriteLine("Enter Student Name:");
            studentName = Console.ReadLine();
            Console.WriteLine("Enter student score:");
            while (!(double.TryParse(Console.ReadLine(), out studentScore))
                    || (studentScore < 0) || (studentScore > 100))
            {
                Console.WriteLine("Score must be between 0 and 100.");
                Console.WriteLine("Reenter student score:");
            }
            // score is valid
            // convert to letter grade
            char letterGrade;
            if (studentScore >= 90)
                letterGrade = 'A';
```

```
        else if (studentScore >= 80)
            letterGrade = 'B';
        else if (studentScore >= 70)
            letterGrade = 'c';
        else if (studentScore >= 60)
            letterGrade = 'D';
        else
            letterGrade = 'F';
        // display result
        Console.WriteLine("Name: {0} Grade: {1}", studentName, letterGrade);
        Console.ReadKey();
        }
    }
}
```

Programming Challenge 7.3

```
using System;

namespace Chapter7MPG
{
    class Program
    {
        static void Main(string[] args)
        {
            try
            {
                // prompt use for miles
                Console.WriteLine("Enter miles driven:");
                int miles = int.Parse(Console.ReadLine());
                // prompt user for gas used for the trip
                Console.WriteLine("Enter gallon of gas used:");
                int gallon = int.Parse(Console.ReadLine());
                // calculate the miles per gallon
                int mpg = miles / gallon;
                // display the result
                Console.WriteLine("You drove {0} miles with {1} gallons of gas. Miles per
gallon is {2}", miles, gallon, mpg);
            }
            catch (DivideByZeroException ex)
            {
                Console.WriteLine(ex.Message);
            }
            catch (OverflowException ex)
            {
                Console.WriteLine(ex.Message);
            }
            catch (ArithmeticException ex)
            {
                Console.WriteLine(ex.Message);
            }
            catch (FormatException ex)
            {
                Console.WriteLine(ex.Message);
```

```
        }
        catch (SystemException ex)
        {
            Console.WriteLine(ex.Message);
        }
        catch (Exception ex)
        {
            Console.WriteLine(ex.Message);
        }
        finally
        {
            Console.ReadKey();
        }
    }
  }
}
```

7.10 Solutions to Test Your Understanding

7.1 A; 7.2 B; 7.3 A; 7.4 B; 7.5 D; 7.6 A; 7.7 B; 7.8 B; 7.9 D; 7.10 C; 7.11 A; 7.12 A; 7.13 B; 7.14 C; 7.15 A; 7.16 B; 7.17 D; 7.18 C; 7.19 A; 7.20 D; 7.21 C; 7.22 B; 7.23 D; 7.24 A; 7.25 B; 7.26 D; 7.27 A; 7.28 A; 7.29 A; 7.30 B; 7.31 B; 7.32 A; 7.33 A;

Chapter 8: C# Windows Forms Application and Agile Summary

8.1 Windows Forms Application

You have learned basic object oriented programming in C# from previous chapters. It's time to use that knowledge to build some Graphical User Interface (GUI) desktop applications.

Example 8.1

Problem:

The Tiny College needs an application that allows instructors to enter student IDs, student names, and numeric test scores between 0 and 100 for the semester. They want these data to be saved in a text file that can be pulled out, displayed, and printed as wanted.

User Stories:

Based on the description and talking to some employees at The Tiny College, you come up with the following user stories.

User Story 1: As an instructor, I want to save my student's ID, name, and score in a text file so that I can keep record.

Acceptance Criteria: Graphical user interface. A score is a whole number between 0 and 100.

User Story 2: As an administrator, I want to see all students' records in one screen with student ID, student name, and corresponding letter grades so that I can have an overall picture of my college.

Acceptance Criteria: Graphical user interface. All students listed on one screen. Letter grade is based on the formula: 90-100 A; 80-89 B; 70-79 C; 60-69 D; Under 60 F.

User Story 3: As a staff member, I want to be able to search a particular student by student ID so that I can decide if the student is qualified for registration.

Acceptance Criteria: Graphical user interface. When the student ID is entered, only that student's name and letter grade are shown. The letter grade formula is the same as in story 2. The Tiny College requires all students to have a grade of C or higher to qualify for registration.

User Story 4: As a user of the application, I want be able to print the student record from the application so that I can give it to the students or for the convenience of discussion with the students.

Acceptance Criteria: Graphical user interface. The administrator wants to print all records in one document with appropriate headers and date time of printing. The staff wants to print just one student record.

Solution:

Start Visual Studio. Create a new "Project" as you did in the past, but don't use "Console Application" as you've used in the previous chapters. This time, on the "Create a new project" window, select "Windows Forms App (.Net Framework)" as shown in Figure 8.1 and click on the "next" button.

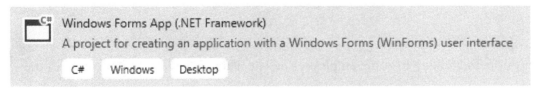

Figure 8.1 Select "Windows Forms App (.NET Framework)

On the "Configure your new project" window, name the project "Chapter8StudentRecord". Make sure the "Place solution and project in the same directory" checkbox is checked. Click on the "Create" button to start a new blank window form application. Refer to Figure 8.2 for an example.

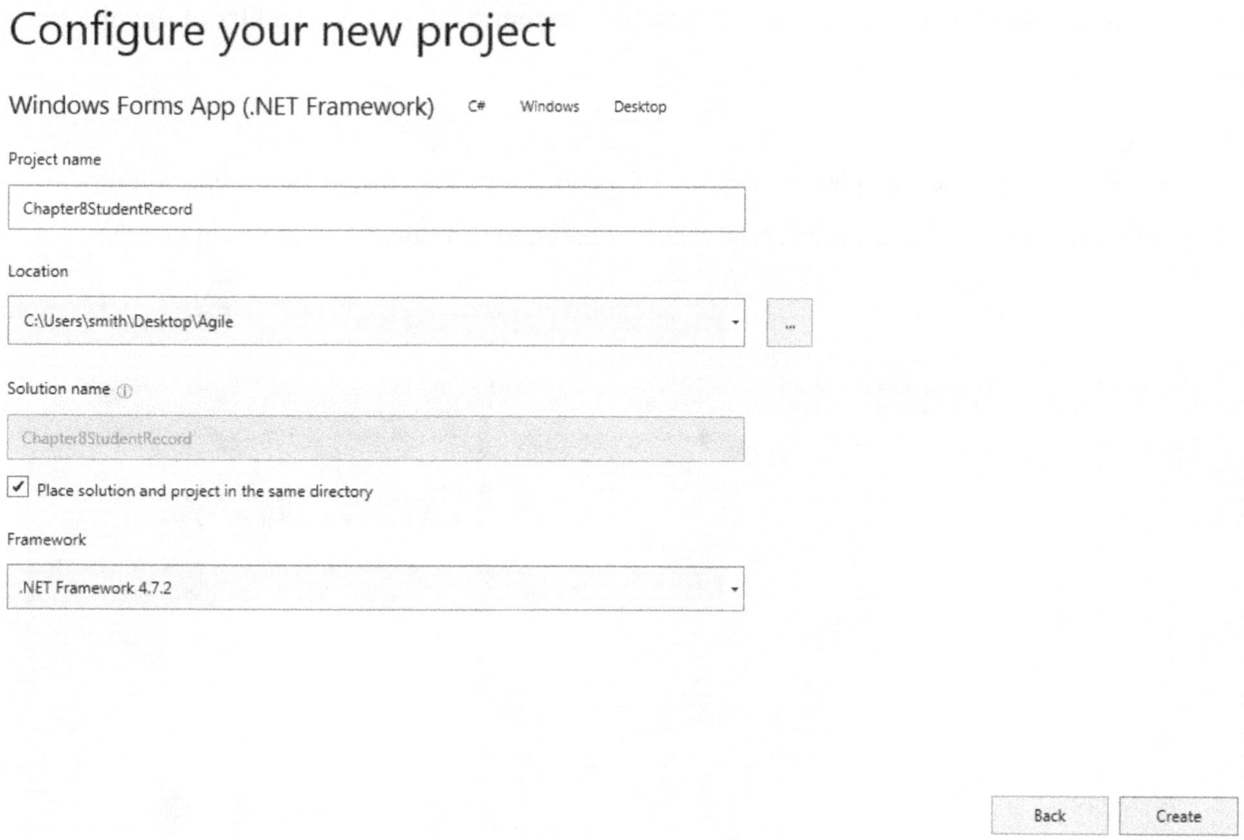

Configure your new project

Windows Forms App (.NET Framework)   C#   Windows   Desktop

Project name

```
Chapter8StudentRecord
```

Location

```
C:\Users\smith\Desktop\Agile                                          ▾
```

Solution name ⓘ

```
Chapter8StudentRecord
```

☑ Place solution and project in the same directory

Framework

```
.NET Framework 4.7.2                                                  ▾
```

Back   Create

Figure 8.2 Configure your new project window.

As you continue to develop the application, pay special attention to the following terms: design view window, controls and toolbox, properties window, solution explorer window, and code window.

Design view window is a Windows form you use during design. Whatever you put on it will be shown when ran.

Controls are object items on a form, like a button, a label, a textbox, a radio button, a checkbox and so on. Toolbox is a place where all those controls are stored. You can drag any controls from toolbox to the form in design view window.

Each control has many properties. Those properties can be found in the property window. For example, a button has the "text" property, which will be the text shown on the button.

Solution Explorer Window is the same one you see throughout the book. All the files of the project can be found there.

Every form has a design view (explained above) and a code view. The design view helps you design the look of a form while the code view allows you to enter code and makes the form interactive.

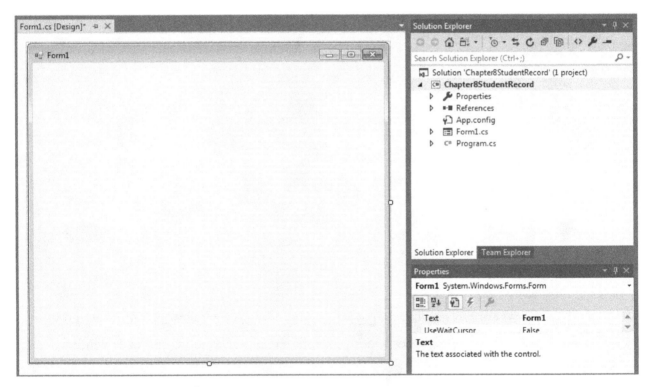

Figure 8.3 Design View Window

Figure 8.3 is the design view window. You can add controls, such as a button, to the form.

To find toolbox, click on "View" on the menu, then "toolbox". Refer to Figure 8.4.

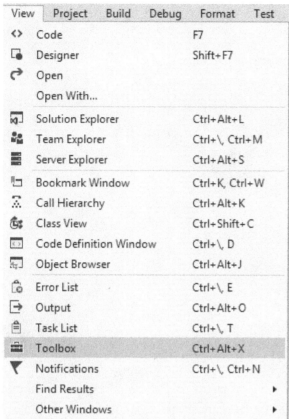

Figure 8.4 Open toolbox.

It may take a few seconds for the first time you open the toolbox. Controls are organized by categories (Figure 8.5). Expand a category by clicking on it (Figure 8.6).

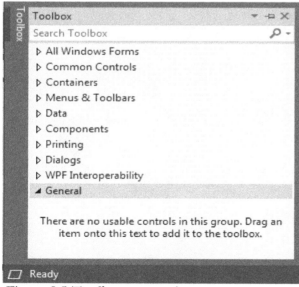

.Figure 8.5 Toolbox categories.

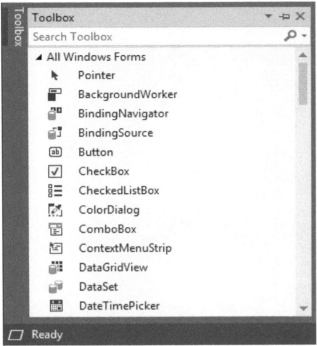

Figure 8.6 A small portion of controls in the All Windows Forms category.

If you want to add a control to the form, you should open the form in design view. Just double click on an item in the toolbox you want to add to the form, or drag and drop the control to the form. Next, let us rename the default Form1.cs file in the project to something more meaningful. In the "Solution Explorer" window (Figure 8.7), right click on the Form1.cs. Select "Rename" as shown in Figure 8.8.

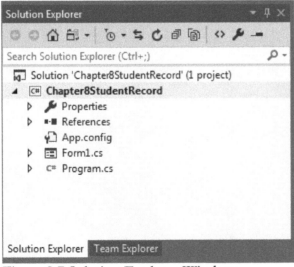

Figure 8.7 Solution Explorer Window.

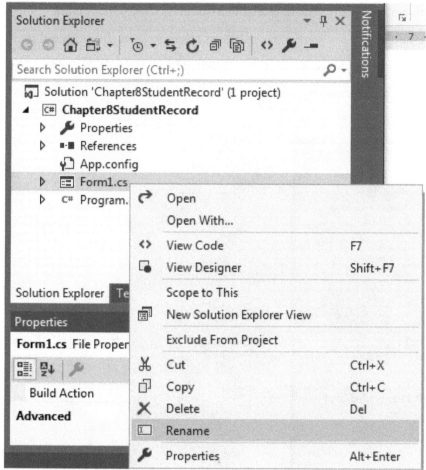

Figure 8.8 Rename Form1.cs

Change the Form1 name to DataEntryForm.cs

A popup will be displayed asking if you want to change the name for all corresponding components (Figure 8.9). Click yes.

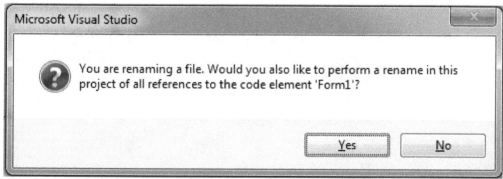

Figure 8.9 Rename popup window

Next, make the title/caption of the DataEntryForm more readable instead of using the default "Form1". First, click (do not double click) on anywhere in the form to select it. You should see the "Properties" window (Figure 8.10). By default, the properties are organized by category. You can click on the "A to Z alphabetical" icon to see a different organization.

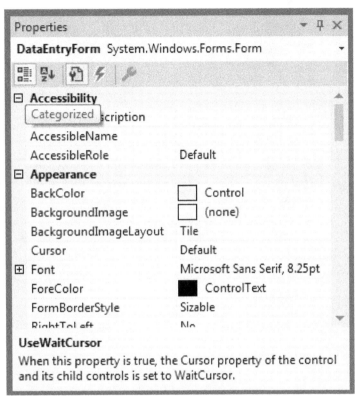

Figure 8.10 the properties window.

Find the "Text" property in the properties window (Figure 8.11). Change its default value from "Form1" to "Data Entry Form" (note the use of space between words for users). If the "Text" property is not shown, you may scroll down the list.

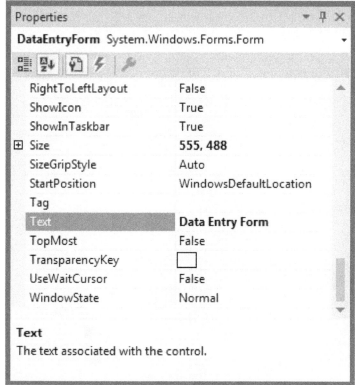

Figure 8.11 "Text" property in the properties window.

Test Your Understanding 8.1
Every windows form in the develop environment has a _____ view and a _____ view
A. design, code
B. user, design
C. code, user
D. developer, user

Test Your Understanding 8.2
A text field you want to add to a form is called a _____.
A. design item
B. user item
C. control
D. property

Test Your Understanding 8.3
Where can you find all the controls you can add to a form in a design view?
A. design view
B. Solution Explorer
C. Properties Window
D. toolbox

Test Your Understanding 8.4
If you want to change the settings of a control, such as the title/caption of a form, where can you find those settings?
A. design view
B. Solution Explorer
C. Properties Window
D. toolbox

Test Your Understanding 8.5
If you want to change the title/caption of a form, what property of the form would you change?
A. Title
B. Caption
C. either Title or Caption
D. Text

8.2 Add Controls to the Form

In this section, you will learn how to add different controls to a Windows form.

Have the "Toolbox" window showing. Add the following controls to the Data Entry Form (must be in design view) by double clicking on each control in the toolbox (each double click adds only one control):

1 GroupBox, 3 Labels, 3 TextBoxes, and 3 Buttons.

Reorganize the "Data Entry Form" so the controls look like Figure 8.8. You can move a control by dragging and moving.

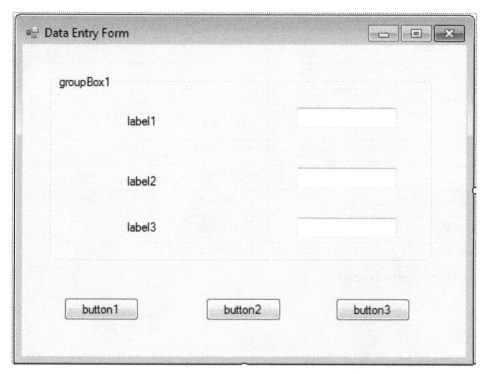

Figure 8.12 Data Entry Form with controls added

Click once on groupBox1, but not on any controls inside the groupBox1, to select it. Go to the "Properties" window and change its "Text" property from "groupBox1" to "Student Data". Once click anywhere to save the change. You should see the "groupBox1" on the form change to "Student Data".

Follow the same rule: click once on the control, go to the "Properties" window and change its properties listed in Table 8.1. The blank cell means no change is necessary. We don't recommend changing a control name when it is never used in the code. The & character makes the button's access key. Users can use alt+letter on the keyboard to click on the button instead of using a mouse.

Click once to select	Change "Text" property to	Change "Name" property to
Label1	Student ID:	
Label2	Student Name:	
Label3	Student Score:	
TextBox1		idTextBox
TextBox2		nameTextBox
TextBox3		scoreTextBox
Button1	&Save	saveButton
Button2	&Clear	clearButton
Button3	E&xit	exitButton

Table 8.1 Properties for Data Entry Form controls

The completed form should look like Figure 8.13 (name property cannot be seen; make sure you did change them).

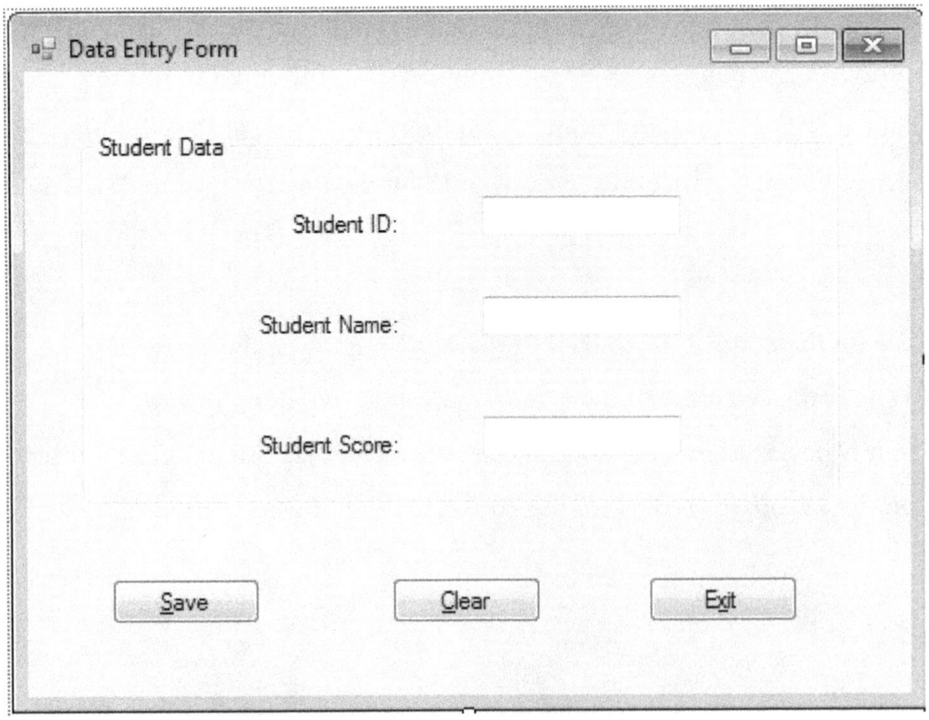

Figure 8.13 Data Entry Form with all controls' properties set

Test Your Understanding 8.6
A control can be added to a form by double clicking on it in the toolbox. However, you still need to organize it on the form by moving it around.
A. True
B. False

Test Your Understanding 8.7
Each control has a name property coming with a default value. We recommend that you change it if the control will appear in the _____.
A. form
B. code
C. design view
D. Solution Explorer Window

Test Your Understanding 8.8
How do you add an underscore to a button in a form?
A. use the underscore key on the keyboard
B. click on the underscore icon on the property window
C. add the & in front of the character of the "Text" property
D. add the _ in front of the character of the "Text" property

Test Your Understanding 8.9
Where can you find all the controls to add to a form?
A. Control window
B. Toolbox window
C. Properties window
D. Design View window

Test Your Understanding 8.10
You need to give a meaningful name to a control used in the statements. Where can you change a control's name?
A. Control window
B. Toolbox window
C. Properties window
D. Design View window

Test Your Understanding 8.11
If you want to view or move the controls on the form. Where can you find the form?
A. Control window
B. Toolbox window
C. Properties window
D. Design View window

8.3 Add Student Class to the Project

The application is about students at The Tiny College. You need a class called Student that has three fields (ID, name, and score) and a method (GetLetterGrade()). Go to the "Solution Explorer" window and right click on the "Chapter8StudentRecord" project and add a new class named Student.cs as you did in the previous chapters. The code for the Student.cs class is as follows:

```csharp
namespace Chapter8StudentRecord
{
    class Student
    {
        // fields
        private string studentId;
        private string studentName;
        private int studentScore;
        // properties
        public string StudentId
        {
            get { return studentId; }
            set { studentId = value; }
        }
        public string StudentName
        {
            get { return studentName; }
            set { studentName = value; }
        }
        public int StudentScore
        {
            get { return studentScore; }
            set { studentScore = value; }
        }
        // constructor
        public Student(string studentId, string studentName, int studentScore)
        {
            this.studentId = studentId;
            this.studentName = studentName;
            this.studentScore = studentScore;
        }
        // method
        public char GetLetterGrade()
        {
            char letterGrade;
            if (StudentScore >= 90)
            {
                letterGrade = 'A';
            }
            else if (StudentScore >= 80)
            {
                letterGrade = 'B';
            }
```

```
        else if (StudentScore >= 70)
        {
            letterGrade = 'C';
        }
        else if (StudentScore >= 60)
        {
            letterGrade = 'D';
        }
        else
        {
            letterGrade = 'F';
        }
        return letterGrade;
    }
    // ToString() method
    public override string ToString()
    {
        string str;
        str = string.Format("ID: {0} Name: {1} Grade: {2}", StudentId, StudentName,
GetLetterGrade());
        return str;
    }
  }
}
```

Test Your Understanding 8.12
Adding a class to a Windows Form project is the same as adding a class to a console project.
A. True
B. False

8.4 Add Event Handler to the Button

In previous chapters of the book, you learned the flow of code execution follows one of three ways: 1. sequential, 2) conditional, and 3) repeating. In this section, you will learn another way. A Windows Form application is event-driven. The flow of the execution of the statements is determined by events such as user actions (e.g. mouse click, key press). In this section, you will write statements to make the buttons on the form work.

Open the data entry form in the "design view" window by double clicking on "DataEntryForm.cs" in the "Solution Explorer" window, if it is not already open. Then double click on the "Exit" button to create a button click event handler. When the user clicks on this button, all statements inside the handler will be executed. For now, you just need one statement to exit the application. Add Close(); inside the handler so that the code will look like Figure 8.14:

```
1    using System;
2    using System.Windows.Forms;
3
4    namespace Chapter8StudentRecord
5    {
6        public partial class DataEntryForm : Form
7        {
8            public DataEntryForm()
9            {
10               InitializeComponent();
11           }
12
13           private void exitButton_Click(object sender, EventArgs e)
14           {
15               Close();          Your code between
16           }                     the braces
17       }
18   }
```

Figure 8.14 Add a statement to the exit button click event handler

Next, click on the "Save all" icon in Visual Studio to save the project. Then click on "Start" to run the application as shown in Figure 8.15. Your Exit button should work as expected.

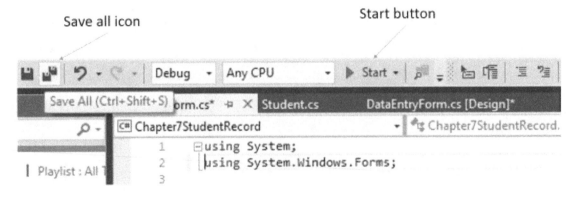

Figure 8.15 Save all icon and start button on Visual Studio

Back in the Designer window of the "Data Entry Form", double click on the "Clear" button to create the "clear button click event handler" and add the following lines inside the "clear button click event handler" as shown in Figure 8.16.

```
1    using System;
2    using System.Windows.Forms;
3
4    namespace Chapter8StudentRecord
5    {
6        public partial class DataEntryForm : Form
7        {
8            public DataEntryForm()
9            {
10               InitializeComponent();
11           }
12
13           private void exitButton_Click(object sender, EventArgs e)
14           {
15               Close();
16           }
17
18           private void clearButton_Click(object sender, EventArgs e)
19           {
20               idTextBox.Clear();
21               nameTextBox.Clear();        Your code inside
22               scoreTextBox.Clear();       the event handler
23               idTextBox.Focus();
24           }
25       }
26   }
```

Figure 8.16 Statements are added to the clear button event handler

Explanation:

Every control in the toolbox is a class which has built-in methods.

Line 20, idTextbox is an object you instantiate from the TextBox class which has a method called Clear(). The method will remove any content in the textbox.

Line 23, Focus() is another method of the TextBox class which will receive the focus of the form (blink cursor).

Save and run the application. You should see that anything typed into the textboxes are gone and the ID field receives the focus once the Clear button is clicked.

Back in the designer window of the "Data Entry Form", double click on the "Save" button to create "save button click event handler". In the "Code View" window at the top of the page, add the following line:

```
using System.IO;
```

This will import all Types inside the System.IO namespace. It is called using directive. You need to import the IO namespace so that the application can save data to an external file. Then, inside the "save button click event handler", type in the following statements as shown in Figure 8.17.

```
27      private void saveButton_Click(object sender, EventArgs e)
28      {
29          using (StreamWriter sw= File.AppendText("student.txt"))
30          {
31              if(!((string.IsNullOrWhiteSpace(idTextBox.Text)) ||
32                  (string.IsNullOrWhiteSpace(nameTextBox.Text)) ||
33                  (string.IsNullOrWhiteSpace(scoreTextBox.Text))))
34              {
35                  // save the textboxes content to the file
36                  sw.WriteLine(idTextBox.Text);
37                  sw.WriteLine(nameTextBox.Text);
38                  sw.WriteLine(scoreTextBox.Text);
39                  // clear the textboses
40                  clearButton.PerformClick();
41              }
42              else
43              {
44                  MessageBox.Show("All fields must be filled.");
45              }
46          }
47      }
```

Figure 8.17 Statements are added to the save button click event handler

Explanation:

Line 29 is a using statement which provides an easy way to open, write, and then close the connection between this application and the text file, and to ensure the correct use of Disposable objects. This line also creates a StreamWriter object named sw which has a WriteLine() method you can use to save the text to the file. The "using" statement is different from the "using" directive you added on top of the code file.

Lines 31 to 33: check to make sure the three textboxes are not empty before you save their contents.

Line 40 calls the "clear button click event handler" you wrote earlier and performs the clearance. This provides good user experience as it makes the form ready for the next input.

Line 44 displays a message to the user if any of the three textboxes are empty.

The complete code for the form should look like the following:

```csharp
using System;
using System.Windows.Forms;
using System.IO;

namespace Chapter8StudentRecord
{
    public partial class DataEntryForm : Form
    {
        public DataEntryForm()
        {
            InitializeComponent();
        }

        private void exitButton_Click(object sender, EventArgs e)
        {
            Close();
        }

        private void clearButton_Click(object sender, EventArgs e)
        {
            idTextBox.Clear();
            nameTextBox.Clear();
            scoreTextBox.Clear();
            idTextBox.Focus();
        }

        private void saveButton_Click(object sender, EventArgs e)
        {
            using (StreamWriter sw= File.AppendText("student.txt"))
            {
                if(!((string.IsNullOrWhiteSpace(idTextBox.Text)) ||
                    (string.IsNullOrWhiteSpace(nameTextBox.Text)) ||
                    (string.IsNullOrWhiteSpace(scoreTextBox.Text))))
                {
                    // save the textboxes content to the file
                    sw.WriteLine(idTextBox.Text);
                    sw.WriteLine(nameTextBox.Text);
                    sw.WriteLine(scoreTextBox.Text);
```

```
            // clear the textboses so the user can enter a new one
            clearButton.PerformClick();
        }
        else
        {
            MessageBox.Show("All fields must be filled.");
        }
    }
  }
 }
}
```

Save and run the application. Add a few student records.

To see the data you just saved, go to the folder where you saved the project and open the bin folder inside your project, then open debug folder. The file with the name student.txt should be inside. You can open it with Notepad or any text editor to view the content.

Test Your Understanding 8.13
The flow of execution of the statements as determined by events, such as user actions, is called _____ programming.
A. sequential
B. conditional
C. repeating
D. event-driven

Test Your Understanding 8.14
Windows Form application is _____.
A. sequential
B. conditional
C. repeating
D. event-driven

Test Your Understanding 8.15
With the form on design view window, double click on a button to generate the button click event handler.
A. True
B. False

Test Your Understanding 8.16
All statements inside a button click event handler will be executed when the user clicks on the button at run time.
A. True
B. False

8.5 Add a Main Form to the Project

In order to have each functionality of the application on its own form, you need a main form or an introduction form that can link to other forms. Add a new form that will serve as the main form for all features.

In the "Solution Explorer" window, right click on the Chapter8StudentRecord project, then "Add" and then "Windows Form...", as shown in Figure 8.18.

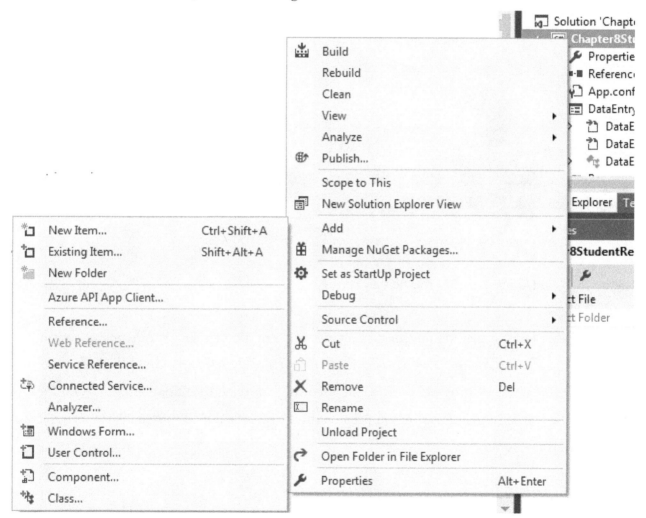

Figure 8.18 Add a new Windows Form from "Solution Explorer" window

The "Add New Form" dialog box will pop up as shown in Figure 8.19. Name this new form as MainForm.cs.

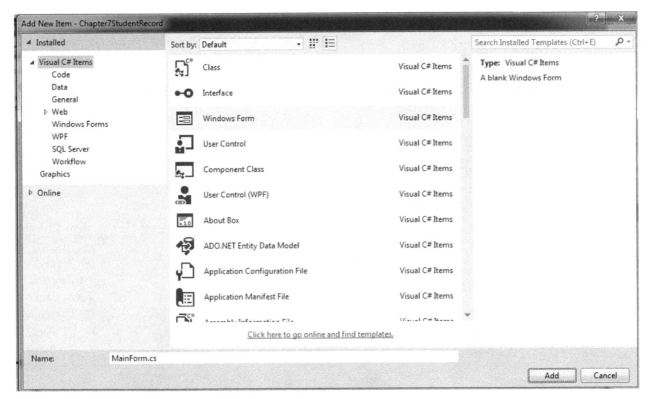

Figure 8.19 The "Add New Form" Dialog window

Click on the "Add" button to add this new form.

After the MainForm is displayed in the designer window, go to the "Toolbox". Add a label control to the form, then click once on the label to select it (if it is not already selected). Go to the properties window, change the "Text" property to "Student Records", then find the "Font" property and click once to select it. Click on the ellipsis button (small button with little dots, Figure 8.20) on the right to open the font dialogue window.

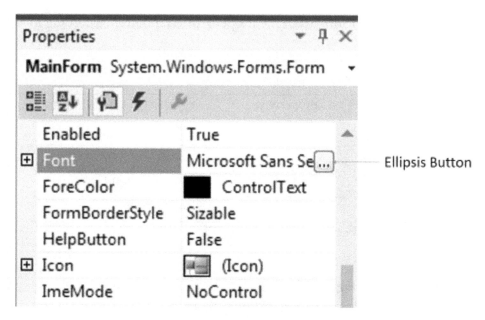

Figure 8.20 Properties window with the Font property displayed

In the font dialog box, select the font, style, and size of your liking. In Figure 8.21, the selected font is "Lucida Handwriting", font style is "Italic", and the size is 24.

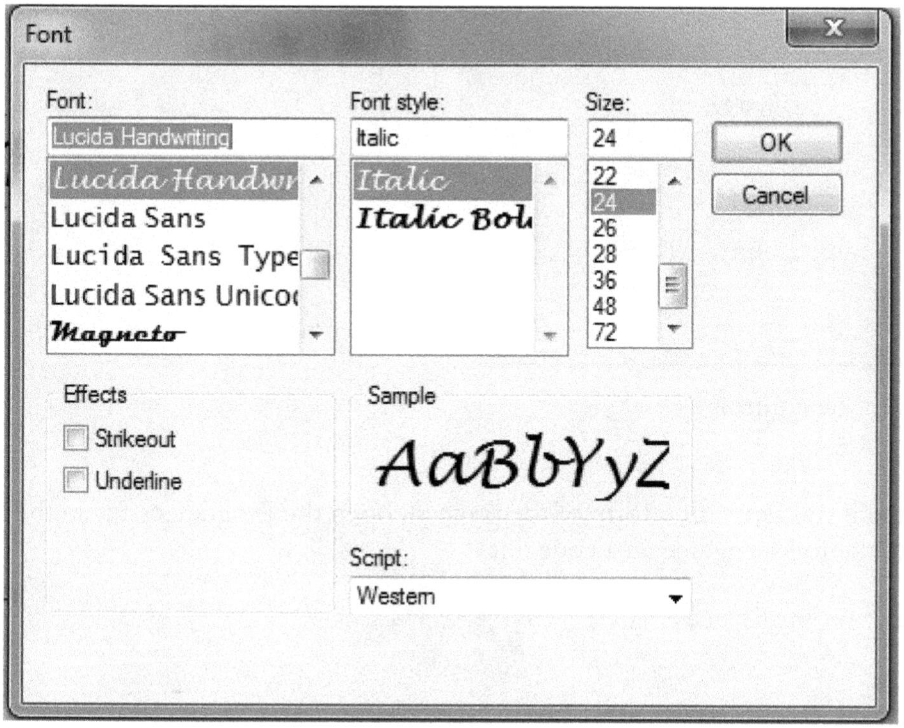

Figure 8.21 Font dialog box

Next, add four buttons to the new form. Make the property of each button according to the values in Table 8.2:

Click once to select	Change "Text" property to	Change "Name" property to
Button1	&Add	addButton
Button2	&Display	displayButton
Button3	&Search	searchButton
Button4	E&xit	exitButton

Table 8.2 Properties for the Main Form buttons

The completed form will look like Figure 8.22.

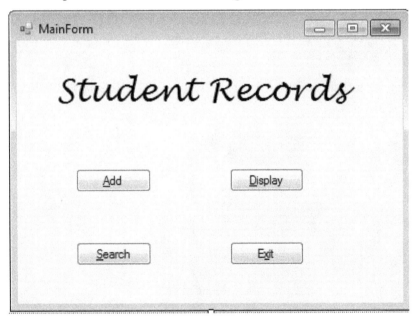

Figure 8.22 The MainForm with the controls

Finally (you don't need this step if this is the first form of the project), open the Program.cs file in the code view window and replace the following line (last code line)

```
Application.Run(new DataEntryForm());
```
with

```
Application.Run(new MainForm());
```

This will change the startup form from DataEntryForm to the MainForm. Save and run the program. You can see the main form, but none of the buttons work yet.

Test Your Understanding 8.17
The process of adding a Windows form to a project is the same as adding a class to a project.
A. True
B. False

Test Your Understanding 8.18
To set a particular form as a start up form, you need to modify the code in _____.
A. MainForm.cs
B. StartUp.cs
C. Form1.cs
D. Program.cs

8.6 Open the Data Entry Form from the Main Form

In this section, you will make the "Add" button on the MainForm work. When the user clicks on the "Add" button, the "data entry form" will popup.

With the MainForm in the designer window, double click on the "Add" button to create "add button click event handler". Type the code in Bold as shown below.

```
namespace Chapter8StudentRecord
{
    public partial class MainForm : Form
    {
        public MainForm()
        {
            InitializeComponent();
        }

        private void addButton_Click(object sender, EventArgs e)
        {
            // Create an instance of DataEntryForm
            DataEntryForm entryForm = new DataEntryForm();
            // call the ShowDialog() method of DataEntryForm
            entryForm.ShowDialog();
        }
    }
}
```

Save and run the program. You should be able to add more students.

Test Your Understanding 8.19
When you have more than one form in your application, make sure you have a main form that introduces all other forms.
A. True
B. False

8.7 User Story 2

You just completed User Story 1. Let's move on to User Story 2:

User Story 2

As an administrator, I want to see all students' records on one screen with student ID, student name, and corresponding letter grades so that I can see an overall picture of my college.

Acceptance Criteria: Graphical user interface. All students listed on one screen. Letter grade is based on the formula: 90-100 A; 80-89 B; 70-79 C; 60-69 D; Under 60 F.

Analysis:

This story requires that every line of data from the student.txt file be retrieved. Every three lines make a record/student. You will put every three lines into a student object. Then, you will add the student object into a List and display the List in a Listbox control. All these should happen when the Form loads.

Solution:

Add a new form named DisplayForm to the project. This form will display all student records.

Right click on the project in the "solution explorer" window. Add a Windows Form. When the new form is displayed, go to the Toolbox window and add a Listbox and two buttons to the form. Set the properties for each control by using the values in Table 8.3.

Click once to select	Change "Text" property to	Change "Name" property to
listBox1		allStudentListBox
Button1	&Close	closeeButton
Button2	&Print	printButton

Table 8.3 Properties for the DisplayForm controls

The completed form design should be similar to Figure 8.23.

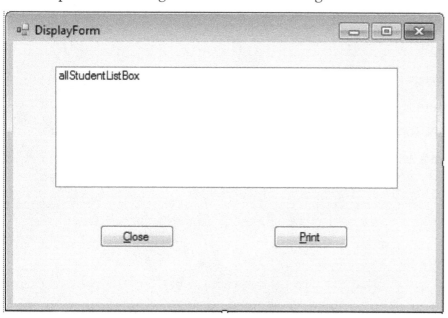

Figure 8.23 DisplayForm with all controls

Next, back in the MainForm designer window, you will make the "Display" button work. Double click on the Display button. Inside the button click event handler, add the two lines of code in bold below:

```
namespace Chapter8StudentRecord
{
    public partial class MainForm : Form
    {
        public MainForm()
        {
            InitializeComponent();
```

```
    }

    private void addButton_Click(object sender, EventArgs e)
    {
        // Create an instance of DataEntryForm
        DataEntryForm entryForm = new DataEntryForm();
        // Call the ShowDialog() method of DataEntryForm
        entryForm.ShowDialog();
    }

    private void displayButton_Click(object sender, EventArgs e)
    {
        // Create an instance of DisplayForm
        DisplayForm displayForm = new DisplayForm();
        displayForm.ShowDialog();
    }
  }
}
```

Now, go to the DisplayForm designer window. Double click anywhere on the form, but not on any controls. This will create the "form load event handler". Any statements written inside this event handler will be executed when the form loads. Type the statements inside the "form load event handler" so they look like Figure 8.24.

```
1    using System;
2    using System.Collections.Generic;
3    using System.Windows.Forms;
4    using System.IO;
5    namespace Chapter8StudentRecord
6    {
7        public partial class DisplayForm : Form
8        {
9            // A list that includes all students
10           List<Student> allStudent = new List<Student>();
11           public DisplayForm()
12           {
13               InitializeComponent();
14           }
15           private void DisplayForm_Load(object sender, EventArgs e)
16           {
17               using (StreamReader sr = new StreamReader("student.txt"))
18               {
19                   string id;
20                   while ((id = sr.ReadLine()) != null)
21                   {
22                       string name = sr.ReadLine();
23                       int score = int.Parse(sr.ReadLine());
24                       // creat the student
25                       Student s = new Student(id, name, score);
26                       // add the student to the list
27                       allStudent.Add(s);
28                       // add the student to the listbox
29                       allStudentListBox.Items.Add(s);
30                   }
31               }
32           }
33       }
34   }
```

Figure 8.24 Code for DisplayForm load event handler

Explanation:

Line 4 uses a directive so that you can use all the types/classes in the System.IO namespace for reading text from a file.

Line 10 declares a List object named allStudent that can hold all students retrieved from the student.txt text file.

Line 17 is a using statement very similar to the StreamWriter you used earlier in this chapter. This time you use StreamReader to retrieve data from student.txt.

Lines 20 to 30 uses a while loop to read three lines of text from the file in each loop; sr.ReadLine() appears three times in the loop, one for reading one line.

Line 25 uses the three values from the text file and creates a student object called s.

Line 27 adds the new student s created in Line 25 to the allStudent List created in Line 10.

Line 29 adds that same student s to the allStudentListBox on the Display Form.

Next, you will make the "Close" button on the DisplayForm work. Double click on the "Close" button on the DisplayForm in the designer window. Add one line of code Close(); inside the "close button click event handler".

This completes user story 2. Save and run the application.

Test Your Understanding 8.20
The built-in _____ class is used to retrieve data from a text file.
A. Stream
B. StreamWriter
C. StreamReader
D. StreamRetriever

Test Your Understanding 8.21
The statement List<Student> allStudent = new List<Student>(); creates a variable allStudent that can hold any type of objects.
A. True
B. False

Test Your Understanding 8.22
Suppose you have a listbox control called allStudentListBox on a form. Which of the following statements will add "Hello" to the listbox?

A. allStudentListBox("Hello");
B. allStudentListBox.Add("Hello");
C. allStudentListBox.Items.Add("Hello");
D. allStudentListBox.Items.Last.Add("Hello");

8.8 User Story 3

User Story 3: As staff member, I want to be able to search a particular student by student ID so that I can decide if the student is qualified for registration.

Acceptance Criteria: Graphical user interface. When the student ID is entered, only that student's name and letter grade is shown. Letter grade formula is the same as in story 2. The Tiny College requires all students to have a grade of C or higher to qualify for registration.

In this section, you will add a search feature to the application.

Go to the "Solution Explorer" window. Right click on the project. Add a new Windows Form. Name it SearchForm.cs

Back in the MainForm in designer view window, double click on the "Search" button. Add the following code in bold inside the "search button click event handler".

```
SearchForm searchForm = new SearchForm();
searchForm.ShowDialog();
```

Next, go to SearchForm in the design view window. Add the necessary controls so that it looks like Figure 8.25.

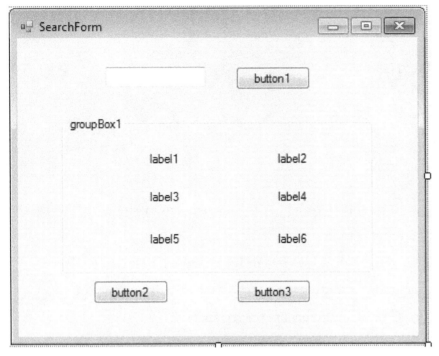

Figure 8.25 SearchForm with necessary controls

Then you set the properties of the controls by following the values in Table 8.4:

Click once to select	Change "Text" property to	Change "Name" property to
textBox1		searchTextBox
Button1	&Search	searchButton
Button2	&Close	closeButton
Button3	&Print	printButton
groupBox1	Student Found	
Label1	Student Id:	
Label2		idLabel
Label3	Student Name:	
Label4		nameLabel
Label5	Letter Grade:	
Label6		gradeLebel

Table 8.4 Properties for the controls on the SearchForm

Change the properties of label2, label4, and label6 so that they look like the ones in Figure 8.26 by following the following instructions for Label2:

Click once on Label2 to select it. Set its "AutoSize" property from "true" to "false". This will make it the same size regardless of the text in it. Next, set its "BorderStyle" property from "none" to "Fixed 3D".

Do the same for label4 and label6.

The completed Search form should look like Figure 8.26.

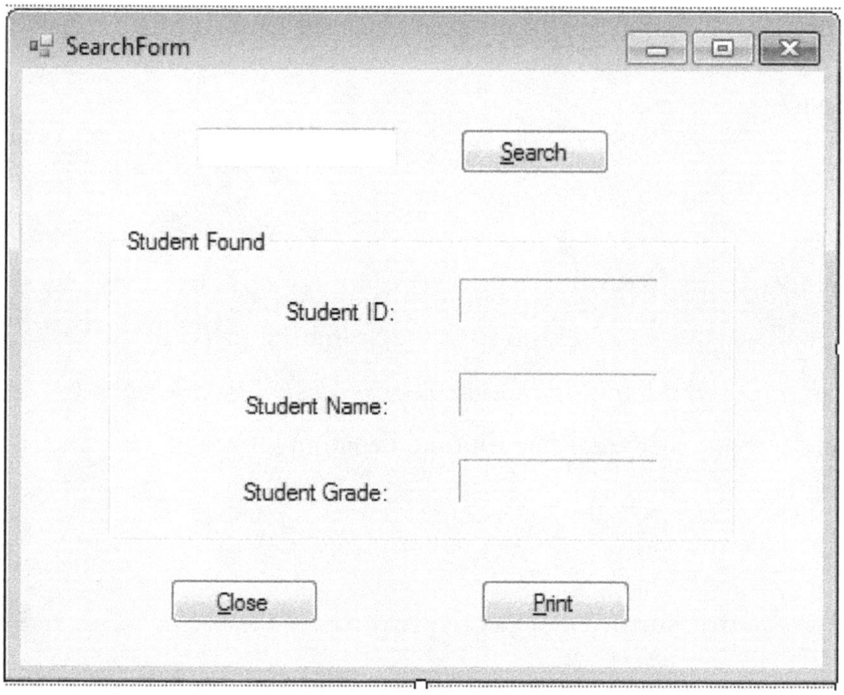

Figure 8.26 The SearchForm with all controls

Analysis:

When this search form loads, you want all data retrieved from the text file to store in a List. When the user types in a student ID and clicks on the "Search" button, the List will be searched. If a match is found, the student data will be displayed in the corresponding labels (the right three labels in Figure 8.26).

Solution:

With SearchForm in the design view window, double click anywhere in the form, but not on any controls. This will create the "form load event handler". Add the following code in bold inside the form load event handler.

```
private void SearchForm_Load(object sender, EventArgs e)
{
    using(StreamReader sr = new StreamReader("student.txt"))
    {
        string id;
        while ((id= sr.ReadLine())!= null)
        {
            string name = sr.ReadLine();
            int score = int.Parse(sr.ReadLine());
            // create a student object
            Student s = new Student(id, name, score);
            // add to the List
            allStudent.Add(s);
        }
    }
}
```

You will notice several red squiggle underscores. You need to insert two lines of code to remove the red squiggle. First, add the following line which creates a List inside the SearchForm. To allow the allStudent list to be used in more than one method, this line should appear as the first line of code inside the SearchForm class and outside of any method, right after the beginning brace of the class{.

```
List<Student> allStudent = new List<Student>();
```

Second, add a using System.IO directive in the directive block at the very top of the file.

```
using System.IO;
```

With all students data in a List, make the search button work next.

Back with SearchForm in the designer window, double click on the "Search" button. Add the following code in bold inside the "search button click event handler".

```
private void searchButton_Click(object sender, EventArgs e)
{
    // search the list, find the student by id
    Student s = allStudent.Find(x => x.StudentId == searchTextBox.Text);
    if (s != null)
    {
        idLabel.Text = s.StudentId;
        nameLabel.Text = s.StudentName;
        gradeLabel.Text = s.GetLetterGrade().ToString();
    }
    else
    {
        MessageBox.Show("No student found.");
        idLabel.Text = string.Empty;
        nameLabel.Text = string.Empty;
        gradeLabel.Text = string.Empty;
    }
}
```

Explanation:

The following line:

```
Student s = allStudent.Find(x => x.StudentId == searchTextBox.Text);
```

The operator => is called Lambda operator. A Lambda expression is a short hand way to write a method. On the left side of the Lambda operator is the input parameter of a method. On the right side are the lambda body statements which correspond to the method body. The lambda statement is to compare a student's StudentId with the search text entered by the user. The whole line will find the first student and store it in a Student object s.

Back with the SearchForm in the design view window, double click on the "Close" button to create the "button click event handler", and add one line of statement inside, Close();

Save and run the application. You should be able to search a student by student ID.

Test Your Understanding 8.23
A List class in C# has a _____ method you can use to search for an element in the List.
A. Search()
B. Find()
C. SearchFor()
D. FindFor()

Test Your Understanding 8.24
A Lambda expression is a shorthand way of writing a method.
A. True
B. False

Test Your Understanding 8.25
The symbol => is a Lambda operator, the left side of the operator corresponding to the _____ of a method.
A. access modifier
B. return type
C. method name
D. parameter list

8.9 User Story 4

User Story 4: As a user of the application, I want to be able to print the student record from the application so that I can give it to the students or use it for the convenience of discussion with students.

Acceptance Criteria: User Story 4: Graphical user interface. The administrator wants to print all records on one document with appropriate headers and date time of printing. The staff wants to print just one student record.

In this section, you will add the print feature to the DisplayForm and SearchForm. First, the DisplayForm:

With the DisplayForm in the design view window, go to the Toolbox, find printDocument control (Figure 8.27), and double click on it to add it to the form's component tray (Figure 8.28).

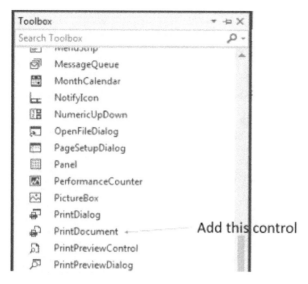

Figure 8.27 PrintDocument control in the Toolbox

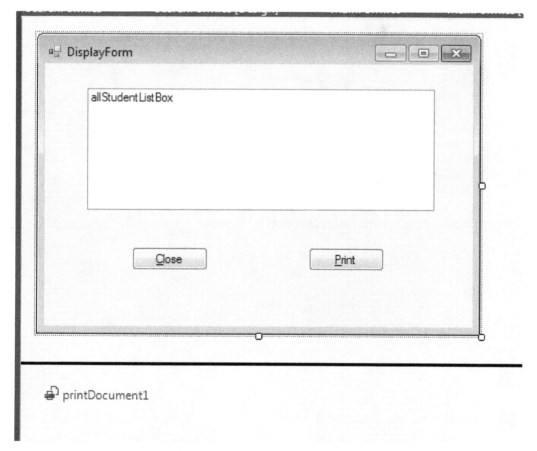

Figure 8.28 printDocument1 in the "Component Tray" of DisplayForm

Double click on the "Print" button. Add one line of code inside the "print button click event handler" as shown in bold below:

```csharp
private void printButton_Click(object sender, EventArgs e)
{
    printDocument1.Print();
}
```

The above statement calls the Print() method of printDocument1 control. Back in the designer window of the DisplayForm, double click on the "printDocument1" in the component tray. Inside its event handler, add the code from Line 43 to 59 in Figure 8.29.

```csharp
35          private void printButton_Click(object sender, EventArgs e)
36          {
37              printDocument1.Print();
38          }
39
40          private void printDocument1_PrintPage(object sender,
41              System.Drawing.Printing.PrintPageEventArgs e)
42          {
43              // print a header
44              e.Graphics.DrawString("Grade Report",
45                  new Font("Courier New", 24, FontStyle.Bold),
46                  Brushes.Black, 200, 100);
47              // print date and time
48              e.Graphics.DrawString(DateTime.Now.ToString(),
49                  new Font("Courier New", 10, FontStyle.Italic),
50                  Brushes.Black, 240, 150);
51              // print each student in a loop
52              int x = 100, y = 200;
53              foreach (Student s in allStudent)
54              {
55                  e.Graphics.DrawString(s.ToString(),
56                      new Font("Courier New", 10, FontStyle.Regular),
57                      Brushes.Black, x, y);
58                  y += 15;
59              }
60          }
```

Figure 8.29 Code for PrintPage event handler.

You may notice multiple red squiggly lines. Point your mouse pointer to any one of them. You will see a yellow light bulb. Click on it and select the first suggestion to add using `System.Drawing;` to the directives. Alternative, you can just type in the line in the directives on the top of the code window.

Explanation:

In Line 46, the first number, 200 indicates the print starts horizontally 200 pixels from the left border of the paper. The second number, 100 indicates, the print starts vertically 100 pixels from the top of the paper. Refer to Figure 8.30 for an example.

Line 58 adds 15 pixels to the vertical distance when printing the next student. This ensures the next line will be further down.

On paper, it will look like the one on Figure 8.30.

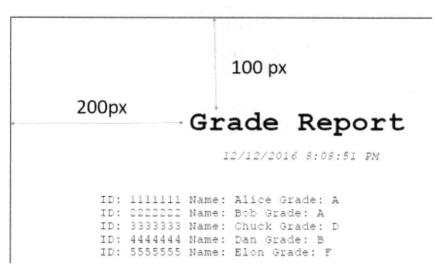

Figure 8.30 Explanation of print positions in DrawString() method.

Save and run the application. You should be able to print all the students in the file if you have a printer connected to your computer.

There is one more task for User Story 4. Make the SearchForm print button work.

Have the SearchForm open in the design view window. Go to the Toolbox. Double click on printDocument control to add a printDocument object to the component tray. Use the default name printDocument1.

Double click the Print button on the searchForm and add a single line of code inside the handler.

```
printDocument1.Print();
```

Back in the SearchForm design view window, double click on the printDocument1 to create the printPage event handler, and add the following code in bold

```
        private void printDocument1_PrintPage(object sender,
System.Drawing.Printing.PrintPageEventArgs e)
        {
            e.Graphics.DrawString("Student ID: " + idLabel.Text,
                new Font("Courier New", 12, FontStyle.Regular),
                Brushes.Black, 100, 200);
            e.Graphics.DrawString("Student Name: " + nameLabel.Text,
                new Font("Courier New", 12, FontStyle.Regular),
                Brushes.Black, 100, 215);
            e.Graphics.DrawString("Student Grade: " + gradeLabel.Text,
                new Font("Courier New", 12, FontStyle.Regular),
                Brushes.Black, 100, 230);
        }
```

Last step for the application: back in the MainForm in the design view window, double click on the "Exit" button and add the Close(); statement inside the "exit button click event handler" to complete the project.

Save and run the program to test all features.

Test Your Understanding 8.26

There are two steps to making a print button on a form work. What are these two steps?
A. the print button click event calls the printDocument's print() method, which will trigger the printDocument's printPage event.
B. the print button click event calls the button's print() method, which will trigger the printDocument's printPage event.
C. the print button click event calls the printDocument's printPage() method, which will trigger the printDocument's printPage event.
D. the print button click event calls the printPage's print() method, which will trigger the printDocument's printPage event.

Test Your Understanding 8.27
The statement printDocument1.Print(); will print everything on the form.
A. True
B. False

Test Your Understanding 8.28
The text you want to print should be included inside the printDocument's printPage event handler.
A. True
B. False

Programming Challenge 8.1
Create an application that allows the user to enter an employee's payroll information. It allows the user to enter a new employee, add hours worked, and display all employee information. A sample MainForm is shown in Figure 8.31.

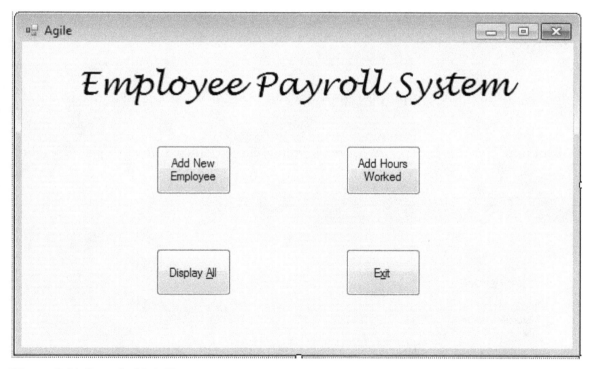

Figure 8.31 Sample MainForm

If the user clicks on the "Add New Employee" button, a new form is displayed, as shown in Figure 8.32.

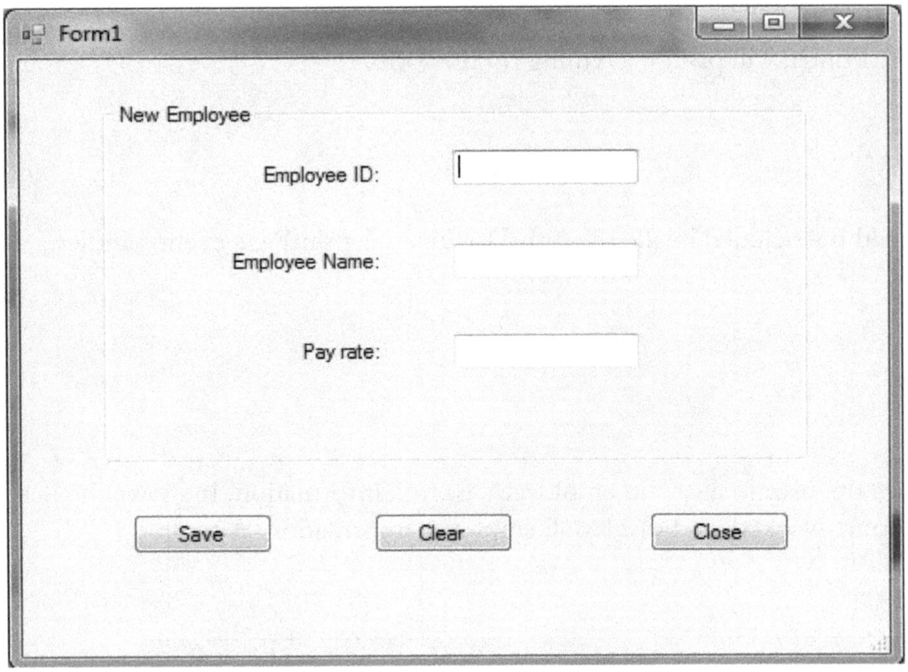

Figure 8.32 Add New Employee Form

The save button on the form will save the new employee into a text file employee.txt in the default debug folder.

Back to the MainForm, if the "Add Hours Worked" button is clicked, a new form is displayed.(Figure 8.33)

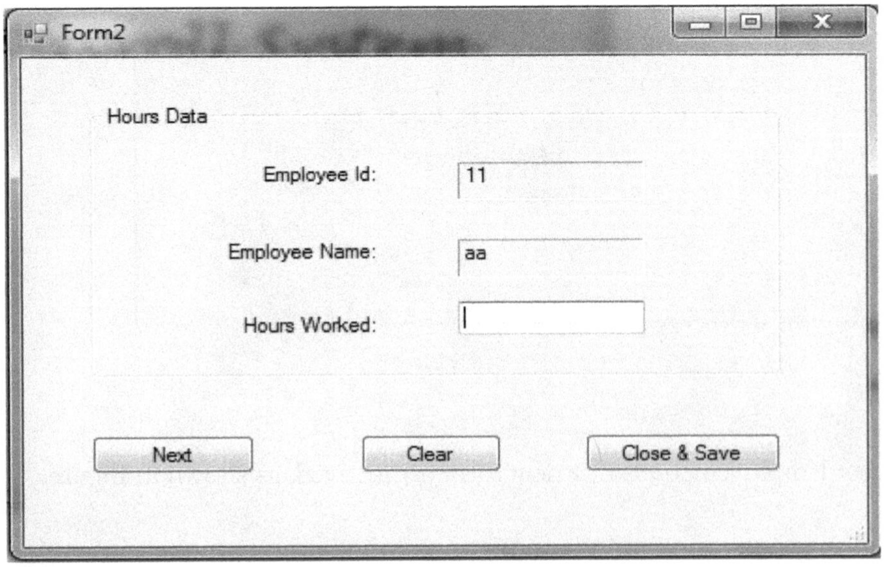

Figure 8.33 Form for entering an employee's hours worked.

In the form, the first employee from employee.txt should be displayed. Then, the user enters hours worked and clicks on the next button. The hours worked should be added to a List of employees, and the second employee data is displayed and expects the user to enter hours worked. When all hours worked data are entered, a pop up will display "no more employees". The user can then click on "Close & Save", which will close the form and save all data to the same employee.txt file.

Back in the MainForm, when the Display All button is clicked, the following form will be displayed (Figure 8.34):

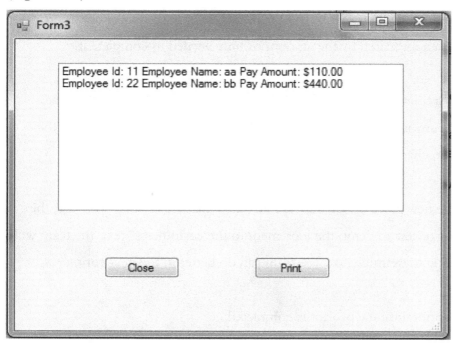

Figure 8.34 Form for displaying all employees.

The "Print" button in Figure 8.34 will print all employee data in a nicely formatted way on paper.

The "Exit" button on the MainForm will exit the program.

8.10 Agile Summary

You have learned the roles, events, and artifacts of agile in the previous chapters. It's time for a summary.

Your agile team starts with the software requirements from the business. Start writing user stories based on the requirements and put the stories in the product backlog. Some stories can be easily written while others may be vague and need clarification from the business. The stories are estimated by the team members for the effort needed to implement each story. Product owner is in charge of the product backlog and the product backlog is updated frequently. Stories in the product backlog are prioritized with different granularity.

Your team will move a certain number of stories from the product backlog to the sprint backlog based on the team velocity. In the sprint planning, the team will break each story into smaller and more manageable tasks. Each task is then estimated by the amount of time needed to complete it.

On a daily basis, the team holds a brief daily scrum meeting to see what each member has done yesterday, plans to do today, and any impediments encountered. Progress may be recorded on the Kanban board and/or burn down chart.

At the end of the sprint, after the new piece of software is integrated into the existing software, the team will hold an informal sprint review to demo the increment to the customers. Next, the team will hold a sprint retrospective meeting to examine how the team can do better in the next sprint.

This brings us back to another sprint until the project is completed.

Test Your Understanding 8.29

Which of the following is the first meeting of a sprint?
A. Sprint planning
B. Daily scrum
C. Sprint review
D. Retrospective

Test Your Understanding 8.30

Which of the following is the last meeting of a sprint?
A. Sprint planning

B. Daily scrum
C. Sprint review
D. Retrospective

8.11 Chapter Summary

In this chapter, you learned how to create a windows forms application, how to write and read from an external text file, how to search a List to find a matching element, how to display a group of elements in a ListBox, and how to print content from a form.

You also learned how to break up a project into sprints and complete one sprint at a time. User requirements are expressed in the form of user stories. Each sprint completes one or more user stories.

8.12 Solution to Programming Challenge

Programming Challenge 8.1 (You must follow the same steps in the Example 8.1. If you just type the code from this section for each form, it will not work.)

Code for Employee.cs

```csharp
class Employee
{
    // fields
    private string employeeId;
    private string employeeName;
    private decimal payRate;
    private decimal hoursWorked;
    // constructor
    public Employee(string employeeId, string employeeName, decimal payRate)
    {
        this.employeeId = employeeId;
        this.employeeName = employeeName;
        this.payRate = payRate;
    }
    public Employee(string employeeId, string employeeName, decimal payRate, decimal
hoursWorked)
    {
        this.employeeId = employeeId;
        this.employeeName = employeeName;
        this.payRate = payRate;
```

```csharp
            this.hoursWorked = hoursWorked;
        }
        // properties
        public string EmployeeId
        {
            get { return employeeId; }
            set { employeeId = value; }
        }
        public string EmployeeName
        {
            get { return employeeName; }
            set { employeeName = value; }
        }
        public decimal PayRate
        {
            get { return payRate; }
            set { payRate = value; }
        }
        public decimal HoursWorked
        {
            get { return hoursWorked; }
            set { hoursWorked = value; }
        }
        // method
        public decimal PayAmount()
        {
            decimal amount = 0.0m;
            amount = PayRate * HoursWorked;
            return amount;
        }
        // toString
        public override string ToString()
        {
            string str;
            str = string.Format("Employee Id: {0} Employee Name: {1} Pay Amount: {2:C}",
                EmployeeId, EmployeeName, PayAmount());
            return str;
        }
    }
```

Code for the MainForm

```csharp
    public partial class MainForm : Form
    {
        public MainForm()
        {
            InitializeComponent();
        }

        private void addButton_Click(object sender, EventArgs e)
        {
            Form1 form1 = new Form1();
```

```
        form1.ShowDialog();
    }

    private void hoursButton_Click(object sender, EventArgs e)
    {
        Form2 form2 = new Form2();
        form2.ShowDialog();
    }

    private void displayButton_Click(object sender, EventArgs e)
    {
        Form3 form3 = new Form3();
        form3.ShowDialog();
    }
}
```

Code for the Add New Employee Form:

```
public partial class Form1 : Form
{
    public Form1()
    {
        InitializeComponent();
    }

    private void saveButton_Click(object sender, EventArgs e)
    {
        Employee emp = new Employee(idTextbox.Text, nameTextbox.Text,
decimal.Parse(payrateTextbox.Text));
        using (StreamWriter sw = File.AppendText("employee.txt"))
        {
            sw.WriteLine(emp.EmployeeId);
            sw.WriteLine(emp.EmployeeName);
            sw.WriteLine(emp.PayRate);
            sw.WriteLine(0);
        }
    }
}
```

Code for Add Employee Hours Form

```
public partial class Form2 : Form
{
    List<Employee> allEmployee = new List<Employee>();

    public Form2()
    {
        InitializeComponent();
    }

    private void Form2_Load(object sender, EventArgs e)
    {
        if (File.Exists("employee.txt"))
        {
```

```csharp
            using (StreamReader sr = new StreamReader("employee.txt"))
            {
                string employeeId = "";
                while ((employeeId = sr.ReadLine())!= null)
                {
                    Employee emp = new Employee(employeeId, sr.ReadLine(),
                        decimal.Parse(sr.ReadLine()));
                    sr.ReadLine();
                    allEmployee.Add(emp);
                }
                // display first employee
                if(allEmployee.Count > 0)
                {
                    idLabel.Text = allEmployee[0].EmployeeId;
                    nameLabel.Text = allEmployee[0].EmployeeName;
                }
                else
                {
                    MessageBox.Show("No employee in the file.");
                    Close();
                }
            }
        }
        else
        {
            MessageBox.Show("Missing employee.txt");
            Close();
        }

    }
    int count = 1;
    private void nextButton_Click(object sender, EventArgs e)
    {
        // add hours worked to the array
        allEmployee[count - 1].HoursWorked = decimal.Parse(hoursWorkedTextbox.Text);

        if (count < allEmployee.Count)
        {
            idLabel.Text = allEmployee[count].EmployeeId;
            nameLabel.Text = allEmployee[count].EmployeeName;
            count++;
        }
        else
        {
            MessageBox.Show("no more record.");
        }
    }

    private void closeButton_Click(object sender, EventArgs e)
    {
        using (StreamWriter sw = File.CreateText("employee.txt"))
        {
            foreach(Employee emp in allEmployee)
            {
                sw.WriteLine(emp.EmployeeId);
```

```
                    sw.WriteLine(emp.EmployeeName);
                    sw.WriteLine(emp.PayRate);
                    sw.WriteLine(emp.HoursWorked);
                }

            }
            Close();
        }
    }
```

Code for Display all employees Form:

```
    public partial class Form3 : Form
    {
        List<Employee> allEmployee = new List<Employee>();
        public Form3()
        {
            InitializeComponent();
        }

        private void Form3_Load(object sender, EventArgs e)
        {
            if (File.Exists("Employee.txt"))
            {
                using (StreamReader sr = new StreamReader("employee.txt"))
                {
                    string employeeId = "";
                    while ((employeeId = sr.ReadLine()) != null)
                    {
                        Employee emp = new Employee(employeeId, sr.ReadLine(),
                            decimal.Parse(sr.ReadLine()), decimal.Parse(sr.ReadLine()));
                        employeeListbox.Items.Add(emp);
                        allEmployee.Add(emp);
                    }
                }
            }
            else
            {
                employeeListbox.Items.Add("No Employees entered yet.");
            }
        }

        private void button2_Click(object sender, EventArgs e)
        {
            // remember to add printDocument1 control to the form
            printDocument1.Print();
        }

        private void printDocument1_PrintPage(object sender,
System.Drawing.Printing.PrintPageEventArgs e)
        {
            // double click on the printDocument1 control to generate this printPage
            //event hander
            int x=75, y=75;
```

```
foreach (Employee emp in allEmployee)
{

    e.Graphics.DrawString(emp.ToString(),
        new Font("Courier", 10, FontStyle.Regular), Brushes.Black, x, y);
    y += 14;
}
}
}
```

8.13 Solutions to Test Your Understanding

8.1 A; 8.2 C; 8.3 D; 8.4 C; 8.5 D; 8.6 A; 8.7 B; 8.8 C; 8.9 B; 8.10 C; 8.11 D; 8.12 A; 8.13 D; 8.14 D; 8.15 A; 8.16 A; 8.17 A; 8.18 D; 8.19 A; 8.20 C; 8.21 B; 8.22 C; 8.23 B; 8.24 A; 8.25 D; 8.26 A; 8.27 B; 8.28 A; 8.29 A; 8.30 D;

Chapter 9: Case Study

9.1 Develop simple C# Windows Form application by following agile principles.

9.1 Case Background

In this chapter, you will be working on an agile team to develop an inventory management system for Mr. Lincoln (introduced in Chapter 1). Find two or three classmates or friends who are interested in agile software development to work together on this case study.

Dragon Phoenix Toy (DPT) LLC is a tiny retailer founded in 1994. It sells about 50 types of toys and most of them are seasonal. The manager wants a simple desktop application that can handle the company's inventory.

A product in DPT has a product ID, product name, product description, sales price, and inventory on hand.

When a shipment of new products arrives, the manager wants to be able to enter the product information into the system.

When a shipment of existing products arrives, the manager wants to be able to update the inventory on hand.

When a purchase is made by a customer, the check-out associate wants to enter the product ID and units sold. One sale can include multiple products. When all sale items are entered, the form should display a receipt which includes the name of each product sold, units sold, line total, subtotal, tax (9%), and total charge. The manager wants the inventory on hand to be updated after each sale. The application should be able to display and print the receipt similar to the following format.

```
Dragon Phoenix Toy (DPT)
       123 Toys St.
    Argentina OK 48451
   11/12/2019 2:30:03 PM
Wooden Train      2        40.00
Doll              1        30.00
Sub total                  70.00
Tax                         6.30
Total                      76.30
```

From time to time, the manager wants to check the product inventory and print it out. The print sheet should include the date and time of when the inventory was checked.

All data should be saved in a text file in its default location.

9.2 Your Tasks

Your tasks as a team:

1. Build the Product Backlog.

2. Write the user stories.

3. Prioritize the stories.

4. Estimate the story points for each story.

5. Build the Sprint Backlog.

6. Start a sprint planning, break each story down to its component tasks.

7. Estimate hours of work needed for each task.

8. Each member picks a task to work for a day or less. Use paired programming if possible.

9. Have daily stand-up meetings, and after the meeting, each member picks tasks to work on.

10. At the end of the sprint, conduct a sprint review/demo the deliverable to the customer.

11. Retrospection. As a team, find out what works and what doesn't. How can you do better in the next sprint?

12. Repeat steps 2 to 11 above for another sprint.

Find a few people to work with before checking the solution.

9.3 User Stories.

1. Possible user stories

User Story 1: As the owner, I want to check the inventory at any time so that I know how the business runs.

Acceptance Criterion 1: Graphical user interface. With a click of a button, the current inventory is displayed.

User Story 2: As the owner, I want to update the inventory when a new shipment arrives so that I have up to date inventory.

Acceptance Criterion 2: User enters the product ID and the new shipment quantity, click on "Update" to update the inventory.

User Story 3: As the owner, I want to enter new product information into the system before a new shipment arrives.

Acceptance Criterion 3: User can enter new product information without the quantity. The quantity can be updated later.

User Story 4: As a cashier, I want to enter order information and the inventory is automatically updated so that I don't need to keep the record on paper.

Acceptance Criterion 4: An order can contain multiple product items with varying quantity. Inventory should be updated as the order is submitted.

User Story 5: As a cashier, I want to print the receipt for an order for the customer so that the customer has the proof of purchase.

Acceptance Criterion 5: The receipt should be similar to the one displayed in the problem description earlier in this chapter.

User Story 6: As the owner, I want to print my inventory on paper so that I can take it anywhere I want.

Acceptance Criterion 6: The inventory print is on the regular print paper and looks professional with the date and time on it.

9.4 Prioritize the Stories

The product owner decides that the priority of the stories should be as follows with the first one as the most important:

Story 3, Story 2, Story 1, Story 4, Story 5, Story 6.

9.5 Estimate the Story Points for each Story

The team plays the Poker Planning Game. If you don't remember the game, you can go back and read it again (in Chapter 5). At first, the members don't know what each number exactly means and are not comfortable with which number to place. All of them know that ½ is the easiest story and 100 is the most difficult one. After a few rounds of play, they decide 8 story points as the estimate for story 1.

The estimate for the next story is easier. If a member thinks story 2 is more difficult than story 1, he or she will place a number larger than 8. Otherwise, a smaller number is placed. After a few rounds of play, they decide story 2 is 40 points.

One benefit of estimating story points is getting to know more about each story. Some stories may be more difficult than they look. For example, Story 2 was first estimated by the members as 5, 5, 5, and 100. Even though the majority estimate it for 5 points, the member who gave 100 points explains that the difficulty is due to the fact that an update on a text file is not as easy as an update on database. It is not difficult to read the specific inventory on hand from the file. Also, it is not difficult to update that number once it is in the program. However, it is difficult to save it back to the original location in the text file. One member suggests that maybe they should retrieve all data instead of just one inventory on hand. This way, after updating, the whole list of data can be saved back to the file without worrying about the original location, since the old one will be completely erased and replaced with the new inventories. Now, they believe they understand the problem better and in the second play, they give the estimate as 40.

The team continues to play and estimates 5 points for Story 3. They believe saving data to a text file is not much different from reading it from the file, as they already learned in Chapter 8.

They estimate 40 points for Story 4. They don't know how to handle an order with multiple items.

They estimate 8 points for Story 5 because they learned how to print from Chapter 8. The only challenge is how to display the date and time.

Finally, they estimate 5 points for Story 6. They believe with the experience from Story 5, they can handle it in less time for the print feature.

9.6 Sprint One (Zero)

The team members have a full time job somewhere and cannot work on this in a full time manner. Each member says he or she can devote about 5 hours per week to the project. They don't want a long sprint. They decide to have a time-box of two weeks for each sprint so that they can get feedback sooner. The total story points are 106 (8+40+5+40+8+5). They pick stories one, two, and three for the first sprint with a team velocity of 53 points.

9.6.1 Sprint Planning

The team identified the tasks for Story 1:

Story 1 user interface(Figure 9.4) (2 hours).

Product class (2 hours).

Make up a text file, read data from the text file, and display on the form (Figure 9.4) (2 hours).

Tasks for Story 2:

Story 2 user interface (Figure 9.3) (2 hours).

Read the inventory from the text file (2 hours).

Update the inventory (8 hours).

Save the updated inventory back to the text file (2 hours).

Story 3 Tasks:

Story 3 user interface (Figure 9.2) (2 hours).

Save data to the text file (1 hour).

9.6.2 Working on the project

They decide to use pair programming. Since they cannot physically meet, they decide to use remote PC access to work on one screen with two members. Each pair picks some tasks to work on.

9.6.3 Sprint Review

At the end of the sprint, they put all applications together and demo it to a friend pretending to be Mr. Lincoln, the store owner, and see how close they meet the requirements.

9.6.4 Retrospective

As a team, they hold a video conference meeting and discuss what works and what does not work, and what new techniques they want to try in the next sprint.

9.7 Sprint Two

In the second sprint, the team works on the remaining stories by following the same pattern as sprint one.

9.8 Release

By the end of the four weeks, they believe they have achieved what Mr. Lincoln wants and deploy the software on Mr. Lincoln's computer.

9.9 Product Class and Order Class

There are two custom classes you will need for this application: a Product class and an Order class. Create a product class which includes product ID, product name, product description, sales price, and inventory on hand.

```csharp
namespace DragonPhoenixToy
{
    class Product
    {
        // fields
        private string productId;
        private string productName;
        private string productDescription;
        private double productPrice;
        private int productOnHand;
        private int unitSold;
        // constructor
        public Product (string productId, string productName, string productDescription,
            double productPrice, int productOnHand)
        {
            this.productId = productId;
            this.productName = productName;
            this.productDescription = productDescription;
            this.productPrice = productPrice;
            this.productOnHand = productOnHand;

        }
        public Product(string productId, int unitSold)
        {
            this.productId = productId;
            this.unitSold = unitSold;
        }
        // properties
```

```csharp
public string ProductId
{
    get { return productId; }
    set { productId = value; }
}
public string ProductName
{
    get { return productName; }
    set { productName = value; }
}
public string ProductDescription
{
    get { return productDescription; }
    set { productDescription = value; }
}
public double ProductPrice
{
    get { return productPrice; }
    set { productPrice = value; }
}
public int ProductOnHand
{
    get { return productOnHand; }
    set { productOnHand = value; }
}
public int UnitSold
{
    get { return unitSold; }
    set { unitSold = value; }
}
// METHOD
public double CalculateProductCost()
{
    double cost = 0.0;
    cost = ProductPrice * UnitSold;
    return cost;
}
public void Sold()
{
    ProductOnHand -= UnitSold;
}
// ToString
public override string ToString()
{
    string str;
    str = string.Format("{0} {1} {2} {3} {4}",
        ProductId, ProductName, ProductDescription, ProductPrice, ProductOnHand );
    return str;
}
    }
}
```

Next, create an order class that includes a List of products, their corresponding quantities ordered, and calculation of subtotal, tax, and total.

```csharp
using System;
using System.Collections.Generic;

namespace DragonPhoenixToy
{
    class Order
    {
        public const double TaxRate = 0.09;
        // fields
        private List<Product> productInOrder = new List<Product>();
        // constructor
        public Order(List<Product> productInOrder)
        {

            this.productInOrder = productInOrder;
        }
        // method
        public double CalculateSubTotal()
        {
            double subTotal = 0.0;
            foreach (Product p in productInOrder)
            {
                subTotal += p.CalculateProductCost();
            }
            return subTotal;
        }
        // calculate tax
        public double CalculateTax()
        {
            double taxAmount = 0.0;
            taxAmount = CalculateSubTotal() * TaxRate;
            return taxAmount;
        }
        // calculate total
        public double CalculateTotal()
        {
            double total = 0.0;
            total = CalculateSubTotal() + CalculateTax();
            return total;
        }
        //ToString
        public override string ToString()
        {
            string str;
            str = string.Format("Dragon Phoenix Toy \n");
            str += string.Format("123 Toy St.\n");
            str += string.Format("Argentina OK 48451 \n");
            str += string.Format(DateTime.Now.ToString() + "\n");
            foreach (Product p in productInOrder)
```

```
        {
            str += string.Format("{0, -15} {1, 5} {2, 5:n2}\n", p.ProductName,
p.UnitSold, p.CalculateProductCost());
        }
        str += string.Format("{0, -20}{1, -10:n2} \n", "Sub total:",
CalculateSubTotal());
        str += string.Format("{0, -20}{1, -10:n2} \n", "Tax:", CalculateTax());
        str += string.Format("{0, -20}{1, -10:n2} ", "Total:", CalculateTotal());
        return str;
    }
  }
}
```

9.10 The Main Form

A MainForm with buttons that will open up new forms for each feature.

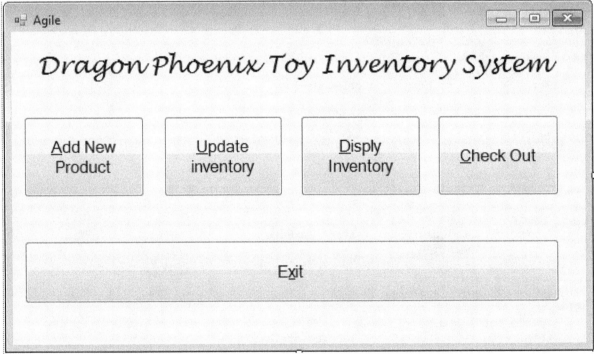

Figure 9.1 The MainForm and its controls

Code for the MainForm.

```
using System;
using System.Windows.Forms;

namespace DragonPhoenixToy
{
```

```csharp
public partial class MainForm : Form
{
    public MainForm()
    {
        InitializeComponent();
    }

    private void addButton_Click(object sender, EventArgs e)
    {
        AddNewProductForm addForm = new AddNewProductForm();
        addForm.ShowDialog();
    }

    private void checkoutButton_Click(object sender, EventArgs e)
    {
        CheckOutForm coForm = new CheckOutForm();
        coForm.ShowDialog();
    }

    private void updateButton_Click(object sender, EventArgs e)
    {
        UpdateProductForm updateForm = new UpdateProductForm();
        updateForm.ShowDialog();
    }

    private void displayButton_Click(object sender, EventArgs e)
    {
        DisplayProductForm displayForm = new DisplayProductForm();
        displayForm.ShowDialog();
    }

    private void exitButton_Click(object sender, EventArgs e)
    {
        Close();
    }
}
```

9.11 The Add New Product Form

When the "Add New Product" button is clicked, this form will open.

An AddNewProductForm that allows the user to enter new product information.

Figure 9.2 Add New Product Form

Code for AddNewProductForm.

```csharp
using System;
using System.Collections.Generic;
using System.Windows.Forms;
using System.IO;

namespace DragonPhoenixToy
{
    public partial class AddNewProductForm : Form
    {
        List<Product> allProduct = new List<Product>();
        public AddNewProductForm()
        {
            InitializeComponent();
        }

        private void saveButton_Click(object sender, EventArgs e)
        {
            using (StreamWriter sw = File.AppendText("product.txt"))
            {
                double price = 0;
                int onHand = 0;
                if (string.IsNullOrEmpty(idTextbox.Text)||
                    (allProduct.Find(x=>x.ProductId == idTextbox.Text)!=null))
                {
                    MessageBox.Show("ID already used or a new ID is required.");
```

```csharp
                idTextbox.Focus();
                idTextbox.SelectAll();
            }
            else if (string.IsNullOrEmpty(nameTextbox.Text))
            {
                MessageBox.Show("Product name cannot be empty");
                nameTextbox.Focus();
            }
            else if (string.IsNullOrEmpty(descriptionTextbox.Text))
            {
                MessageBox.Show("Description cannot be empty");
                descriptionTextbox.Focus();
            }
            else if (string.IsNullOrEmpty(priceTextbox.Text) ||
!(double.TryParse(priceTextbox.Text, out price)))
            {
                MessageBox.Show("Price is required and must be a number.");
                priceTextbox.Focus();
                priceTextbox.SelectAll();
            }
            else if (!(string.IsNullOrEmpty(onHandTextbox.Text)) &&
!(int.TryParse(onHandTextbox.Text, out onHand)))
            {
                MessageBox.Show("Qunatity must be a number of empty");
                onHandTextbox.Focus();
                onHandTextbox.SelectAll();
            }
            else
            {
                sw.WriteLine(idTextbox.Text);
                sw.WriteLine(nameTextbox.Text);
                sw.WriteLine(descriptionTextbox.Text);
                sw.WriteLine(priceTextbox.Text);
                if (string.IsNullOrEmpty(onHandTextbox.Text))
                {
                    sw.WriteLine("0");
                }
                else
                {
                    sw.WriteLine(onHandTextbox.Text);
                }

                MessageBox.Show("Record saved.");
                clearButton.PerformClick();
            }
        }
    }

    private void clearButton_Click(object sender, EventArgs e)
    {
        idTextbox.Clear();
        nameTextbox.Clear();
        descriptionTextbox.Clear();
        priceTextbox.Clear();
        onHandTextbox.Clear();
```

```
        idTextbox.Focus();
    }

    private void AddNewProductForm_Load(object sender, EventArgs e)
    {
        using (StreamReader sr = new StreamReader("product.txt"))
        {
            string id;
            while ((id = sr.ReadLine()) != null)
            {
                Product p = new Product(id, sr.ReadLine(), sr.ReadLine(),
                    double.Parse(sr.ReadLine()), int.Parse(sr.ReadLine()));
                allProduct.Add(p);
            }
        }
    }

    private void closeButton_Click(object sender, EventArgs e)
    {
        Close();
    }
    }
}
```

9.12 The Update Product Form

An UpdateProductForm that allows the user to update the inventory on hand by searching the product ID. The user can then enter the quantity in the shipment for that product.

Figure 9.3 Update Product Form

Code for UpdateProductForm.

```
using System;
using System.Collections.Generic;
using System.Windows.Forms;
using System.IO;

namespace DragonPhoenixToy
{
    public partial class UpdateProductForm : Form
    {
        List<Product> allProduct = new List<Product>();
        public UpdateProductForm()
        {
            InitializeComponent();
        }
        private void UpdateProductForm_Load(object sender, EventArgs e)
        {
            using (StreamReader sr = new StreamReader("product.txt"))
            {
                string id;
                while ((id = sr.ReadLine()) != null)
                {
                    Product p = new Product(id, sr.ReadLine(), sr.ReadLine(),
                        double.Parse(sr.ReadLine()), int.Parse(sr.ReadLine())));
                    allProduct.Add(p);
                }
            }
        }

        private void findButton_Click(object sender, EventArgs e)
        {
            Product p = allProduct.Find(x=>x.ProductId == idTextbox.Text);
            if (p != null)
            {
                idTextbox.Text = p.ProductId;
                idTextbox.ReadOnly = true;
                nameTextbox.Text = p.ProductName;
                descriptionTextbox.Text = p.ProductDescription;
                priceTextbox.Text = p.ProductPrice.ToString();
                onHandTextbox.Text = p.ProductOnHand.ToString();
            }
            else
            {
                MessageBox.Show("No product with that ID found.");
                idTextbox.Focus();
                idTextbox.SelectAll();
            }
        }

        private void updateButton_Click(object sender, EventArgs e)
        {
            int index = allProduct.FindIndex(x => x.ProductId == idTextbox.Text);
            double price = 0;
            int onHand = 0;
```

```csharp
            int newArrival = 0;
            if (string.IsNullOrEmpty(nameTextbox.Text))
            {
                MessageBox.Show("Product name cannot be empty");
                nameTextbox.Focus();
            }
            else if (string.IsNullOrEmpty(descriptionTextbox.Text))
            {
                MessageBox.Show("Description cannot be empty");
                descriptionTextbox.Focus();
            }
            else if (string.IsNullOrEmpty(priceTextbox.Text) ||
!(double.TryParse(priceTextbox.Text, out price)))
            {
                MessageBox.Show("Price is required and must be a number.");
                priceTextbox.Focus();
                priceTextbox.SelectAll();
            }
            else if ((string.IsNullOrEmpty(onHandTextbox.Text)) ||
!(int.TryParse(onHandTextbox.Text, out onHand)))
            {
                MessageBox.Show("Qunatity is required and must be a number.");
                onHandTextbox.Focus();
                onHandTextbox.SelectAll();
            }
            else if ((string.IsNullOrEmpty(newArrivalTextBox.Text))||
!(int.TryParse(newArrivalTextBox.Text, out newArrival)))
            {
                MessageBox.Show("New arrival quantity is required and must be a number.");
                onHandTextbox.Focus();
                onHandTextbox.SelectAll();
            }
            else
            {
                allProduct[index].ProductId = idTextbox.Text;
                allProduct[index].ProductName = nameTextbox.Text;
                allProduct[index].ProductDescription = descriptionTextbox.Text;
                allProduct[index].ProductPrice = price;
                allProduct[index].ProductOnHand += newArrival;
                MessageBox.Show("Product updated.");
                clearButton.PerformClick();
                idTextbox.ReadOnly = false;
            }
        }

        private void closeButton_Click(object sender, EventArgs e)
        {
            using(StreamWriter sr = File.CreateText("product.txt"))
            {
                foreach(Product p in allProduct)
                {
                    sr.WriteLine(p.ProductId);
                    sr.WriteLine(p.ProductName);
                    sr.WriteLine(p.ProductDescription);
                    sr.WriteLine(p.ProductPrice);
```

```
                sr.WriteLine(p.ProductOnHand);
            }
        }
        Close();
    }

    private void clearButton_Click(object sender, EventArgs e)
    {
        idTextbox.ReadOnly = false;
        idTextbox.Clear();
        nameTextbox.Clear();
        descriptionTextbox.Clear();
        priceTextbox.Clear();
        onHandTextbox.Clear();
        newArrivalTextBox.Clear();
        idTextbox.Focus();
    }
  }
}
```

9.13 The Display Product Form

A DisplayProductForm that will show all products in the inventory. The form will also allow the user
to print the inventory.

Figure 9.4 Display Product Form

Code for DisplayProductForm.

```csharp
using System;
using System.Collections.Generic;
using System.Drawing;
using System.Windows.Forms;
using System.IO;

namespace DragonPhoenixToy
{
    public partial class DisplayProductForm : Form
    {
        List<Product> allProduct = new List<Product>();
        public DisplayProductForm()
        {
            InitializeComponent();
        }

        private void DisplayProductForm_Load(object sender, EventArgs e)
        {
            using (StreamReader sr = new StreamReader("product.txt"))
            {
                string id;
                while ((id = sr.ReadLine()) != null)
                {
                    Product p = new Product(id, sr.ReadLine(), sr.ReadLine(),
                        double.Parse(sr.ReadLine()), int.Parse(sr.ReadLine()));
                    allProduct.Add(p);
                    displayListBox.Items.Add(p);
                }
            }
        }

        private void closeBbutton_Click(object sender, EventArgs e)
        {
            Close();
        }

        private void printButton_Click(object sender, EventArgs e)
        {
            printDocument1.Print();
        }

        private void printDocument1_PrintPage(object sender,
System.Drawing.Printing.PrintPageEventArgs e)
        {
            int x = 100, y = 100;
            foreach(Product p in allProduct)
            {
                e.Graphics.DrawString(p.ToString(), new Font("Courier New", 12,
FontStyle.Regular),
                    Brushes.Black, x, y);
                y += 15;
            }
        }
```

```
    }
}
```

9.14 The Check Out Form

A CheckOutForm that allows the cashier to enter each product ID and item quantity of an order. On this form, an order should be printed when all purchased items are entered.

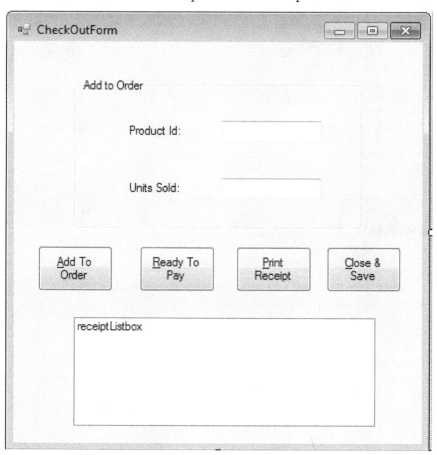

Figure 9.5 CheckOut Form

Code for CheckOutForm.

```
using System;
using System.Collections.Generic;
using System.Drawing;
using System.IO;
using System.Windows.Forms;
```

```csharp
namespace DragonPhoenixToy
{
    public partial class CheckOutForm : Form
    {
        List<Product> productInOrder = new List<Product>();
        List<Product> allProduct = new List<Product>();
        public CheckOutForm()
        {
            InitializeComponent();
        }

        private void addMoreButton_Click(object sender, EventArgs e)
        {
            int unitSold;
            if (string.IsNullOrEmpty(idTextbox.Text) ||
        (allProduct.Find(x => x.ProductId == idTextbox.Text) == null))
            {
                MessageBox.Show("ID does not exists.");
                idTextbox.Focus();
                idTextbox.SelectAll();
            }
            else if ((string.IsNullOrEmpty(unitSoldTextbox.Text)) ||
        !(int.TryParse(unitSoldTextbox.Text, out unitSold)))
            {
                MessageBox.Show("Unit Sold must be a whole number");
                unitSoldTextbox.Focus();
                unitSoldTextbox.SelectAll();
            }
            else
            {
                int index = allProduct.FindIndex(x => x.ProductId == idTextbox.Text);
                if (allProduct[index].ProductOnHand > unitSold)
                {
                    allProduct[index].UnitSold += unitSold;
                    allProduct[index].ProductOnHand -= unitSold;
                    productInOrder.Add(allProduct[index]);
                    idTextbox.Clear();
                    idTextbox.Focus();
                }
                else
                {
                    MessageBox.Show("Not enough inventory.");
                    unitSoldTextbox.Focus();
                }
                unitSoldTextbox.Clear();
            }

        }

        private void CheckOutForm_Load(object sender, EventArgs e)
        {
            using (StreamReader sr = new StreamReader("product.txt"))
            {
                string id;
                while ((id = sr.ReadLine()) != null)
```

```csharp
                {
                    Product p = new Product(id, sr.ReadLine(), sr.ReadLine(),
                        double.Parse(sr.ReadLine()), int.Parse(sr.ReadLine())));
                    allProduct.Add(p);
                }

            }
        }
        Order myOrder;
        private void readyButton_Click(object sender, EventArgs e)
        {
            receiptListbox.Items.Clear();
            myOrder = new Order(productInOrder);
            receiptListbox.Items.AddRange(myOrder.ToString().Split('\n'));
            addMoreButton.Enabled = false;
        }

        private void closeButton_Click(object sender, EventArgs e)
        {
            using (StreamWriter sr = File.CreateText("product.txt"))
            {
                foreach (Product p in allProduct)
                {
                    sr.WriteLine(p.ProductId);
                    sr.WriteLine(p.ProductName);
                    sr.WriteLine(p.ProductDescription);
                    sr.WriteLine(p.ProductPrice);
                    sr.WriteLine(p.ProductOnHand);
                }
            }
            Close();
        }

        private void printButton_Click(object sender, EventArgs e)
        {
            printDocument1.Print();
        }

        private void printDocument1_PrintPage(object sender,
System.Drawing.Printing.PrintPageEventArgs e)
        {
            if (myOrder == null)
            {
                MessageBox.Show("Sorry, cannot print receipt without pay the order.");
            }
            else
            {
                e.Graphics.DrawString(myOrder.ToString(), new Font("Courier New", 12,
FontStyle.Regular),
                    Brushes.Black, 50, 100);
            }
        }
    }
}
```

9.15 Save and Test the Application

After you type all the code, correct any compiler errors. You should test the application with valid inputs and invalid inputs.

Programming Challenge 9.1

The Tiny College is a small college with less than 100 students at any time. It offers a handful of courses in Math and English to help those who want to go back to college, but are not academically ready.

The college needs a simple GUI desktop application that can help them keep track of the course registration. All course registrations must go through the secretary with a paper form filled out by a student. The college already has a student record system that takes care of all student data, so this new system will keep track of who (a student ID) registers what class. The application is just about the courses and corresponding student ID who registered the course.

A course has a course ID, course title, course description, available seats, and student IDs who registered the course. The application should allow the administrators to add new courses or remove a course with no students enrolled. It should also allow the administrators to add more seats to a class that is already open for registration. The data about courses should be stored in an external text file.

When the secretary registers a new student, the student ID is added to the course and the available seat should be deducted by 1. When the class is full, no more students can be registered (the administrator can add more seats though).The application should let the administrators print all course information. The application should let the secretary print a registration record for a student (the student may register for more than one course at the time).

Your Tasks as a team:

Same as the twelve tasks listed in Section 9.2.

Programming Challenge 9.2

The Tiny College is a small college with less than 100 students at any time.

The college needs a simple GUI desktop application that can allow an instructor to create, update, or delete a quiz question through the application. It also allows students to take the quiz with feedback.

When a student completes a quiz, there is a summary form displaying the student's correct and incorrect answers. For the incorrect response, it should also show the correct answer. It also shows the student's percentage of correct and total time taken for the quiz.

A quiz is saved in an external text file and contains several quiz questions. Each quiz question contains a question and four possible answers, and ends with the key. For example,

```
What is the capital of the state of Indiana?
Indianapolis
Fort Wayne
Bloomington
Terre Haute
Indianapolis
```

The last line is the correct answer. It must be one of the four options.

Your Tasks as a team:

Same as the 12 tasks listed in Section 9.2

Programming Challenge 9.3

The Tiny Library need an application to keep track of its books.

A book has a title, author name(s) (all in one string separated by a semicolon ;), original number of copies, and available copies.

A librarian should be able to add a new book into the library and update its original number of copies when a new copy of an existing book is purchased, or a copy is reported missing.

When a book is checked out, the number of available copies of that book is deducted by one. One cannot check out a book if its available copies are zero. When a book is returned, the number of available copies is increased by one.

The lilbrary does not keep track of its borrowers.

The book data should be kept in a text file.

Your Tasks as a team:
Same as the twelve tasks listed in Section 9.2.

Programming Challenge 9.4

The Tiny Airline needs an application to keep track of its flights.

A flight has a date, flight number, total seats, number of available seats, and the ticket price.

A manager can add a new flight and update the ticket price.

A customer can purchase tickets or refund tickets. When a customer purchases a ticket, he or she should enter the date, flight number and number of tickets desired. The application should display the total price and deduct the number of available seats if it is more than the number requested. A ticket should be printed for the customer with the date, flight number, number of tickets for that flight, and total price on it. A customer can purchase more than one flight in one order.

A customer can refund the tickets through the help desk with the receipt. The help desk manager enters the flight number and number of seats returned. The number of available seats should be updated, and a new receipt is printed with the updated data.

The flights data should be kept in a text file.

Your Tasks as a team:
Same as the twelve tasks listed in Section 9.2.

Programming Challenge 9.5
The Tiny bank needs an application to keep track of monthly statement for customers.

A monthly statement has an account number, customer name, statement beginning date, beginning balance, total deposit made, total withdraw made, annual interest rate, and ending balance.

A customer can make a deposit, withdraw cash, and check the balance from his or her account. A deposit will increase the total deposit made, and a withdraw will increase the total withdraw made. Checking the balance will just display the ending balance.

A bank manager can search the monthly statement by customer account number and print one if found. A manager can also process the account, which will calculate the interest amount (annual interest rate divided by 12 and multiplied by the ending balance) and update the ending balance. After the balance update, the statement beginning date is updated to current date and time, beginning balance is replaced by the ending balance, total deposit made and total withdraw made are reset to zero. A manager can change the annual interest rate at any time.

The monthly statement data should be kept in a text file.

Your Tasks as a team:
Same as the twelve tasks listed in Section 9.2.

Programming Challenge 9.6

Update The Tiny Bank's application from Programming Challenge 9.5 so that each withdraw and deposit amount and date and time of the transaction is kept for the account. These data is just for the current month. Once a statement is processed, the transaction history is cleared. The transaction history for the month should be included in the monthly statement.

The account data should be kept in a text file.

Your Tasks as a team:
Same as the tasks listed in Section 9.2.

9.16 Chapter Summary

In this chapter, you applied what you learned in the previous eight chapters in problem solving. You followed the process of building an inventory management system for Mr. Lincoln's toy retail store. You read how a team works on writing user story, estimating stories and tasks, planning sprints, reviewing sprints, and team retrospective. You are encouraged to do similarly with the Programming Challenges provided in this chapter.

CPSIA information can be obtained
at www.ICGtesting.com
Printed in the USA
LVHW101043170821
695493LV00008B/237